Insights into Teaching and Learning Writing

Writing is one of the most challenging skills for a language learner to acquire due its sheer complexity, and language teachers are faced with a demanding task in the teaching and testing of writing. A great deal of research on different aspects of writing has been carried out to date, however despite the abundance of publications in this field, few books aim to offer insights into teaching and learning writing for early career teachers that shed light on writing instruction in jargon-free discourse. This book aims to fill this perceived gap through presenting relevant conceptual and theoretical frameworks of second language writing research and shedding light on the implications of the recent research findings in a clear and practice-oriented style. In this way, it is intended as a companion book for language teachers who include writing as a part of their courses, in particular, new teachers as they embark on their teaching careers.

Hassan Mohebbi holds a PhD in TESOL. His main research interests are writing instruction, individual differences, assessment literacy, and teacher's pedagogical knowledge. He has published extensively in refereed journals of the field. He co-edited *Research Questions in Language Education: A Reference Book* (Springer) with Christine Coombe and co-edited special issues with Christine Coombe for *Language Teaching Research Quarterly* and *Language Testing in Asia*. He is on the editorial board of several top journals on language teaching and research.

Yijen Wang is an Assistant Professor in the School of International Liberal Studies at Waseda University. She holds a PhD in applied linguistics with a focus on computer assisted language learning (CALL). She has published a number of research articles and book chapters in the field, specifically looking at learner and teacher motivation and the development of autonomy through technology. She is currently editor-in-chief of *Technology in Language Teaching & Learning*, and she regularly reviews for multiple journals in the field.

Language Teaching Insights Series
Series Editors: David Nunan & Glenn Stockwell

Burston & Arispe: *Mobile-Assisted Language Learning and Advanced-level Second Language Acquisition*

Eginli: *Insights into Emotional Well-Being of Language Teachers*

Farrell: *Insights into Professional Development in Language Teaching*

Horwitz: *Becoming a Language Teacher (2nd ed.)*

Jitpaisarnwattana, Reinders, & Chong: *Insights into Language MOOCs*

Khezrlou: *Insights into Task-Based Language Teaching*

Lai: *Insights into Autonomy and Technology in Language Teaching*

Leis: *Insights into Flipped Classrooms*

Mohebbi & Wang (Eds.): *Insights into Teaching and Learning Writing*

Son: *Insights into Digital Literacy and Language Teaching*

Tanaka-Ellis: *Insights into Teaching and Learning with Technology*

More information about titles in this series can be found at
https://www.castledown.com/academic-books/book-series/language-teaching-insights/

Insights into Teaching and Learning Writing

A Practical Guide for Early-Career Teachers

Edited by

Hassan Mohebbi
European Knowledge Development Institute

Yijen Wang
Waseda University

Melbourne – London – Tokyo – New York

4th Floor, Silverstream House, 45 Fitzroy Street Fitzrovia, London W1T 6EB, United Kingdom
Ground Level, 470 St Kilda Road, Melbourne, Victoria 3004, Australia
2nd Floor Daiya Building, 2-2-15 Hamamatsu-cho, Minato-ku, Tokyo 105-0013, Japan
447 Broadway, 2nd Floor #393, New York NY, 10013, United States

First published 2023 by Castledown Publishers, London

Information on this title:
www.castledown.com/reference/9781914291159

DOI: 10.29140/9781914291159

Insights into Teaching and Learning Writing: A Practical Guide for Early-Career Teachers

© Hassan Mohebbi & Yijen Wang (Editors), 2023

All rights reserved. This publication is copyright. Subject to statutory exception and to the provisions of relevant collective licencing agreements, no reproduction, transmission, or storage of any part of this publication by any means, electronic, mechanical, photocopying, recording or otherwise may take place without prior written permission from the author.

Typeset by Castledown Design, Melbourne
ISBN: 978-1-914291-15-9 (Paperback)
ISBN: 978-1-914291-16-6 (Digital)

Castledown Publishers takes no responsibility for the accuracy of URLs for external or third-party internet websites referred to in this publication. No responsibility is taken for the accuracy or appropriateness of information found in any of these websites.

This book is dedicated to Michael Hugh Long (1945–2021). Michael's outstanding contribution to second language teaching and learning is with us forever.

Endorsements

Developing the ability to write effectively in English often presents challenges both for those whose mother tongue is English as well as others for whom English is an additional language and who need to be able to write a variety of different kinds of texts for academic as well as professional purposes. Many students worldwide study through the medium of English or plan to study abroad in English-medium tertiary institutions and universities and need to develop effective writing skills for academic purposes. With the emergence of a global economy, written texts also play an increasingly important role in many businesses and organizations. Effective communication within organizations involves paper and electronic memos, reports and other written texts, while communication with customers and clients depends on letters, brochures, sales materials and other documents. In addition, the growth of social-media communications tools has also greatly influenced the amount of written communication people make use of, as well as the form of their written communication.

This book provides a comprehensive overview of current theory and pedagogy in the teaching and assessment of L2 writing. Rich in theoretical insights and practical examples it provides a valuable resource for teachers, curriculum designers, graduate students and others interested in approaches to the teaching of writing.

— *Jack C Richards, Victoria University Wellington and University of Sydney*

As the two editors of this important collection make clear, writing is largely recognised as among the most challenging skills for language learners to acquire. The fields of writing pedagogy and writing assessment would benefit from straightforward and practice-oriented publications that can help guide and support what happens in classrooms. This timely and broad-based collection promises to provide key insights in and for the fields, written by an array of experts working in diverse locations. Deliberately presented in a jargon-free and teacher-friendly way, each chapter follows a similar pattern and offers ideas that teachers can immediately try out in their own classrooms. The book will appeal to a wide audience, in particular early career teachers. It will also be of interest to undergraduate and postgraduate students who want to gain a deeper understanding of some of the fundamental issues when it comes to writing practices, and also those who work in teacher education and are preparing teachers to teach and assess writing in a range of contexts.

— *Martin East, Professor of Language Education, The University of Auckland*

Learning to write effectively is a high-stakes skill for language learners all over the world. Their ability to write well is likely to determine their success in both general and academic language courses and has implications for their further entry into the courses they wish to pursue in the future. Consequently, the quality of the knowledge, guidance and support that writing teachers bring to the classroom is of paramount importance. In order to gain and expand their knowledge of teaching writing, teachers, particularly those at an early-career stage, need resources for professional development that offer both theoretical and practical ideas.

Insights into Teaching and Learning Writing: A Practical Guide for Early-Career Teachers, edited by Hassan Mohebbi and Yijen Wang is one such resource. However, in contrast to many books on writing, it succeeds in highlighting a comprehensive range of topics highly relevant to current trends in writing. Moreover, it combines in a clear and teacher-friendly way discussions of current theory and their implications for practice. This combination is in itself invaluable for teachers, but it then goes further by suggesting what kinds of classroom investigations teachers could pursue (action research or case study) for their own professional development. This is a volume which is likely to be very warmly welcomed by teachers and teacher educators.

— *Anne Burns, University of New South Wales and Curtin University*

Insights into Teaching and Learning Writing is a comprehensive companion for second language writing practitioners and scholars. Its breadth of scope and clear connection between theoretical perspectives, research findings, and pedagogical implications are truly impressive. The contributors are a constellation of multifaceted expertise; together, their chapters demystify the art of writing instruction and make the book an insightful guide for novices as well as for those who embark on theoretically grounded classroom-based research into second language writing. Importantly, even though the material covered is rather complex, this book is written in a very accessible way. Exposing readers to diverse topics and teaching contexts and providing so many important take-aways, it will help early-career writing practitioners in multiple ways. Not only will they be able to teach more effectively by adopting, adapting, and developing new teaching strategies; they will also become more aware of teaching and learning needs and challenges – whether those are related to writing genres, language features, collaborative writing, feedback, assessment, individual differences, and more.

— *Elena Cotos, Associate Professor of Applied Linguistics, Iowa State University*

Contents

List of contributors ix

Preface xiii

Chapter 1 1
Teaching writing for academic and specific purposes
Helen Basturkmen

Chapter 2 13
Integrating awareness of academic reading into teaching writing in an additional language
Mahmoud Altalouli & Mary Jane Curry

Chapter 3 27
Complexity, accuracy, and fluency in writing
Lee McCallum & Niall Curry

Chapter 4 45
Teachers' pedagogical knowledge and assessment literacy
Deborah Crusan, Ali Panahi, & Hassan Mohebbi

Chapter 5 56
Testing issues in writing
Chengyuan Yu

Chapter 6 71
Teacher cognition, pedagogical practice, and meeting student needs in L2 writing
K. James Hartshorn

Chapter 7 87
Individual differences and writing instruction
Olena Vasylets & Rosa M. Manchón

Chapter 8 101
Learner autonomy and writing
Rachael Ruegg

Chapter 9   114
Collaborative writing: Theory, research, and implications
Tomohito Hiromori

Chapter 10   127
Written corrective feedback
Minh Thi Thuy Nguyen & Willy Renandya

Chapter 11   139
Dynamic written corrective feedback
Kendon Kurzer

Chapter 12   155
Feedback on student writing for early career teachers: Effective strategies for teacher, peer, and self-feedback
Grant Eckstein

Chapter 13   167
Technology and second language writing instruction
Yijen Wang & Ali Panahi

Chapter 14   180
Future directions in writing research
Rosa M. Manchón & Ronald P. Leow

Index   *194*

List of contributors

Mahmoud Altalouli teaches academic writing and academic presentation courses to graduate students at the English for International Students department, Duke University. His publications include, *More surefire ways to increase the breadth and depth of vocabulary knowledge* (2020); *Agency and accountability in the academic reading practices of graduate students using English as an additional language* (2021). With Curry, he is a co-author of *An A-W of academic literacy: Key concepts and practices for graduate students* (2021).

Helen Basturkmen has written and researched extensively in ESP and EAP. Her books include works on ESP (Routledge, 2006; Palgrave Macmillan, 2010) and the edited, multi-volume work *English for Academic Purposes*, in the *Critical Concepts in Linguistics* series (Routledge, 2015.) Her latest book is *Linguistic Description in English for Academic Purposes* (Routledge, 2021). Her research has been published in international journals, including *Language Learning, Language Teaching, Language Awareness, Applied Linguistics, TESOL Quarterly, Modern Language Journal, English for Specific Purposes* and *Journal of English for Academic Purposes*.

Deborah Crusan is professor of TESOL/Applied Linguistics at Wright State University, Dayton, OH. Her work has appeared in academic journals and in edited collections about second language writing. Her newest book, *Linking assignments to assessments: A guide for teachers* (with Todd Ruecker) is in press from University of Michigan Press. Crusan formerly served on the TESOL International Association Board of Directors and is a frequent keynote speaker at national and international conferences.

Books produced by **Mary Jane Curry** include *An A-W of Academic Literacy: Key Concepts and Practices for Graduate Students* (2021), *Global Academic Publishing* (2018), *A Scholar's Guide to Getting Published in English* (2013); *Academic Writing in a Global Context: The politics and practices of publishing in English* (2010); and *Teaching Academic Writing* (2002). Co-editor of the Multilingual Matters series, Studies in Knowledge Production and Participation, Curry was a Fulbright scholar in Chile in 2014.

Niall Curry is an Assistant Professor and ASPiRE Fellow at Coventry University. His research spans a range of areas in applied linguistics, including corpus linguistics, contrastive linguistics, academic writing and metadiscourse in English, French, and Spanish, language change, discourse analysis, TESOL, and language teaching materials development. He is Managing Editor of the *Journal of Academic Writing* and a Géras International Correspondent. Further details of his work can be found at: https://niallcurry.com/

Grant Eckstein is a professor of linguistics at Brigham Young University where he teaches graduate academic writing and teacher training courses. His research interests include second language reading and writing development and pedagogy. He is the associate editor of *Journal of Response to Writing* and has published in venues such as Journal of Second Language Writing, *Journal of English for Academic Purposes, Research in the Teaching of English,* and *TESOL Quarterly.*

K. James Hartshorn received his Ph.D. in instructional psychology with a specialization in second language acquisition. He has been involved in second language education in the USA and Asia for more than three decades. As a faculty member in the Brigham Young University's Linguistics Department, James teaches a variety of courses where he mentors new TESOL professionals to optimize the efficacy of their ESL teaching and research.

Tomohito Hiromori is a Professor of Applied Linguistics at Meiji University, Japan. His research interests include second language motivation, learner engagement, and pair/group work dynamics. He is particularly interested in the mechanisms underlying motivation contagion among learners. His research has been published in journals such as *International Review of Applied Linguistics in Language Teaching, System, RELC Journal,* and *Journal for the Psychology of Language Learning.*

Kendon Kurzer is a lecturer at the University Writing Program at the University of California, Davis. He is primarily interested in supporting multilingual students throughout their educational experiences and beyond. His research interests include the intersection of Writing Across the Curriculum and L2 writing and written corrective feedback. He has published in the *TESOL Quarterly, Assessing Writing,* and *Foreign Language Annals,* as well as in various other journals and edited collections.

Ronald P. Leow is Professor (Applied Linguistics) in the Department of Spanish and Portuguese at Georgetown University, USA. A leading proponent of the use of concurrent verbal reports, he has been promoting a process-oriented and curricular approach to Instructed Language Learning studies and has recently proposed a Feedback Processing Framework (2020) that provides a cognitive explanation for the role of corrective feedback, whether oral or written, in L2 development in direct relation to how L2 learners or writers process such feedback.

Rosa M. Manchón is Professor of Applied Linguistics at the University of Murcia, Spain. Her main research interest is the connection between L2 writing and L2 learning. She has been a key agent in the development of the research on writing as a site for language learning, to which she has contributed with numerous publications and diverse professional initiatives. Her latest book is the *Handbook of SLA and writing* (co-edited with Charlene Polio, Routledge, 2021).

List of Contributors xiii

Lee McCallum is a Lecturer and ASPiRE Fellow at Coventry University. She holds an M.Sc in TESOL and Applied Linguistics from the University of Stirling and an Ed.D. in TESOL from the University of Exeter. Her research focuses on exploring the production and assessment of academic written language in learner and professional writing. Further details of her work can be found at: https://leemccallum.net

Hassan Mohebbi holds a Ph.D. in TESOL. His main research interests are writing instruction, individual differences, assessment literacy, and teacher's pedagogical knowledge. He has published extensively in refereed journals of the field. His co-edited book with Christine Coombe *Research Questions in Language Education: A Reference Book* (+150 Chapters) is published by Springer. He has co-edited special issues with Christine Coombe for Language Teaching Research Quarterly and Language Testing in Asia. He is an editorial board member of *Asian-Pacific Journal of Second and Foreign Language Education (Springer), Language Testing in Asia (Springer), Language Teaching Research Quarterly (EUROKD), Australian Journal of Applied Linguistics (Book Reviews Editor), and Technology in Language Teaching & Learning (Book Reviews Editor)*.

Minh Thi Thuy Nguyen, PhD, teaches TESOL and second language acquisition at the University of Otago. Her research interests and publications are in the areas of instructed pragmatics, including the use of feedback to enhance L2 pragmatics, interactional competence development and second language acquisition. Dr. Nguyen is currently serving on the editorial board of *Applied Pragmatics* (John Benjamins).

Ali Panahi (also known as Ali Panahi Masjedlou) has been working and researching in ELT and language assessment since 1998. His Ph.D. focused on Validity Argument of IELTS Listening. His three newest works include *Reflecting on Jack C. Richards' 60 Years in TESOL: A Systematic Review* (Richards, J. C., Panahi, A, Mohebbi, H.), *Glenn Fulcher's Thirty-Five Years of Contribution to Language Testing and Assessment: A Systematic Review* (Fulcher, G., Panahi, A., Mohebbi, H.) and *Teacher Training in ELT* (Panahi, 2023). He received *Train the Trainer Certificate* from Cambridge and two Diplomas (*Dip. in TESOL* and *Dip. in Teacher Training*) from London. He has so far published 15 textbooks and a number of research articles and has widely presented at conferences. At present, he supervises and educates teachers at Iranian Foreign Languages Institute, Ardebil (Ardabil), Iran.

Willy A. Renandya is a language teacher educator currently teaching language education courses at the National Institute of Education, Nanyang Technological University, Singapore. His research interests include second language pedagogy, second language reading and listening and teacher professional development. He has given numerous keynote presentations at international conferences in Asia and beyond.

Rachael Ruegg is a Senior Lecturer in the School of Linguistics and Applied Language Studies and Director of the Academic and Professional Writing programme at Victoria University of Wellington, New Zealand. She has 14 years of experience teaching writing at universities in Japan and New Zealand. Her research interests include teaching and assessment of academic writing, EAP, EMI and the development of learner autonomy.

Olena Vasylets is an Associate Professor at the University of Barcelona, Spain. Her primary research interests are L2 writing, individual differences, and the role of mode (oral versus written) in second language acquisition. Her most current research centers on the specificity of L2 learning in paper-based versus digital writing. She has published articles in such top-rated journals as *Language Learning*, *Journal of Second Language Writing*, and *Annual Review of Applied Linguistics*.

Yijen Wang is an Assistant Professor in the School of International Liberal Studies at Waseda University. Her Ph.D. focused on the factors affecting the adoption of technology by teachers and students in language teaching. She is co-editor of the *Cambridge Handbook of Technology in Language Teaching and Learning* with Glenn Stockwell (Cambridge University Press) and has published a number of research articles and book chapters in the field of technology and language education, specifically looking at learner and teacher motivation and the development of autonomy. She is currently editor-in-chief of *Technology in Language Teaching & Learning*, and she regularly reviews for multiple journals in the field.

Chengyuan Yu has recently received his Ph.D. in Linguistics (English) from University of Macau and is now pursuing his second doctorate in Communication and Information (Human Information Behavior). He is interested in writing assessment, academic writing, and information literacy. He is currently conducting interdisciplinary research on the relationship between writing and information literacy by designing integrated writing assessment instruments. His publications have appeared in *Language Testing*, *Asia Pacific Education Review*, *Journal of Academic Librarianship*, *International Journal of Qualitative Studies in Education*, and *Asian-Pacific Journal of Second and Foreign Language Education*.

Preface

Hassan Mohebbi
Yijen Wang

Writing is widely recognized as one of the most challenging skills for language learners to acquire, particularly due to its inherent complexity. As such, language teachers face a demanding task when it comes to teaching and assessing writing. While there exists an abundance of publications on various aspects of writing, few books offer insights into teaching and learning writing for early career teachers in a manner that is clear and free of technical jargon. New teachers and pre-service teachers may have limited experience teaching second/foreign language (L2) writing, which can make them feel uncertain about the best approaches to use.

Particularly relevant to writing is that there has been a shift in the processes and products of writing. What used to be a relatively solitary process where learners engaged in activities individually, changes in approaches to language teaching in general have also impacted upon the teaching of writing, where collaboration has come to be seen as playing an important role. Similarly, the tools through which writing takes place have also evolved, with assistance provided by sophisticated word processing software and artificial intelligent systems such as machine translation and ChatGPT. Word processors have been in use for decades, but functionality such as spell checking has become an indispensable part of writing (Bangert-Drowns, 1993; O'Rourke et al., 2020), and artificial intelligent machine translation is having a broad pedagogical and ethical influence on writing (Lee, 2022). These digital writing tools can also contribute to the development of learner autonomy (see Godwin-Jones, 2018), which can allow learners more opportunities to engage in writing in the target language.

An essential part of teaching writing, the provision of corrective feedback, has also been the focus of research and practice (see Mao & Lee, 2020), and this has been related to teacher beliefs and practice in teaching writing (Mao & Crosthwaite, 2020). This has affected—and been affected by—the products of writing. Where essays that were submitted to the teacher were the mainstream, learners are producing writing that will be seen by their peers or even the wider community using a broad range of electronic platforms in addition to the more traditional writing forums. Further topics related to the teaching of writing are the position of writing in testing, the development of learner identity, and the position of writing in instructed second language acquisition (see Manchón, 2020). These diverse topics come together in this volume to prepare early career teachers to be effective in the teaching of writing in their individual teaching and learning contexts.

The purpose of this book is to bridge this perceived gap by presenting relevant conceptual and theoretical frameworks of second language writing research and providing a fresh perspective on the implications of recent research findings in a clear, practical style. In doing so, it aims to serve as a useful companion for language teachers who include writing as a part of their courses, particularly for new teachers embarking on their teaching careers. Each chapter follows the structure of introducing the topics, theocratical framework, literature review, practical implications for early-career teachers, suggestions for action research or case study, and suggestions for further reading. Easy-to-follow guidelines are also provided for teachers to apply immediately in their writing instruction practices.

There are three main features of this book. First, it is reader friendly. The book is written in a clear practice-oriented style, which is accessible to a wide range of readers, including but not limited to early-career and practicing teachers, undergraduate and postgraduate students, and teacher educators. It is designed to be easy and enjoyable to read, even for people who may not have a background in the subject matter. This allows readers to gain a more comprehensive understanding of L2 writing education. It aims to convey information through simple and direct language, so that readers can quickly grasp the main points and apply them to their own situations. Second, it is based on research, theory, and practice, which are regarded as the three foundational pillars of education. As each chapter outlines related conceptual and theoretical framework of second language writing research, we encourage teachers to conduct action study and/or case study in their teaching practices. Identifying problems and finding the solutions through conducting classroom-based research, it empowers both students and teachers to improve the current teaching and learning. By being able to relate to the theories and research, teachers can gain insights into how they can adapt and reflect their own teaching strategies to better suit their students' needs and create a more effective and engaging language learning environments. Thirdly, the diversity of the contributors. The contributors of this book come from a variety of L2 educational backgrounds. This diversity provides a rich and varied perspectives on L2 writing pedagogy that is beneficial for readers of the book because they can relate their own teaching contexts to the similar conditions.

The book consists of 14 chapters whose contributors have researched writing instruction extensively, providing a wealth of knowledge and expertise on the topics. Through their research and experience, the contributors share their insights and strategies in a clear and engaging way.

In Chapter 1, Helen Basturkmen provides an introduction to the teaching of English for Specific Purposes (ESP) and English for Academic Purposes (EAP). The chapter explores the distinctive needs of learners in these contexts and the importance of identifying those needs through careful analysis of writing genres and linguistic features. The author also discusses the challenges faced by teachers transitioning from general English instruction to EAP and ESP and offers guidance on developing effective curricula and instructional strategies for these settings.

In Chapter 2, Mahmoud Altalouli and Mary Jane Curry present a discussion on the relationship between academic reading and writing for English as an additional language (EAL) education. Reading for writing (RFW) is a challenging practice for EAL writing, and many EAL students may struggle with academic reading due to linguistic and sociocultural differences. The chapter discusses the theoretical foundations of cognitive and social perspectives on reading for writing and provides strategies for instructors to improve student success.

In Chapter 3, Lee McCallum and Niall Curry shed light on the relationship of complexity, accuracy, and fluency in writing by tracing the origins of the theoretical framework and discussing the complex concept of language proficiency. The chapter guides teachers to have a picture of the Common European Framework of Reference (CEFR) and understand how it is used to measure language proficiency, particularly in writing.

In the following chapter, Deborah Crusan, Ali Panahi, and Hassan Mohebbi focus on teachers' pedagogical knowledge of assessment literacy, regarding why to assess (purposes), what to assess (scales), how to assess (methods), and who (stakeholders) are involved in the assessment. This chapter raises the awareness of assessment practices, knowledge, and pedagogy to enhance student learning.

Chapter 5 is devoted to testing issues in writing, written by Chengyuan Yu. The chapter provides practical guidance for using standardized writing tests for learning-oriented purposes, drawing on various models of learning-oriented assessment and approach. The chapter also reviews the historical evolution of writing testing, including pre-scientific direct essay tests, psychometric-structuralist indirect tests, and integrative-sociolinguistic direct writing tests, and the adoption of prompt-based writing tasks and scoring rubrics by influential international English language tests.

In Chapter 6, James Hartshorn outlines the place of teacher cognition in writing instruction. The author guides us to explore the complexity of teachers' beliefs classroom practice. Providing practical ideas, this chapter is helpful for practitioners to understand their beliefs about writing education and learners' needs, which also helps teachers to engage in metacognitive practice in their teaching.

Olena Vasylets and Rosa M. Manchón discuss the recent interest in exploring how individual differences (IDs) affect L2 writing. The chapter highlights the theoretical, empirical, and pedagogical relevance of studying IDs in SLA and reviews the main research findings on the connection between IDs and writing. The chapter also covers the impacts of working memory, writing motivation, self-efficacy, self-regulation, and anxiety on L2 writing.

Chapter 8, written by Rachael Ruegg, explicates the development of learner autonomy in L2 writing. This chapter presents practical suggestions on writing instruction to encourage students to take control of their learning, and it outlines manageable pedagogical changes that can be applied in writing instruction and other educational contexts.

Tomohito Hiromori, in Chapter 9, discusses the theoretical framework and literature review on collaborative writing in second/foreign language (L2) learning contexts. The chapter explains how collaborative writing promotes communication abilities and enhances language acquisition through mutual engagement and coordinated effort. The chapter also explores the sociocultural aspects of collaborative writing and how it matches with current teaching methods and provides insights into the key factors that influence the nature of collaborative writing and its outcomes.

Chapter 10 focuses on written corrective feedback (WCF) in L2 writing classrooms, by Minh Thi Thuy Nguyen and Willy Renandya. While feedback is critical for learning, there is controversy regarding the effectiveness of WCF in improving L2 writing. The chapter explores the various types and forms of WCF, and the challenges faced by teachers in providing effective feedback.

Then, in Chapter 11, Kendon Kurzer elaborates on Dynamic Written Corrective Feedback (DWCF), a promising method for enhancing the writing accuracy of multilingual students. The chapter explains how DWCF adheres to the principles of cognitive and second language acquisition theories and established best practices of written corrective feedback. The author discusses the effectiveness of DWCF from theoretical aspects, providing with practical practices and his professional teaching experience.

Chapter 12 covers the three sources of feedback (teacher, peer, and self-feedback) and their effectiveness for L2 learners. Grant Eckstein discusses the complexities involved in providing feedback on student writing and explores pedagogical practices and innovations for early career teachers to support student writing development.

Yijen Wang and Ali Panahi, in the penultimate chapter, present discussion about the interplay of technology, teachers, and learners in second language writing instruction. The chapter how technology has changed the writing process and formats, enabling multimodal composition and access to a wider range of information. The use of technology in writing instruction has been found to enhance students' writing outcomes, creativity, and engagement, and also provides opportunities for collaboration and feedback. The chapter also provides an overview of cognitive and sociocultural theories of writing and how technology can be integrated into writing instruction based on these theories.

In the final chapter, Ronald P. Leow and Rosa M. Manchón summarized recent shifts in the focus of L2 writing research, including the perspective of writing in an additional language as a potential for learning, the need for a process-oriented approach to the study of writing, and the location of writing research designs within an instructed second language acquisition (ISLA) framework. Directions of future research in writing and written corrective feedback WCF are also suggested.

Our hope is that this book can equip language teachers with the necessary knowledge and skills to facilitate their students' success in writing. Regardless of pre-service teachers, new teachers or experienced instructors who are seeking new teaching ideas, this book would be a valuable resource that can be referenced time and again. Ultimately, our goal is to facilitate teachers' autonomy to improve their instruction and further help their students become better writers.

Finally, we would like to express our sincerest gratitude and appreciation to the authors for their hard work and dedication in contributing to this book. It is through their expertise, knowledge, and research that this publication has been made possible. We would also like to extend our heartfelt thanks to the series editors, Dr. David Nunan and Dr. Glenn Stockwell, for their valuable feedback on the book. Their commitment to advancing the field and sharing their insights with others is admirable and has undoubtedly enriched the content of this book. We hope that their contributions will inspire and benefit many readers, and we once again express our deepest gratitude to them.

References

Bangert-Drowns, R. L. (1993). The word processor as an instructional tool: A meta-analysis of word processing in writing instruction. *Review of Educational*

Research, 63(1), 69–93. https://doi.org/10.3102/00346543063001069

Godwin-Jones, R. (2018). Second language writing online: An update. *Language Learning & Technology, 22*(1), 1–15. https://dx.doi.org/10125/44574

Lee, S. -M. (2022). L2 learners' strategies for using machine translation as a personalized writing assisting tool. In J. Colpaert, & G. Stockwell (Eds.), *Smart CALL: Personalization, contextualization, & socialization* (pp. 184–206). Castledown Publishers. https://doi.org/10.29140/9781914291012-9

Manchón, R. M. (Ed.) (2020). Writing and language learning: Advancing research agendas. John Benjamins.

Mao, S. S., & Crosthwaite, P. (2020). Investigating written corrective feedback: (Mis)alignment of teacher's beliefs and practice. *Journal of Second Language Writing, 45*, 46–60. https://doi.org/10.1016/j.jslw.2019.05.004

Mao, Z., & Lee, I. (2020). Feedback scope in written corrective feedback: Analysis of empirical research in L2 contexts. *Assessing Writing, 45*, 100469. https://doi.org/10.1016/j.asw.2020.100469

O'Rourke, L., Connelly, V., Barnett, A., & Afonso, O. (2020). Spellcheck has a positive impact on spelling accuracy and might improve lexical diversity in essays written by students with dyslexia. *Journal of Writing Research, 12*(1), 35–61. https://doi.org/10.17239/jowr-2020.12.01.03

1
Teaching writing for academic and specific purposes

Helen Basturkmen

Introduction

In ESP, English has long been viewed as a set of language varieties or registers (Bloor & Bloor, 1986). Academic, workplace or professional communities are understood to use the language in distinctive ways, draw on different kinds of texts and engage in differing language-based events in their work or study pursuits. Over time, disciplines or a particular profession or occupation develop their own language conventions, forms of expression and practices which new members need to acquire rather than general English.

Many English as a Second Language (ESL) teachers currently work in teaching English for academic purposes (EAP) and English for specific purposes (ESP). This is particularly the case for ESL teachers at adult and tertiary levels. Globally, increasing numbers of tertiary education institutions provide courses in writing academic English, rather than general English writing skills. Private language schools are increasingly offering English for Specific Purposes type courses, such as English for Business, English for Banking and English for Hotel Managers, which often include a focus on writing for workplace or professional needs. This trend towards specific purposes English language instruction has led to a demand for ESL teachers with the requisite skills and knowledge base that can enable them to determine a specific purpose writing curriculum and develop ESP or EAP writing lessons and materials.

ESL teachers often transition from teaching general English to teaching EAP and ESP at a later stage in their careers (Bocanegra-Valle & Basturkmen, 2019), although some novice ESL teachers start their professional teaching careers within EAP and ESP. Those who transition from teaching general English to teaching EAP and ESP soon come to realise that they need to majorly revise their writing pedagogy to meet the new situation and the distinctive demands of the EAP or ESP setting. This transition often involves a shift away from focusing their teaching on the development of writing skills to focusing instruction on raising awareness of language knowledge—knowledge of the linguistic features of the written registers in academic, professional and workplace settings and of the written genres required in those settings. To develop their own and their learners' understanding of genres, EAP and ESP teachers consider the social purposes of the genres, that is, the goals they fulfil in the target environment and the typical communicative functions involved, as well as their typical linguistic patterning and organisation.

Specific purpose courses are provided because learners often have a clear workplace, professional or academic setting in mind and wish to develop their English with that setting as a target. They thus require targeted writing instruction and a carefully delineated program of study that will help them develop knowledge and competencies to produce the kinds of written texts and genres associated with study or work in those fields. To illustrate, a general academic writing course would target the academic written register (linguistic features of academic writing) and the kinds of genres that students typically produce in their tertiary level disciplinary study, such as *essays* and *assignment reports*. For a workplace/professional setting, a course such as English for Engineering would likely focus on the genres that the learners need to produce in their work, such as *feasibility reports* or *design specification* documents.

English for academic purposes courses can be categorised into two distinct strands - English for General Academic Purposes (EGAP) and English for Specific Academic Purposes (ESAP). In EGAP settings learners are typically students from a mix of disciplines in tertiary education or students who have not yet determined their majors or disciplines. Therefore, EGAP writing instruction targets the general academic English register and the genres that are understood to be common across disciplines. In ESAP settings, learners are typically from one discipline or disciplinary area, such as Health Sciences or Social Sciences, and writing instruction targets the genres that students are required to produce in their disciplinary study, such as *laboratory reports* (science students) or *case study reports* (students studying business or social work).

EAP and ESP are distinctive settings for teaching ESL writing. The learners have specific writing needs. In these settings, teachers need to be able to devise targeted writing curriculums and instruction that will help their learners develop an understanding of key features of the registers and genres that the learners are required or will be required to produce in their study areas, work settings or professional lives.

Literature

Identifying writing needs

Central to EAP and ESP writing instruction is the goal of targeting the specific needs of the group or class of learners in question. One of the first tasks of the teacher is to identify what the learners' needs are. There are various ways that teachers can investigate their leaners' needs. Possibilities include the use of questionnaires and interviews and examining writing samples from the target settings. To illustrate, a questionnaire can be devised to ask students, teachers/faculty teaching staff, workplace managers, employees and employers to list (and rank) the writing tasks (genres)of importance in their study, workplace or professional settings, and to specify which of these writing tasks typically present writing difficulties for novices.

It is important that the teacher/course developer bears in mind that asking respondents about needs can potentially be problematic. Respondents may lack language awareness or metalanguage to describe needs in any meaningful way. Pre-experienced EAP or ESP learners (those with limited or no experience of work or study in the target setting) cannot meaningfully be asked about writing needs in a situation in which they have limited or no direct experience (Basturkmen, 2010). A teacher preparing a writing course for prospective students of Health Sciences, for example, might interview graduate Health Science students or undergraduate students who are already in year-one or later years of study or faculty to inquire about the writing tasks students are required to produce and to comment on any writing difficulties they have perceived in students' writing. Graduate students (or other experienced students) may be willing to provide samples of the kinds of writing or assignments they completed in their disciplinary courses and faculty may have collected samples too that they are able (with student permission) to discuss. Faculty can provide the titles and specifications of the writing assignments they set on their papers so that the EAP writing teacher can get a clear picture of the kind of writing tasks (genres) that the students need to produce.

In some cases, the perspectives of what the needs are of the different stakeholders may have vary (Lin & Morrison, 2021) and perceptions may not reflect reality (Abouzeid, 2021). Lin and Morrison (2021) investigated the perspectives of teaching faculty and ESL postgraduate students of Engineering in Hong Kong about the academic writing challenges the students faced. Findings indicated the perspectives of the writing challenges varied between students and faculty. Whereas the students were mostly concerned with sentence level writing difficulties, faculty perceive the challenges at macro, discourse level of writing. Abouzeid (2021) interviewed instructors about their perceptions of students' academic writing challenges in an English Medium Instruction psychology programme in a Lebanese university. The perceptions data were compared to findings from an analysis of students' writing in disciplinary assignments. The comparison revealed that the instructors' perceptions aligned with students' writing performance on two out of the three perceived challenges they had identified in the interviews.

In planning a writing curriculum, EAP writing teachers consider which genres their learners need. Genre demands can vary by discipline. To illustrate, students in various disciplines may be required to essays and the teacher may target essays in the curriculum. However, there is considerable variation across a university in essay writing practices and what is expected (as an essay) in one discipline, such as history, may be very different from what is expected in another, such as sociology. To provide relevant instruction, EAP teachers needs to identify the essay writing practices in the discipline or disciplines their students are currently or will be studying to design course material that is relevant to their leaners' needs.

A study of assessed writing across over 30 disciplines in different universities in the UK (Nesi & Gardner, 2012) revealed the range of genres that students in years one to four were required to produce. The study collected a large corpus of samples of student writing, which the students contributed voluntarily to the research. The study identified 13 families of genre writing and made an analysis of how each genre family was typically structured rhetorically. The study also included interviews with university teaching staff and with students and examination of course descriptions and written assignment tasks from a range of disciplines to throw light on and the educational functions of the genres. The 13 genre families were *case study, design specification, critique, empathy writing, essay, exercise, explanation, literature survey, methodology recount, problem question, proposal and research report*.

As well as considering their learners' disciplines, EAP writing teachers also need to consider their learners' stage of study, that is, what genres the learners need in the different years of study. Nesi and Gardner (2012) found that *explanation* and *exercise* type assignments, which function as a means for students to develop and demonstrate their understanding, tended to be set in the initial years of disciplinary study. The EAP writing teacher would likely target in the writing curriculum the genres that their learners' most immediate needs.

In ESP courses for workplace, professional and commercial purposes there can sometimes be difficulties in gathering information on the genres and writing tasks and especially difficult to gather authentic samples of writing and observe writing practices. Workplaces and businesses may be reluctant to share information or samples of writing due to client confidentiality issues. If the teacher's ESP class members are already working in the business or commercial area, the teacher can draw on their knowledge of what written genres are typically used and the class members may (with permission) be able to provide some samples of writing. In this case, the ESP class members can provide details on the purposes of the genre and how they are produced and used, and the ESP teacher can provide additional insights based on his or her observations of language in the samples. If the learners have not yet entered the professional or workplace, they are much less likely to know about the genres and genre practices in them.

Studies of learners' needs in workplace and commercial settings are sometimes possible (Arias-Contreras & Moore, 2021). One recent study (Al Hilali & McKinley, 2021) investigated writing needs and practices on-site at five private sector companies in Oman where English was used as the official means of communications. The study participants included engineering college graduates working in the companies and their line managers. Amongst various findings, the study revealed that writing in those settings was often collaborative in nature.

Genre-based instruction

Genre-based writing instruction has generally become a major if not the major teaching approach in EAP and ESP. In this approach, instruction focuses on genres of relevance to learners' current or future needs, one genre at a time. In preparation for instruction, the EAP or ESP teacher needs to develop his or her own understanding of the genre's social context of use, how it is typically structured rhetorically (communicative moves and steps) and its salient linguistic features. The latter involves a focus on lexical and grammatical uses of language in the text. The importance of the latter stage has been highlighted in recent literature (Cheng, 2021).

Hyland (2018) describes genre-based writing instruction as often initially teacher-led and centred on analysis of model texts. Modelling, argues Hyland, is a visible pedagogy that enables students to see clearly what is to be learned and how it is to be assessed. Hyland identifies a typical instructional cycle of modelling, learners and the teacher co-constructing texts through joint negotiation and then learner independent text construction. This cycle includes a role for expert support (the teacher or more experienced/knowledgeable peer) to assist and support the learner (the learner or novice) until he or she has the knowledge and skills to create the genre independently. Cotos (2018) identified the characteristics of the instructional sequence typically used in genre-based instruction as follows – the learners or novices are explicitly introduced to the move and step structure of the targeted genre usually through the use of a model text, provided with authentic texts to identify the communicative moves and steps, are guided to explore languages use choices in those moves and steps and the functional meanings these convey, and are led to consider to the possible reasons for patterns and features.

Linguistic features of the academic written register

Teaching of EAP writing, especially in English for General Academic Purposes, often includes a focus on the linguistic features of the academic written register, that is, the lexical, grammatical and discourse features that are distinctive in academic written text regardless of genre. A considerable body of corpus linguistic inquiry has brought to light linguistic features that are more pervasive in academic writing than in other registers of English (Basturkmen, 2021). The inquiry has used corpus analysis techniques to identify key features that distinguish academic language use from English language use in other settings, such as everyday conversation or to compare academic writing with academic speaking (Biber, 2006; Biber & Grey, 2010; Liu & Myers, 2020) and findings can be used to provide to descriptions of the academic register for applications in teaching EAP writing. Many linguistic features appear to be characteristic of the written academic register including the high use of specialised vocabulary and technical terms, hiding personal opinions with third-person expressions (such as *it is interesting to note that)*, and hedging to show caution when making claims (such as *it would appear that)*. These kinds of linguistic features can be targeted in teaching writing. The teacher can draw attention to the linguistic forms and expressions and their functions during instruction and when correcting learners' writing.

Materials development

ESP and EAP teachers are often heavily involved and spend a good deal of time in developing in-house materials, including materials for writing lessons- see for example, reports of in-house materials in Bosher (2010) and Flowerdew (2010). Generally, ESP and EAP teachers cannot rely as much on published coursebooks as their counterparts in general ELT. Although some published course materials are available for certain highly popular domains, such as English for general academic purposes, publishers are often not keen to publish materials for limited specialist audiences (Basturkmen, 2021). Even if teaching a general academic English writing course, the teacher may wish to include some focus on the writing of the different disciplines represented by the learners in the class. Matheson and Basturkmen (2015) report a writing course design in which a focus on disciplinary genre practices was embedded within a teaching approach that was primarily focused on general academic writing content. The focus on disciplinary genre practices involved the teacher designing materials which engaged the learners in making observations of student writing from their disciplines. To prepare the course, the teacher had developed a text bank (corpus) of samples of student year-one disciplinary writing at the university.

Corpus-based tools

As illustrated in the Matheson and Basturkmen (2015), genre-based writing instruction and materials can be used in conjunction with corpus-based applications. A recent example of this is reported in Labrador and Ramón (2020), which describes a corpus-based text-generating tool to help ESL professionals working in business and international marketing in the Spanish dairy industry. In building the tool, a corpus of online product descriptions in English and Spanish was compiled and was tagged for move/step structure. The application included an inventory of linguistic expressions and an English-Spanish glossary of specialized vocabulary. Hocking (2021) reports a study of the *artist's statement* genre, a genre which provides a written description of an artist's creative work that can be used in exhibitions, funding applications and the artist's website. The study combined a genre-based analysis that identify the genre's move structure with a corpus-based analysis to identify associated lexical features. The findings were compared to the information found in 'how to write an artist's statement' websites, a comparison that highlighted the limitations of the website guide materials.

Corpus-based ESP/EAP teaching approaches are often discussed in relation to the concept of data-driven learning (Anthony, 2019; Karpenko-Secommbe, 2021). The corpus or corpora provide data to the learners that is used in instruction. Teaching activities guide learners to making observations and investigate the ways language is used in the texts that make up the corpus or corpora.

Practical implications for teacher education

Teachers new to ESP and EAP teaching, whether novice ESL teachers or experienced ESL teachers who are transitioning to teaching ESP and EAP, require information and know-how on how to develop effective specific purposes writing instruction. This section identifies three topics for teacher education in this area.

Firstly, as described above, knowing how to investigate learners' writing needs is critical for the development of carefully delineated ESP/EAP writing curriculum. There is little point in providing an EAP or ESP course if course content is not well matched to the actual needs (present or future) of the class or individual student in question. Most general works on ESP or EAP include a section on needs analysis and introduce techniques that can be used. See for example, Anthony (2018), which is listed in the Recommended Reading section below. Even if a needs analysis has previously conducted by another teacher for a past cohort of students, each group is unique. Needs vary and change over time. Having some practical know-how about how to develop a needs analysis strategy will stand the new ESP/EAP teacher in good stead for future eventualities.

Secondly, new ESP/EAP teachers need knowledge in the basics of how to do a genre analysis and how to develop a genre-based instructional approach. If learners need to write a type of report or document in their work or study setting (for which no ready description and materials are currently available), the teacher will need to make some attempt at demystifying this genre for their students. Information on genre analysis is included in most introductory works on EAP and ESP (see Recommended Reading list below) as well as works dedicated exclusively to this topic—see, for example, Samraj (2017) in the recommended reading section below.

New EAP teachers need to develop their understanding of the linguistic features of the academic written register. The teachers may be able to write academic English well (they may have good tacit knowledge of the register) but this does not mean that they have the kind of a meta-awareness of the register that will enable them to highlight the register's features, target relevant features in instruction and generally support their learners who are struggling to produce register-appropriate expression. See sections on corpus analysis and features of academic writing in Charles and Pecorari (2017) in the recommended reading section at the end of this chapter.

Suggestion for a case study

Information on teaching strategies and methods has generally come into the ESP and EAP literature by means of case study reports of practice, including innovative practice in a specific setting (Basturkmen, 2020). This is usually in the form of a report by a teacher or teachers who have developed a curriculum, materials or a new approach for their specific group of learners. A case study approach is, however, also a useful means also for a new ESP or EAP teacher to directly observe the practice of an experienced practitioner and learn from it.

The new teacher, who is about to teach (writing) to learners in a specific area, such as English for General Academic Purposes or English for Specific Academic Purposes (such as nursing or engineering studies), or in English for an industry sector (such as, the healthcare sector or engineering) may be able to locate another teacher who is currently already teaching in the area. If this is not possible, the new teacher might locate an EAP or ESP teacher teaching in any domain area. What is essential is that the teacher is willing to discuss his/her practice with the new teacher and allow the new teacher to observe his or her classroom practice and/or material designs. Graduate students, such as those on MTESOL programmes might also find the case study suggestion here of interest. The case study might be set as an investigative assignment and the student may be required to write a report of the case study findings. There are three parts to the case study, and according to interests, one, two or all three parts could be used.

The case study would provide a means by which a novice can gain a window onto one practitioner's practical approach to teaching ESP or EAP writing. As part of the case study, the new teacher (or postgraduate MTESOL student) engages the experienced ESP practitioner in a conversion that addresses topics relating to teaching writing, such as:

1. The place of writing in the overall EAP or ESP curriculum (how much of the curriculum is dedicated to writing and why?)

2. How the learners' writing needs were identified (was a formal or informal needs analysis conducted, what kind of information was collected and how, who was consulted?)
3. What writing needs were identified? (what do the learners need to know about the written register, what genres and writing tasks do/will the leaners need to produce, what writing challenges do they typically encounter?)
4. What is/are the aims of the writing curriculum?
5. What content does the writing curriculum include? (which written genres and linguistic features, are writing skills included?)
6. Did the teacher determine the aims and content or the writing curriculum (was this in the hands of the teacher or were they determined in accordance with school, departmental, workplace requirements?)
7. How would the teacher describe his or her approach to teaching writing (one approach or mixed, why this/these approaches?)
8. Does the teacher draw on published or ready writing materials (either to adopt or adapt them, has the teacher developed his or her own materials?)

In the second part of the case study, the new teacher (or postgraduate MTESOL student) makes observations of the experienced teacher's practices:

1. Observing writing instruction in the classroom (what teaching/learning activities are used, how are the activities introduced or set up, what techniques does the teacher use?)
2. Observing materials design - ask the teacher to select sample materials he/she has adapted or developed from scratch (what does the material targeted for instruction, why are the teaching/learning activities are as they are, what are the learners are expected to learn about writing from using them, how did the teacher go about developing or adapting the material?)

The practising ESP or EAP teachers can be invited to select samples which they felt had worked well in the classroom and one or two that had not worked well. It is possible to learn from observing successful as well as less successful examples (Basturkmen & Bocanegra-Valle, 2018).

The third part of the case study focuses on learning how to teach writing for specific purposes.

1. *Personal experiences* (how did you learn, did you have opportunities for teacher education or observing/working with a more experienced colleague, have you attended relevant conferences or read useful literature on the topic?)
2. *Advice* (what would be your top three suggestions for a teacher who is

about to start teaching writing for specific purposes for the first time?)

Some caveats are in order. Firstly, the case study suggested here is intended to have descriptive aims only. It aims to help the new teacher find out about teaching writing, the curriculum and materials design practices of an ESP or EAP practitioner and the practitioner's learning. It does not have an evaluative aim. Secondly, the novice would need to obtain any of the permissions and consents for the case study that are required in their context. It cannot be assumed that teacher practitioners are necessarily willing or able to share any details of their teaching or the case setting or learners with others. In the New Zealand university context, where I work, classroom observations, for example, require the informed consent of both the teacher and the students.

Further reading

Anthony, L. (2018). *Introducing English for specific purposes.* Routledge.

This is an up-to-date and general introduction to the field of ESP.

Charles, M., & Pecorari, D. (2016). *Introducing English for academic purposes.* Routledge.

The book provides a general introduction to EAP. It describes the types of linguistic inquiry on which EAP teaching draws.

Gollin-Kies, S., Hall, D. R., & Moore, S. H. (2015). *Language for specific purposes.* Palgrave Macmillan.

This work gives readers a broad overview of the main topics in ESP.

Hyland, K. & Wong, L.C. (Eds.) (2019), *Specialised English: New directions in ESP and EAP research and practice.* Routledge.

The volume includes chapters from different ESP and EAP researchers who describe individual studies that represent emerging research directions in ESP and EAP.

Samraj, B. (2017). *Introducing genre and English for specific purposes.* Routledge.

This work focuses on genre analysis in ESP. It introduces concepts and approaches to genre analysis as a form of research inquiry and as an approach to teaching writing.

References

Abouzeid, R. (2021). Aligning perceptions with reality: Lebanese EMI instructor perceptions of students' writing proficiency. *English for Specific Purposes, 63,* 45–58. https://doi.org/10.1016/j.esp.2021.03.001

Al Hilali, T. S. & McKinley, J (2021). Exploring the socio-contextual nature of workplace writing: Towards preparing learners for the complexities of English L2 writing in the workplace. *English for Specific Purposes, 63*, 86–97. https://doi.org/10.1016/j.esp.2021.03.003

Anthony, L. (2019). Tools and strategies for data-driven learning (DDL) in the EAP classroom. In K. Hyland & L. C. Wong (Eds.), *Specialised English: New directions in ESP and EAP research and practice* (pp. 179–94). Routledge.

Arias-Contreras, C., & Moore, P.J. (2022). The role of English language in the field of agriculture: A needs analysis. *English for Specific Purposes, 65*, 95–106. https://doi.org/10.1016/j.esp.2021.09.002

Basturkmen, H. (2021). *Linguistic description in English for academic purposes.* Routledge.

Basturkmen, H. (2010). *Developing courses in English for specific purposes.* Palgrave Macmillan.

Basturkmen, H., & Bocanegra-Valle, A. (2018). Materials design processes, beliefs and practices of experienced ESP teachers in university settings in Spain. In Y. Kirkgoz & K. Dikilitas (Eds.) *Key issues in English for specific purposes in higher education* (pp. 13–27). Springer.

Biber, D. (2006). *University language: A corpus-based study of spoken and written registers.* John Benjamins Publishing Company.

Biber, D. & Gray, B. (2010). Challenging stereotypes about academic writing: Complexity, elaboration and explicitness. *Journal of English for Academic Purposes, 9*, 2–20. https://doi.org/10.1016/j.jeap.2010.01.001

Bloor, M. & Bloor, T. (1986). *Languages for specific purposes: Practice and theory.* Trinity College Dublin.

Bocanegra-Valle, A. & Basturkmen, H. (2019). Investigating the teacher education needs of experienced ESP teachers in Spanish universities. *Ibérica, 38*, 127–151.

Bosher, S. (2010). English for nursing: Developing discipline-specific materials. In N. Harwood (Ed.), *English language teaching materials: Theory and practice* (pp. 346–394). Cambridge University Press.

Cheng, A. (2021). The place of language in the theoretical tenets, textbooks, and classroom practices in the ESP genre-based approach. *English for Specific Purposes, 64*, 26–36. https://doi.org/10.1016/j.esp.2021.07.001

Cotos, E. 2018. Move analysis. In C.A. Chapelle (Ed.) *Encylcopedia of applied linguistics.* John Wiley & Sons. https://doi.org/10.1002/9781405198431.wbeal1485

Flowerdew, L. (2010). Devising and implementing a business proposal module: Constraints and compromises. *English for Specific Purposes, 29*, 108–20. https://doi.org/10.1016/j.esp.2009.06.003

Hocking, D. (2021). Artist's statements, 'how to guides' and the conceptualisation of creative practice. *English for Specific Purposes, 62*, 103–116. https://doi.org/10.1016/j.esp.2020.12.006

Hyland, K. (2018). Genre and second language writing. In C. A. Chapelle (Ed.) *Encyclopedia of applied linguistics.* John Wiley & Sons. https://doi.org/10.1002/97811187844235.eelt0535

Karpenko-Seccombe, T. (2021). *Academic writing with corpora: A resource book for data-driven learning.* Routledge.

Labrador, B. & Ramón, N. (2020). Building a second-language writing aid for specific purposes: Promotional cheese descriptions. *English for Specific Purposes, 60,* 40–52. https://doi.org/10.1016/j.esp.2020.03.003

Lin, L.H.F. & Morrison, B. (2021). Challenges in academic writing: Perspectives of Engineering faculty and L2 postgraduate research students. *English for Specific Purposes, 63,* 59–70. https://doi.org/10.1016/j.esp.2021.03.004

Matheson, N., & Basturkmen, B. (2015). Developing a research-informed academic writing curriculum using a text bank of student writing. In P. N. Shrestha (Ed.), *Current developments in English for academic and specific purposes* (pp. 139–156). Garnet Education.

Nesi, H., & Gardner, S. (2012). *Genres across the disciplines: Student writing in higher education.* Cambridge University Press.

2
Integrating awareness of academic reading into teaching writing in an additional language

Mahmoud Altalouli
Mary Jane Curry

Introduction

Students using English as an additional language (EAL) who attend higher education institutions in English-speaking countries or who take English-medium instruction courses in other contexts often need to learn English academic literacy practices to be successful in higher education. As a key literacy practice, reading has received insufficient attention in discussions of teaching writing, despite the fact that reading for writing (RFW) can be a challenging practice for EAL writing (Grabe & Stoller, 2019). As reading plays a foundational role across academic disciplines and levels, in this chapter we explore the relationship between academic reading and writing. We concur with Kroll's (1993, p. 75) argument that "teaching writing without teaching reading is not teaching writing at all."

In RFW, students engage in a variety of complex reading and writing tasks including writing responses to readings and summarizing texts. In completing these tasks, students typically paraphrase information from a text or synthesize information from multiple texts. Here we adopt a broad definition of text, including not only print texts but also those produced through oral and multimodal modes. Many instructors, especially in higher education, may assume that EAL students arrive equipped to engage in academic reading in English, yet for several reasons students may struggle with academic reading. Both undergraduate and graduate students may be underprepared for the literacy demands of a new academic context because of linguistic and sociocultural differences between students' former and new educational institutions and contexts. These demands may include the purposes of reading (i.e., knowledge production versus knowledge consumption); the uses for academic vocabulary; the amount of reading required; and learning new academic genres (Curry et al., 2021). Additionally, expectations for academic reading are often implicit and can be difficult for instructors to articulate. Below we explain useful approaches to providing explicit RFW instruction that can support students in dealing with these differences (Altalouli, 2021).

In this chapter we first summarize the key theoretical foundations underpinning our discussion of the integration of academic reading into teaching writing, drawing from cognitive and social perspectives. Briefly, the cognitive perspective on reading views it as a decontextualized set of skills that can be acquired in one context and applied to tasks in another context (Hudson, 2007). In contrast, the social perspective argues that reading is embedded in and shaped by the social practices of particular academic contexts (Hirano, 2015). Then, we highlight key findings from literacy research to glean important take-aways about RFW practices instructors can draw on to improve student success, and how writers can develop reading practices to support their academic writing. We conclude by providing implications from the research literature and suggestions for action research that instructors could undertake to improve their teaching practice.

Theoretical framework: Cognitive and social perspectives on reading for writing

The cognitive view of reading primarily focuses on what happens in an individual's brain—cognition—while the social perspective broadens the scope to consider interactions among texts, their creators, and their readers as situated within specific contexts. In the cognitive perspective, reading is seen as a decontextualized set of skills that can be acquired in one context and applied to another. It assumes that readers employ bottom-up and top-down strategies to create meaning (e.g., Lee, 2015). In this view, these bottom-up strategies (e.g., parsing letters and words) and top-down strategies (e.g., using background knowledge to predict and evaluate information) can be applied across contexts (Hudson, 2007). The skilled use of these strategies is believed to be closely related to readers' language proficiency (Li, 2014).

In the social perspective, reading and writing are seen as practices that emerge from the social context of academic settings (Lea & Street, 2006). The social view highlights the reading-writing connection, providing an understanding of how readers are informed by their social and cultural experiences and use these experiences as they construct meaning from texts. Students typically read to achieve different purposes such as reading to write and reading to speak (Altalouli, 2021). In addition, students read discipline-specific genres, including textbooks, books, book chapters, and journal articles (Curry & Oh, 2011). Such texts are constructed for specific purposes by writers who belong to particular social groups (instructors, researchers, disciplines, global regions). Individual genres exhibit patterns of structure, language, and register that engage with how other writers have responded to recurring similar situations in previous texts (Hyland, 2008). Knowledge about a specific genre does not emerge from a reader's head but rather is learned by participating in the literacy practices of particular contexts. In sum, the purposes for which students read and the contexts in which they read influence how they read. In other words, reading is not only a cognitive process but also a socially situated literacy that is more or less effective based on specific situations.

Literature review: Academic reading for writing strategies

As university students are often expected to write based on what they have read, they can benefit from using reading-to-write strategies. Engaging with academic texts is a process of meaning-making in which readers use background knowledge to recreate the meaning of the text in interactions with the author(s). To do so, student writers deploy a number of RFW strategies to glean information to use in producing their texts.

Many academic RFW tasks include the practices of summarizing and synthesizing. Summary is commonly defined as a short version or synopsis of the main points of a text in which the writer does not include their perspective or use evaluative language (Curry et al., 2021); in synthesis, writers create a discussion that weaves together information on a topic from several sources (Grabe & Stoller, 2019). A synthesis often involves selecting from sources (by notetaking), making connections among sources (by identifying similarities and differences), and organizing sources (by making tables, matrices, and outlines). In both practices, writers paraphrase major points from source texts. EAL students with previous experience with RFW in English may feel comfortable with paraphrasing as they write summaries and syntheses, whereas students without previous knowledge of these practices may heavily quote source texts (Zhao & Hirvela, 2015) or resort to copying source text, resulting in plagiarism (Pecorari & Petrić, 2014).

To summarize and synthesize effectively and to avoid inappropriate quotation or plagiarism, EAL students can use several RFW strategies. Hirvela (2016, p. 36) identifies "mining" and "writerly reading" approaches to RFW: Mining involves "culling information" from a text to gain knowledge about a topic; in writerly reading, readers engage with texts with an eye to improving their writing, for example, through examining word and phrase use or text structure. Drawing on her study of EAL undergraduate and graduate students writing two argumentative essays, Plakans (2009) categorized five additional RFW strategies: 1) goal-setting for reading source texts (e.g., checking the task to integrate sources) to help writers understand how to fulfill the writing assignment; 2) cognitive processing (i.e., slowing down, re-reading); 3) global strategies (e.g., skimming, scanning, asking questions, recognizing text structure, summarizing main ideas); 4) metacognitive strategies (i.e., identifying what they don't understand, confirming understanding); and 5) mining source texts for information to use in writing (rereading the text, paraphrasing, checking for plagiarism). Plakans found that students use more cognitive RFW strategies (i.e., slowing down) and global strategies (i.e., summarizing main ideas) in pre-writing stages, whereas they use more metacognitive strategies (i.e., confirming understanding) and mining strategies (i.e., checking for plagiarism) while writing and revising.

Studies have shown that students with different amounts of experience tend to approach RFW assignments differently. Overall, more experienced students use more RFW strategies in the stages of pre-writing and drafting than do less experienced students, and students who use more RFW strategies generally perform better on reading-writing tasks (McCulloch, 2013; Zhao & Hirvela, 2015). These strategies lead to practical implications for teaching writing to EAL students, which we provide next.

Practical implications

The complexity of the reading for writing tasks involved in academic writing lies in both what writing entails and how students with varying experiences approach writing assignments. To support students' approaches to RFW tasks, instructors can explicitly highlight reading-writing practices in their course syllabi and integrate iterative activities in which students work with exemplary texts, engage in peer review, and/or analyze personal corpora using a software analysis tool.

Focusing on reading-writing practices on the syllabus

Many students have concerns about not knowing how to read lengthy assigned readings or complete source-based assignments (Singh, 2015). When presenting a syllabus at the start of the course, instructors can highlight the role of reading in course activities and requirements. For example, on the first day of the master's level course examined in Altalouli (2021), the instructor went over the major assignments explained on the syllabus and intentionally drew students' attention to academic reading-writing practices. She highlighted that the journal assignment required students "not merely [to] summarize the readings; [but to] use this journal as a critical synthesis task—what issues, topics, questions arise?" (p. 939). The instructor distinguished between a summary and a synthesis because, as an international student herself, she was aware that students do not always know the difference (see Zhao & Hirvela, 2015).

In addition, explicit instruction can increase students' understanding of requirements and help them to avoid plagiarism in their writing (Du, 2022). The syllabus can also include dedicated readings about RFW strategies that can be discussed in class and taught as scaffolding for particular assignments. For instance, the instructor in Altalouli (2021) showed students a slide labeled "academic reading" to explain the strategies of skimming and scanning as a way to cope with large quantities of reading assigned in their courses. Indeed, pedagogy for reading to write can help students understand the relationship between their literacy practices and the social context (Grabe & Stoller, 2019). To prepare students to write a literature review, for example, instructors can use activities on identifying research findings/results, recognizing text structure, paraphrasing, quoting, drawing on sources, and avoiding plagiarism.

Using exemplars and personal corpus

In this section we describe three RFW activities that can support students' academic writing: 1) reading and analyzing exemplary papers written by previous students, alongside an evaluation guide (Appendix A); 2) reading and analyzing another student's draft paper in peer review, using the evaluation guide in Appendix A; and 3) constructing and analyzing a personal corpus compiled from texts in students' disciplines via a digital tool (Bercuci & Chitez, 2019). Instructors may also weave in explicit teaching about discoursal and linguistic features before and during these activities.

Analyzing exemplary papers

The use of a range of exemplary papers by previous students (with their permission) can provide current students with a sense of what is expected. Exemplars from other students may feel more accessible to students than do professional samples (e.g., published abstracts or literature reviews). For the first time an instructor teaches a particular course, colleagues may have samples available. If the course involves literacy practices across disciplines, students from similar disciplinary backgrounds or topics of interest can work in groups to read and analyze an exemplar from a close discipline or related topic. For students to analyze the sample paper with a clear purpose, instructors should provide the specific evaluation tool that was used to assess the exemplars (e.g., a rubric or set of benchmarks) or they can create a rubric that evaluates components such as the organizational and linguistic features of the text. At a minimum, instructors can offer questions or prompts for students to use in analyzing the exemplar (as in Appendix A), related to features such as: citation style and format (e.g., from the American Psychological Association, the Association of Computing Machinery, or the American Institute of Physics); the rhetorical moves (Swales, 1990) made in different sections of the text (e.g., the hook or thesis statement in an introduction); and linguistic aspects such as verb tenses and transitions and other metadiscoursal markers (e.g., however, therefore). Instructors may also ask students to analyze an exemplar in terms of its content (e.g., ideas, importance of topic, background information, argument). Depending on the focus of the course, the accuracy or relevance of content may or may not be evaluated.

If students are working in groups, each group can present its analysis to the whole class. By using various RFW strategies such as taking notes, re-rereading, skimming, and recognizing text structure, students can increase their awareness of the task and their ability to produce writing that meets the established criteria.

Analyzing peer texts

Peer review is a common feature of writing courses designed to help students learn to provide and receive formative feedback and to negotiate meaning as they develop their texts. After learning how to do peer review and create a positive environment in which to provide feedback (see Eckstein, this volume; Yu & Lee, 2016), students can share a draft of their paper with partners. Each student reads their partner's paper or section and provides feedback based on specific assessment criteria (i.e., rubric) that may include content-related aspects (information included, argument, evidence) and linguistic features (lexical, grammatical, and mechanical issues). In addition to applying the rubric, each partner ideally provides formative comments on the text to enable the author to address specific comments as they revise. Peer review feedback can be provided on paper or using electronic texts and comments. If the instructor desires, students can submit the peer review draft with comments and rubric along with the final version. Through engaging in peer review, providers of feedback gain experience in evaluating others' writing, which can help them become aware of their own writing in terms of organization, cohesion, vocabulary, grammar, and citation practices (Cho & MacArthur, 2011; Greenberg, 2015).

Analyzing a personal corpus

Another useful activity for reading to write is analyzing a personal corpus, or a collection of texts on the student's topic that the student compiles from articles available in online databases. Students can enter keywords and phrases into database search boxes to find and choose their articles. A librarian can be invited to class to teach students how to search academic databases for credible sources including peer-reviewed research articles. The corpus serves as a personalized resource to help students gain content knowledge and analyze the conventions of academic writing in their discipline such as the use of reporting verbs, verb tenses, hedging and boosting words, frequently used words and phrases, and typical collocations. The corpus can comprise the number of required sources for a writing assignment and be kept in a folder on students' computers.

After downloading a particular digital tool for use with their personal corpus, students load and import their corpus data into the tool. Available free digital tools including LancsBox (Brezina et al., 2021) provide user guides. Instructors can choose among digital tools according to each tool's affordances and requirements (e.g., corpus size produced, computer specifications). By annotating and visualizing language data, these tools can help users analyze texts (Bercuci & Chitez, 2019). After completing a writing assignment, students can upload their text to compare how they used language with how authors of the published texts in their corpora draw on language and, if desired, revise their text according to the results of the analysis (see Doval & Nieto, 2019).

Presenting how reading is interwoven in the syllabus and incorporating text analysis activities as we have discussed here are instructional approaches that can help raise students' awareness of the crucial academic reading-writing connection. For support in explaining the role of reading in writing practices and teaching RFW activities, instructors may also invite into the classroom academic consultants such a librarian or a writing consultant to help teach these approaches.

Suggestions for action research

Action research studies can help instructors answer specific questions about their teaching practice (Bissonnette & Caprino, 2014). Before starting any study, instructors should identify relevant institutional research policies and procedures to ensure the ethical conduct of research (Nolen & Vander Putten, 2007). This section presents three action research projects that can be adapted according to the experience level of the instructor, the course, mode of teaching, class size, course objectives, evaluation measures, and students' backgrounds, goals, and needs. Each project can be used in relation to one of the RFW activities discussed in Practical Implications: sample papers, partner peer review, and personal corpora. For each project, we propose a research question, needed resources, and data collection and analysis methods.

Project 1. The effectiveness of exemplary papers

Research question

How effective is the analysis of exemplary papers in supporting students' RFW practices?

Resources and tools

Four to five exemplary papers; evaluation guide (Appendix A); laptop for each student; video camera if instructor wants to record group work

Data collection

In a class session that involves students in analyzing exemplary papers, instructors can divide students into groups of three or four. Each group receives an electronic version of an exemplar. Individually, each student analyzes the assigned exemplar using the evaluation guide (Appendix A) then shares the results with the group. Each group can then share specific gleanings with the whole class.

Before the activity begins, with student permission, the instructor can set up a video camera to record one or more group's interactions during the group sharing. The instructor can also organize and audio-record individual conferences to elicit information about the influence of the exemplar analysis on the student's understandings and possibly on specific written assignments.

Data analysis

As soon after the class meeting as possible, the instructor should watch the videotape of one group to take notes on how students draw on their reading practices and use the evaluation guide to analyze and discuss the exemplar text. These responses can be compared to the recordings of individual conferences to explore whether and how students' RFW practices align during and after the exemplar analysis. Instructors may also compare these findings to aspects of students' submitted assignments, depending on genre, time frame, and guidelines.

Project 2. The use of peer review

Research question

To what extent does peer review support students' RFW practices?

Resources and tools

Student paper drafts; Evaluation Guide (Appendix A); laptop for each student, audio recorders

Data collection

During a class that includes a peer feedback activity, students work in pairs based on their topics of interest or disciplines. Before the activity, the instructor can set up an audio-recorder near where one pair is working, with their permission. Peer review partners share their papers, then each student reads and analyzes their partner's paper using the evaluation guide. Each student then verbally shares their responses with their partner. If desired, students can write a reflection paper on the activity and include it with their submitted assignment.

Data analysis

As soon after class as possible, the instructor listens to the audio-recording to take notes on the areas that each partner shared. After assignments (and optional reflection) have been submitted, the instructor can compare students' comments made during the feedback activity and explore whether their discussion has resulted in changes in their writing.

Project 3. The use of LancsBox in analyzing personal corpora

Research question

How can the use of a corpus analysis tool and evaluation guide support teaching RFW?

Resources and tools

Personal corpora, Evaluation Guide (Appendix A); Corpus Analysis Matrix (Appendix B); laptop for each student; LancsBox

Data collection

During at least one class session after students have compiled a personal corpus of five or more published articles on their topic, depending on the assignment, students analyze their corpus in terms of organizational/rhetorical moves and content features using the evaluation guide (Appendix A). They then use LancsBox to analyze their corpus in terms of linguistic features (Appendix B). In LancsBox, they use the Key Words in Context (KWIC) feature (Brezina et al., 2021) to analyze word classes (e.g., adjectives), semantic categories (e.g., booster), and grammatical patterns (e.g., passive voice). The instructor collects written assignments and the results of students' analyses of the features in appendices A and B. After assignments have been submitted and graded, the instructor can invite one or more students to participate in an audio-recorded interview about their perceptions of whether and how their corpus analysis activity helped their writing.

Data analysis

After the submission of the written assignment, the instructor compares the organizational/rhetorical moves and language aspects in the assignment and the results of the students' analyses of the features in appendices A and B. The interview data may help the instructor understand students' perspectives and experiences with using the tools.

These three action research projects can be used to explore how students connect their academic reading and writing practices. The research questions and procedures for data collection and analysis can be adapted according to course variables and instructors' needs, interests, and available time.

Conclusion

This chapter has outlined the value we see in reading-for-writing instruction for EAL students. It provides in-class RFW activities that can be used and adapted by both new and experienced instructors. The suggested activities—analyzing sample papers, peer's papers, and personal corpora—aim to help instructors support students in developing their understanding of writing tasks and improving their writing. These activities may require the explicit teaching of RFW strategies such as recognizing text structure, taking notes, and re-reading. The outcomes of these activities will ideally help prepare both undergraduate and graduate students for the literacy demands of their academic and disciplinary contexts.

Further reading

Grabe, W., & Stoller, F. L. (2019). *Teaching and researching reading* (3rd ed.). Routledge.

This book comprises 10 chapters that present empirical studies on the effective reading practices of EAL students and teaching practices for this population. It offers action research ideas on reading-related topics including pre-, during-, and post-reading activities. In pre-reading, instructors start classes by using questions that tap into students' background knowledge and teach key vocabulary items. During reading, instructors aim to connect readings to students' experiences and lives and/or the texts they have read earlier. Post reading, instructors can ask questions about content, rhetorical strategies, and use of language.

Hirvela, A. (2016). *Connecting reading and writing in second language writing instruction* (2nd ed.). University of Michigan Press.

Hirvela explores several connections between reading and writing, including the principles of reading/writing connections; knowledge telling versus knowledge transforming; reading for writing/writing for reading; the integration of reading and writing along a continuum; and pedagogy related to reading/writing connections. This edition provides instructors with related theoretical foundations and approaches to teaching.

Morley, J. (2014). *Academic phrasebank.* University of Manchester. https://www.phrasebank.manchester.ac.uk/

This free online resource introduces phrases that are organized according to the main sections of a research paper or dissertation (i.e., introduction, related literature, methodology/methods, results, discussion, and conclusion) and more general functions of academic writing (e.g., being critical, defining terms, describing trends, giving supporting examples, and signaling transitions). It notes characteristics of academic style (e.g., using academic words, transforming verbs into nouns, avoiding contractions) and sentence structure (e.g., simple, compound, complex).

Swales, J. & Feak, C. B. (2012). *Academic writing for graduate students: Essential tasks and skills* (3rd ed.). University of Michigan Press.

This book explains many academic reading and writing topics, such as audience and genre. This edition explores the organizational and rhetorical moves of a research paper. It provides Language Focus sections with adaptable exercises on linguistic elements such as vocabulary, linking words and phrases, active and passive voice, and verb tenses.

The Writing Center. (2021). *Tips and tools*. University of North Carolina at Chapel Hill. https://writingcenter.unc.edu/tips-and-tools/

This website, like most of many other writing centers, provides free handouts on "Writing the Paper," "Citation, Style, and Sentence Level Concerns," "Specific Writing Assignments or Contexts," and "Writing for Specific Fields." The Additional Resources page offers strategies for effective reading such as annotating texts, understanding diagrams and graphs, taking notes, reading different genres, and skimming.

Acknowledgment

We would like to thank Dr. Mary Jane Curry's doctoral student advising group, First Friday Group, for their insightful and constructive suggestions.

References

Altalouli, M. (2021). Agency and accountability in the academic reading of international graduate students using English as an additional language. *Journal of International Students, 11*(4), 932–949.

Bercuci, L., & Chitez, M. (2019). A corpus analysis of argumentative structures in ESP writing. *International Online Journal of Education and Teaching, 6*(4), 733–747.

Bissonnette, J. D., & Caprino, K. (2014). A call to action research: Action research as an effective professional development model. *Mid-Atlantic Education Review, 2*(1), 12–22. https://doi.org/10.2478/jtes-2020-0008

Brezina, V., Weill-Tessier, P., & McEnery, A. (2021). #LancsBox v. 6.x. [software]. http://corpora.lancs.ac.uk/lancsbox

Cho, K., & MacArthur, C. (2011). Learning by reviewing. *Journal of Educational Psychology, 103*(1), 73–84. https://doi.org/10.1037/a0021950

Curry, M. J., He, F., Li, W., Zhang, T., Zuo, Y., Altalouli, M., & Ayesh, J. (2021). *An A-W of academic literacy: Key concepts and practices for graduate students*. University of Michigan Press.

Curry, M. J., & Oh, H. (2011). Teaching academic literacies: Raising genre awareness in a graduate school of education. In H. P. Widoyo & A. Cirocki (Eds.), *Innovation and creativity in ELT methodology* (pp. 108–122). Nova Science Publishers.

Doval, I., & Nieto, M. T. S. (Eds.). (2019). *Parallel corpora for contrastive and translation studies: New resources and applications*. John Benjamins.

Du, Y. (2022). Adopting critical-pragmatic pedagogy to address plagiarism in a Chinese context: An action research. *Journal of English for Academic Purposes, 57.* https://doi.org/10.1016/j.jeap.2022.101112

Eckstein, G. (2023). Feedback on student writing for early career teachers: Effective strategies for teacher, peer, and self-feedback. In H. Mohebbi & Y. Wang (Eds.), *Insights into teaching and learning writing: A practical guide for early-career teachers* (pp. 155–166). Castledown Publishers.

Grabe, W., & Stoller, F. L. (2019). *Teaching and researching reading* (3rd ed.). Routledge.

Greenberg, K. P. (2015). Rubric use in formative assessment: A detailed behavioral rubric helps students improve their scientific writing skills. *Teaching of Psychology, 42*(3), 211–217. https://doi.org/10.1177/0098628315587611

Hirano, E. (2015). "I read, I don't understand": Refugees coping with academic reading. *ELT Journal, 69*(2), 178–187. https://doi.org/10.1093/elt/ccu068

Hirvela, A. (2016). *Connecting reading and writing in second language writing instruction* (2nd ed.). University of Michigan Press.

Hudson, T. (2007). *Teaching second language reading.* Oxford University Press.

Hyland, K. (2008). Genre and academic writing in the disciplines. *Language Teaching: Surveys and Studies, 41*(4), 543–562. https://doi.org/10.1017/S0261444808005235

Kroll, B. (Ed.). (1993). *Reading in the composition classroom: Second language perspectives.* Cambridge University Press.

Lea, M. R., & Street, B.V. (2006). The "academic literacies" model: Theory and applications. *Theory Into Practice, 45*(4), 368–377. https://doi.org/10.1207/s15430421tip4504_11

Lee, J. Y. (2015). Language learner strategy by Chinese-speaking EFL readers when comprehending familiar and unfamiliar texts. *Reading in a Foreign Language, 27*(1), 71–95.

Li, L. (2014). Language proficiency, reading development, and learning context. *Frontiers: The Interdisciplinary Journal of Study Abroad, 24,* 73–92. https://doi.org/10.36366/frontiers.v24i1.337

McCulloch, S. (2013). Investigating the reading-to-write processes and source use of L2 postgraduate students in real-life academic tasks: An exploratory study. *Journal of English for Academic Purposes, 12*(2), 136–147. https://doi.org/10.1016/j.jeap.2012.11.009

Nolen, A. L., & Vander Putten, J. (2007). Action research in education: Addressing gaps in ethical principles and practices. *Educational Researcher, 36*(7), 401–407. https://doi.org/10.3102/0013189X07309629

Pecorari, D., & Petrić, B. (2014). Plagiarism in second-language writing. *Language Teaching, 47*(3), 269–302. https://doi.org/10.1017/S0261444814000056

Plakans, L. (2009). The role of reading strategies in integrated L2 writing tasks. *Journal of English for Academic Purposes, 8*(4), 252–266. https://

doi.org/10.1016/j.jeap.2009.05.001

Singh, M. K. M. (2015). A qualitative perspective of academic reading practices and overcoming strategies used among international graduate students in Malaysia. *Malaysian Journal of Languages and Linguistics*, *4*(1), 55–74.

Yu, S., & Lee, I. (2016). Peer feedback in second language writing (2005–2014). *Language Teaching*, *49*(4), 461–493. https://doi.org/10.1017/S0261444816000161

Zhao, R., & Hirvela, A. (2015). Undergraduate ESL students' engagement in academic reading and writing in learning to write a synthesis paper. *Reading in a Foreign Language*, *27*(2), 219–241.

Appendix A: Evaluation Guide

Student name:
Field/topic:

Organizational and Rhetorical Moves

1. Identify the sections of the paper and their order (e.g., headings).
2. Identify the length of each section (e.g., number of paragraphs/sentences/words).
3. Identify how the author begins each section.

Language Aspects

1. Identify the verb tenses used in the paper (e.g., present simple, past simple) and where they may change.
2. Identify examples of hedging and boosting words (e.g., modal verbs such as *may*, emphasis words such as *indeed*) and how they affect the strength of claims the author makes.
3. Identify key technical terms used in the paper and whether they are defined or explained sufficiently.

Content

1. What is the main idea(s)? Where is it presented in the text?
2. How does the author support their claims (e.g., with what types of evidence)?

Additional Comments:

Appendix B: Corpus Analysis Matrix

Student name:
Field/topic:

Search term	Frequency	Example	Source Text
Adjective			
Adverb			
Pronoun			
Booster			
Modal			
Linking adverb			
Time adverb			
Passive voice			
Present tense			
Past tense			
Contraction			
Phrasal verb			
Negation			
Superlative			
Comparative			

3
Complexity, accuracy, and fluency in writing

Lee McCallum
Niall Curry

The theoretical framework of CAF in L2 writing

The origins of CAF can be traced back to definitions and ideas of what it means to be proficient in a language (in this chapter we focus on second and foreign language writing proficiency). Generally, early-career teachers need to be aware of the range of definitions and ideas that have been expressed about proficiency, which is a complex concept in language education (see Leclercq & Edmonds, 2014 for an overview). Following Hulstijn (2011), we consider learners to have a degree of proficiency when they have some recognised ability to function in a particular *communicative situation* in a particular *modality* (emphasis ours). It is important to highlight, for teachers beginning their careers, that we envisage "a particular communicative situation" to be wide-ranging and thus, a degree of reflexivity is required to effectively unpack and understand learners' proficiency.

Getting to grips with how to evaluate the competence a learner might have in a given language or skill has led to the creation of many proficiency frameworks (e.g., The American Council on the Teaching of Foreign Languages (ACTFL, 2021); The Association of Language Testers in Europe (ALTE)'s "Can Do statements" (2021). Typically, such frameworks are cyclical in the sense that they also inform teaching materials, syllabi and wider curriculum designs, and there is an expectation that teachers will be able to place learners into proficiency levels or bands and that they can distinguish between learners who are more or less proficient than others. This therefore assumes another key tenet of (writing) proficiency: that it can be articulated and measured. One widely used set of pioneering criteria for articulating and measuring language proficiency is the Common European Framework of Reference (Council of Europe, 2018).

The CEFR has been at the heart of understanding how a learner might function in communicative situations and has been a source of inspiration and development for many local assessment frameworks (e.g., early career teachers may be interested in the fairly recent China English Standards (Jin, Wu, Alderson & Song, 2017), or the earlier Japanese implementation of the CEFR (e.g., see Negishi & Tono, 2014). The communicative situations in these frameworks are wide ranging and span all skills and levels of education.

For example, at university levels of education, communicative writing situations in the CEFR might include:

- Writing an argumentative essay.
- Responding to a friend or professor by email.
- Taking notes in a university lecture.
- Writing a summary of a research paper.
- Writing a research proposal.

These communicative situations also span different modalities and involve the use of different aspects of the language system (e.g., grammatical structures, vocabulary items).

The components of proficiency are often mapped onto a grading scale or rubric that teachers use to place learners in a particular level or band (Green, 2012). This scale is an ordered set of levels with a set of characteristics that describe each level. These grading scales are often influenced by the CEFR with assessment stakeholders adopting the CEFR levels for assessment and evaluation purposes (e.g., see Curry & Clark, 2020; McCallum, 2020).

We now turn to consider each of the CAF dimensions in terms of their definitions, manifestations, and operationalisations in some of the common grading scales and proficiency examinations to and of which we believe teachers will gain exposure and experience.

Complexity

The CAF dimensions have often been vaguely defined and operationalised across contexts and research studies (Housen, Kuiken & Vedder, 2012). For the sake of brevity, we capture the most prominent definitions and operationalisations in the sections that follow.

Complexity has been defined by several key scholars as at least one of the following:

- The ability to use an elaborate and varied range of sophisticated grammatical structures and vocabulary (Ellis & Barkhuizen, 2005; Housen et al., 2012).
- Cognitively demanding or challenging, taxing language which may or may not be acquired late by learners (Hulstijn, 1995; Skehan, 2009; Pallotti, 2009).

Complexity is said to possibly impact which linguistic features are acquired later in the language learning process. Early career teachers will see this complexity "in action" as they browse learning materials, with textbook contents and syllabi in general being organised according to some form of either linguistic complexity, cognitive complexity or a mixture of both. This organisation is underpinned by the premise that learners acquire the structures that are least taxing and/or least linguistically complex first. However, complexity is not the only guiding criterion in materials development and, as Hulstijn (1995) notes, these features may simply be introduced late because they are infrequent and not necessarily because they are cognitively demanding. Likewise, we may see complex features introduced early in the language learning process owing to their utility. Therefore, early career teachers need to bear in mind that the usefulness of the structure being practised and taught is also a primary consideration for teaching and assessment.

Complexity involves both grammatical structures and vocabulary items with researchers and assessment specialists interested in aspects of grammar such as clauses, phrases, and sentence types. They are also interested in lexical or vocabulary complexity with many researchers, assessment specialists and teachers themselves interested in presenting learners with lists of frequent or infrequent vocabulary items. These items are thought to be valuable for learning if the learners wish to be successful in a particular communicative situation (e.g., including completing sentences in an exercise, writing a story in class for peers to read, writing a piece of coursework at school, college, or university, or writing an extended project/dissertation).

Accuracy

Accuracy has most often been thought of as the simplest CAF dimension to define and pin down in practice. It has often been defined as "the ability to be free from errors while using language to communicate" (Wolfe-Quintero et al., 1998, p. 33). However, different theoretical and practical understandings of error and how it is evaluated exist. Housen et al. (2012) equate accuracy with correctness and in this respect, there are two central tenets of traditional understandings of accuracy. First, that accuracy is bound up in native speaker language use, and second, that accuracy is bound up in how much and in what ways a non-native speaker's language use varies from that native norm. Housen et al. (2012) follow a markedly different view of accuracy to the advice from the CEFR which is explicit in not judging language use produced by learners against language produced by native speakers. Instead, the CEFR judges language according to what a "successful user" produces.

It must be said here to early career teachers that although alignment with native speaker language use continues to persist in proficiency literature, there is a paradigm of thought and research that now challenges the notion of a norm in twenty-first century language use. This is especially prominent with English as it is used by more non-native speakers in the form of a lingua franca than being used by native speakers. This is a point we encourage early career teachers to reflect on and question in their contexts.

Fluency

In contrast to accuracy, fluency has often been difficult to pin down and articulate in writing. Fluency has been said to involve "the ease, eloquence, smoothness and native-likeness of speech or writing" (Housen et al., 2012). Fluency encapsulates easy access to linguistic knowledge (Wolfe-Quintero et al., 1998) and has been operationalised as "the number of words or structural units a writer is able to include in their writing within a particular period of time" (Wolfe-Quintero et al., 1998, p. 14).

We see a cross-over between the dimensions of accuracy and fluency here. Equally, operating under these definitions, early career teachers need to be aware that different learning contexts, institutions and individuals will place different degrees of importance on each of the CAF dimensions (Housen & Kuiken, 2009). At the same time, it is important that teachers recognise that CAF dimensions do not develop linearly or equally over a learner's learning journey (Larsen-Freeman, 2006). The dimensions are known to operate under an analogy of a game of snakes and ladders where learners can advance in one dimension but fall behind in another (Glaser, 1963). However, all three generally form part of views on how proficiency can be articulated, measured and brought to life in everyday language assessment practices.

We now move on in the next section to consider how CAF has been operationalised, contested, and refined across some of the key learning and assessment contexts in which we expect early career teachers to work in.

Literature review

In this brief literature review, we discuss CAF from the perspective of evaluative assessment models and then follow with a discussion on how CAF dimensions have been captured in empirical research studies.

How does CAF present itself in a common second/foreign language writing scale?

Many assessment stakeholders have drawn on CAF in designing proficiency grading scales. As mentioned in the first section, arguably the most prominent of these has been the CEFR. The CEFR determines learner language proficiency by evaluating learners' capacity to use language in a range of real-life communicative situations. Its proficiency levels/bands operate on A, B and C bands. A1/A2 are beginner levels, B1/B2 are intermediate and upper-intermediate levels and C1/C2 levels

CEFR Level	CEFR Can Do Statement Example
Pre-A1	Can provide basic personal information in writing (e.g., name, address, nationality), perhaps with the use of a dictionary.
A1	Can give information in writing about matters of personal relevance (e.g., likes and dislikes, family, pets) using simple words and basic expressions. Can write simple isolated phrases and sentences.
A2	Can write a series of simple phrases and sentences linked with simple connectors like 'and,' 'but' and 'because'.
B1	Can write straightforward connected texts on a range of familiar subjects within his/her field of interest, by linking a series of shorter discrete elements into a linear sequence.
B2	Can write clear, detailed texts on a variety of subjects related to his/her field of interest, synthesising, and evaluating information and arguments from a number of sources.
C1	Can write clear, well-structured texts of complex subjects, underlining the relevant salient issues, expanding, and supporting points of view at some length with subsidiary points, reasons, and relevant examples, and rounding off with an appropriate conclusion. Can employ the structure and conventions of a variety of written genres, varying the tone, style and register according to addressee, text type and theme.
C2	Can write clear, smoothly flowing, complex texts in an appropriate and effective style and a logical structure which helps the reader to find significant points.

Figure 3.1 *CEFR descriptors for overall written production (summarised from the Council of Europe, 2018)*

are the most proficient levels which are associated with highly successful writers (language users more broadly) and how effective their language control is; not benchmarking to native speaker language users.

In its original 2001 form, the CEFR was developed by asking assessment stakeholders for their views on how they would determine a language user's proficiency and distinguish it from the proficiency of another language user. The result was a set of "Can Do" statements which specified what language users were able to do with the language in particular communicative situations/simulated tasks. These "Can Do" statements have also been used in approaches to giving learners feedback on their work (e.g., see the pedagogic approach by Abatayo, 2020). Figure 3.1 summarises some of these "Can Do" statements in the revised CEFR (2018) framework for the skill of writing.

A close examination of how the CEFR has been used to inform examinations across Cambridge English Assessment exams highlights the role CAF dimensions play in guiding evaluators in their judgements. The

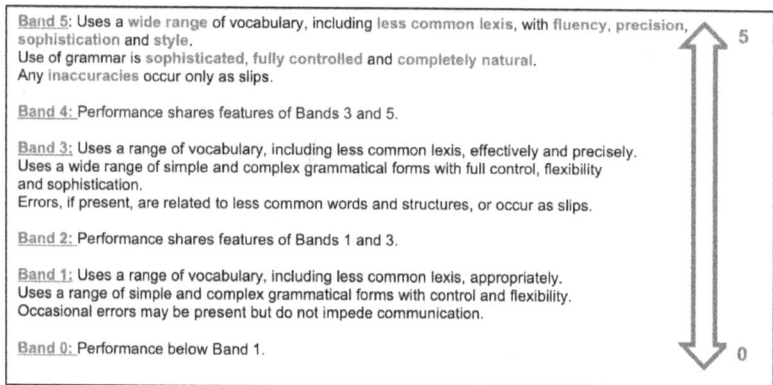

Figure 3.2 *Presence of CAF Dimensions and Sub-Dimensions in the CPE Language Component (based on the Cambridge CPE Handbook for Teachers, 2021, p. 26).*

prominence of these dimensions is perhaps best clear when looking at how the C2 Proficiency exam from Cambridge English Assessment has been presented (C2 Proficiency Handbook for Teachers, 2021). This exam is for candidates wishing to undertake high levels of academic study (e.g., postgraduate or Ph.D. level programmes) and/or lead businesses and take on management roles (C2 Proficiency Handbook for Teachers, 2021). Traditionally, candidates have been expected to produce multiple different genres (e.g., newspaper articles, proposals, reviews, and letters) and in doing so, it is expected they will show the characteristics in Figure 2 across different 0-5 score levels:

In commentaries that accompany sample answers, evaluators draw attention to phrases such as "stifling," "critically reviewed," and "leapfrog towards" as evidence which shows the candidate's range and level of style and sophistication (C2 Proficiency Handbook for Teachers, 2021, p. 31). The terms highlighted in Figure 3.2 (e.g., "wide range of vocabulary," "less common lexis," "fluency," "precision," "sophistication," and "style") are connected to the underpinnings of the CAF dimensions and are open to interpretation and debate. As such, it is worth bearing in mind their importance for teacher training in this regard. We emphasise here that these terms need orientation for teachers and a common understanding needs to be reached between assessors as to how these terms are articulated and ultimately operationalised in their context. At the same time, teachers have a responsibility to unpack these terms for learners who are preparing for internationally recognised language examinations. This is especially important, as learners need to know what is being expected of them in an examination that has the power to determine so much of their future.

The fact the CEFR was intended to be used across different European languages has meant that its underspecified nature left it open to criticism. Criticism focused on how the CEFR lacked specific reference and exemplification of language users' language in use (O'Keefe & Mark, 2017). This lack of authenticity led to substantial work being started by Cambridge University Press/Cambridge Assessment under the banner of "The English Profile" project and later continued by affiliated researchers (e.g., see Capel, 2010; Harrison & Baker, 2015; O'Keefe & Mark, 2017). This profiling project aimed to establish the language that became "criterial" or prominently used at particular CEFR bandscales in English. The project had clear goals towards language learning as it allowed teachers and assessors opportunities to understand what characterised language use at these levels and how this language might contribute to the judgements being made about language users' proficiency levels.

In an influential study, O'Keefe and Mark (2017) used the Cambridge Learner Corpus to examine the use of different grammatical features across the CEFR categories. The corpus contains over 55.5 million words in 266, 600 Cambridge English exams, taken by test takers speaking 143 different first languages. Among their main observations, they illustrate what a "Can Do" statement might look like for past perfect simple, as evidenced by actual language use in candidates' scripts. They determine that candidates at CEFR B1 (intermediate level) can:

- Use the affirmative form of the past perfect simple.
- Use the past perfect simple with a limited range of adverbs (e.g., including never, ever, just, always, already) in the normal mid-position.
- Use the past perfect simple to talk about a time before another time in the past.

The work in the English Profile project reminds us of the importance of transparency in understanding what lies behind the grade score that a learner is awarded. The work also serves as a reminder that there needs to be a cyclical relationship between grade banding, the language being used within these bands and CAF dimensions.

How has CAF been measured in empirical research which aims to understand the proficiency judgements evaluators make?

In the discussion above, many CAF dimensions and sub-dimensions have been illuminated. These include complexity and its sub-dimensions of range and sophistication, accuracy and fluency. A connected branch of research that early career teachers can use to engage with CAF dimensions further is statistical research that aims to understand the extent that these language dimensions have a relationship or association with the grade awarded. In this sense, the research aims to acknowledge the role of already established CAF dimensions but also uncover other sub-dimensions and aspects of language that may have a "hidden" association that is not currently captured in the assessment scales being used.

This work has been built around the notion that the frequency and type of language being used will have an association with how evaluators judge pieces of writing. In other words, this work is grounded in understanding what shapes a score linguistically and how the use of frequency and language type information can allow grading scales to become more illustrative and empirically informed. This work also plays a role in training automated grading and feedback systems which grade and give feedback on actual authentic writing samples.

In the sub-sections that follow we give a broad overview of how grammatical and lexical complexity, accuracy and fluency have been captured in research studies. In doing so, we draw readers' attention to key patterns and findings in this work but also remind them of the nuanced differences that have emerged in this work.

An overview of grammatical and lexical complexity

The most comprehensive overview of studies in second language writing studies has been the corpus linguistics informed systematic review by Durrant et al. (2021). Grammatical complexity has been split into an understanding of the range of grammatical or syntactical structures used and also a focus on their sophistication. Although range and sophistication have been operationalised in a wealth of ways, for the sake of economy and simplicity, early career teachers should essentially know that range and sophistication have been operationalised via large-grained and fine-grained measures. Large-grained measures have included units of analysis that operate at sentence level (e.g., number of sentences; number, length, and type of clauses (e.g., t-units, dependent clauses) and/or phrases) while fine-grained measures often operate at part of speech levels (e.g., number of adjective, adverb and verb phrases). Researchers have made inferences about how differences in these features across proficiency levels may play some role in evaluators' decision making.

The most pertinent results found in Durrant et al.'s (2021) review are shown in Figure 3.3. Figure 3.3 shows large-grained measures which operate at sentence and clause levels (e.g., a t-unit is a main clause and any dependent clause attached to it) while more fine-grained measures operate at different part-of-speech levels. Figure 3.3 highlights features with positive associations with writing proficiency scores across different contexts.

Amongst the strongest results for lexical complexity from Durrant et al. (2021) are that:

- Lexical diversity or range is overall positively correlated with writing quality scores across second language contexts.

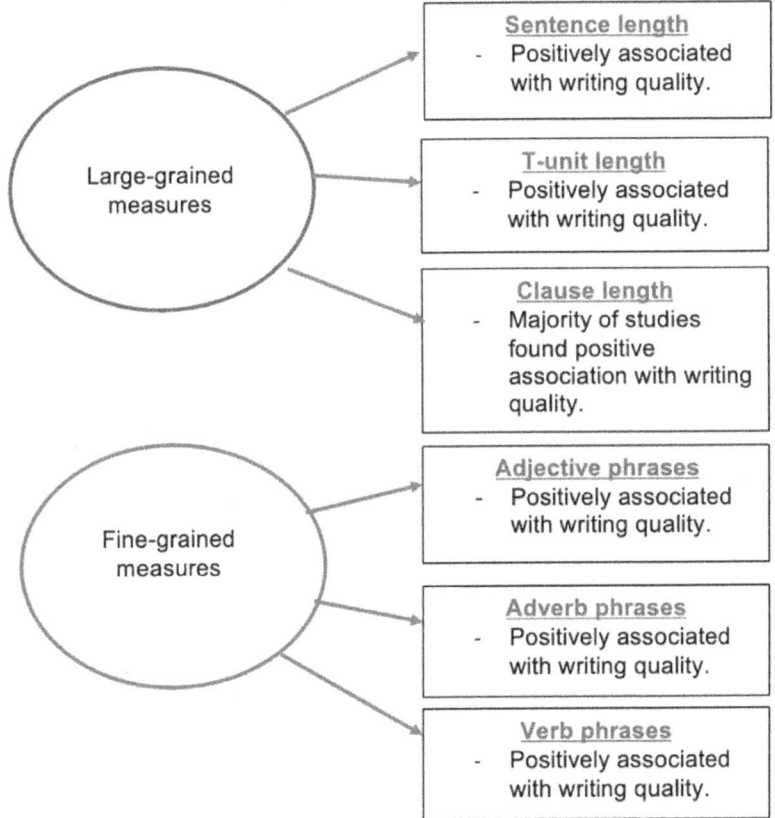

Figure 3.3 *Selected key grammatical complexity trends from L2 literature*

- Learners who use lower-frequency words tend to be perceived as more proficient, but this depends on genre and level of study.

Much like grammatical complexity, lexical complexity results have been equally varied and although some patterns appear to have some consistency, teachers are encouraged to interpret and use them cautiously with consideration for how these findings may or may not align with their own unique contexts.

An overview of accuracy and fluency

Both accuracy and, to a greater extent, fluency have been far less studied than complexity. Focusing first on accuracy, its less frequent study has meant that concrete robust inferences have been hard to pin down. However, some key trends from a scoping review of the literature are shown in Figure 3.4.

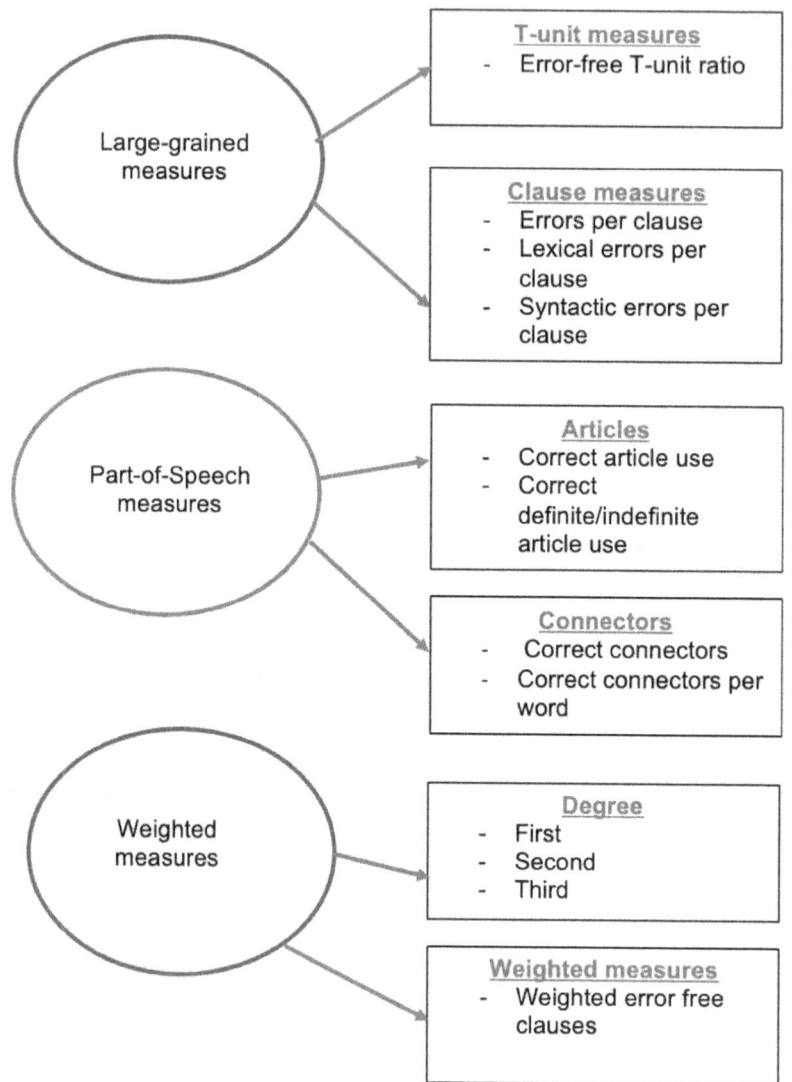

Figure 3.4 *Selected key accuracy measures from L2 literature*

As Figure 4 shows, studies have focused on different types of large-grained measures which use clauses as their starting point for counting accurate stretches of language. Other studies have focused on the accurate use of different parts of speech or looked at the severity of errors on communicating intended meaning. In the latter, first degree errors are judged as completely understandable, second-degree errors are judged to be understandable from context, and third degree errors are those judged

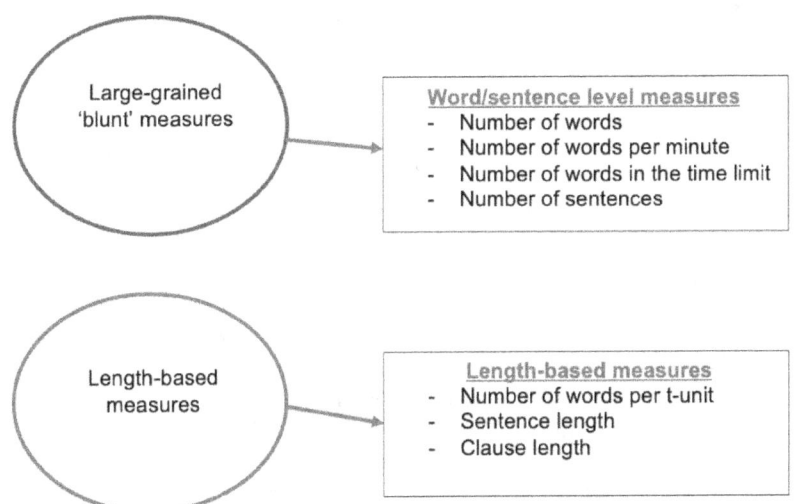

Figure 3.5 *Selected key fluency measures from L2 literature*

to interfere with comprehension (Wolfe-Quintero et al., 1998).

Studies using these measures have produced mixed results. These include that:

- The error-free t-unit ratio (the number of error free t-units divided by the number of t-units in total) has mixed statistical associations with writing quality grades.
- The correct use of articles and connectors have both had weak to non-significant associations with writing quality grades.
- The degree of error has moderately significant associations with writing quality grades.

Turning to fluency, some key trends from our scoping review are shown in Figure 3.5. Blunt text length focused measures have been shown to have mixed associations with writing quality grades as have the length-based measures.

From this overview, two important questions emerge:

- How should teachers use CAF dimensions to advise students on writing development? and
- How should teachers approach learning and assessment tasks which draw out CAF dimensions in student writing?

We address these questions in the next section.

Practical implications and suggestions

How should early career teachers use CAF knowledge to advise students on writing development?

To develop students' writing, teachers can reflect on the affordances of learner autonomy. Developing learner autonomy requires that we equip students with the capacity to understand and manage their own learning process (Najeeb, 2013). Guiding students to reflect on their learning process, to interrogate their engagement with CAF dimensions in their writing explicitly and to seek out ways to address gaps in their knowledge and writing competences will allow them to take ownership of their writing development. With this in mind, it will be of critical importance that, as teachers, we ensure our students understand exactly what the CAF dimensions mean for them.

For complexity, students can be encouraged to use tools such as Write & Improve (Cambridge English, 2021) which can give them space to use automated feedforward and feedback technologies to help them to produce more complex sentences and thus more complex texts (Curry & Riordan, 2021). Likewise, for accuracy, Write and Improve can also offer support in drawing attention to inaccurate patterns of language use. Finally, from a fluency perspective, we can encourage students to complete tasks with different expected word counts, with a view to starting with smaller word counts and building up the capacity to write more as they develop (e.g., Fellner & Apple, 2006). Tools with embedded writing tasks, like Write & Improve, facilitate this well; however, these targets could also be self-imposed by learners (e.g., see Datchuk et al., 2021). Irrespective of the approach we take to developing students' understandings of CAF dimensions, a foundational facet of this development is their autonomy for recognising weaknesses in their own writing and using resources available to them to address these.

How should early career teachers approach learning and assessment tasks which draw out CAF evidence in student writing?

From a learning and assessment perspective, teachers can facilitate CAF development in a number of ways. Recognising the critical role corpus linguistics has played in the recent development of complexity studies in the field, a data-driven learning approach is worth consideration. Data-driven learning is a language teaching approach that involves students directly engaging with corpora to investigate authentic language use (Johns, 1994). Bringing corpora into the classroom and guiding students to exploit them to search for patterns in new language being learned can support their acquisition of new features of written language.

Similarly, using corpus-informed feedback on writing, such as the BAWE Quicklinks project (Vincent & Nesi, 2021), can offer another

Figure 3.6 *CAF questions to promote action research*

means to give students direct access to corpora and means to develop their language complexity in a personalised manner. For accuracy, it is important that students understand how accuracy is determined. Therefore, a focus on assessment literacy whereby students are made aware of assessment rubrics and are encouraged to unpack and personalise their understanding of accuracy criteria will be of value. It is important to couple this with self-assessment tasks, in which students are encouraged to focus on and measure their own accuracy development and areas in need of attention. Finally, for fluency, creating free-writing tasks and incorporating timed or word count scaled writing tasks can be used to facilitate writing fluency development (Divya, 2019). However, it is important that students understand why they are being asked to write under time and length constraints, as this will help them to understand what skills they are developing when completing such tasks.

Questions to promote action research projects

We recommend teachers engage with the following questions in their contexts to promote action research projects which may alter or question their existing understandings of CAF dimensions. Figure 3.6 encourages teachers to consider institutional presentations of CAF as well as student CAF development.

Further reading

The five resources below will help guide teachers in their understanding of how CAF dimensions present themselves in assessments. The five resources encourage teachers to engage with social and contextual issues that might spring to mind as they engage with CAF dimensions in their contexts.

An essential starting point for early-career teachers is engagement with the interactive and comprehensive guide on "How language assessment works" by the British Council. https://www.britishcouncil.org/exam/aptis/research/assessment-literacy

The resource includes a glossary of assessment terms and guidance on assessing writing. The resource is particularly useful for early career L2 writing teachers who want to develop rigorous, clear and engaging assessment tasks for their students. The resource is particularly important because it helps teachers put into practice some of the key constructs of good writing assessment such as reliability and validity.

The next four resources originate as Cambridge Research Notes. These notes allow teachers a glimpse into the background, evolution and continuation of the CEFR and its applications to Cambridge English Assessment's suite of exams. We recommend notes 5, 6, 33 and 49.

The first two notes are important resources for different reasons. Hawkey's (2001) offering considers whether or not we can assume a common understanding of what good writing is and whether or not such a common scale across contexts is feasible. We believe these thoughts continue to be important for early career and experienced L2 writing teachers because the issue of nuance and commonality is an important one across different L2 writing contexts.

Hawkey, R. (2001). Towards a common scale to describe L2 writing performance (pp. 9-13). *Cambridge Research Notes, 5.* https://www.cambridgeenglish.org/Images/22644-research-notes-5.pdf

Shaw's (2001) offering in the next Research Note refers back to the common scale Hawkey (2001) deals with but also illuminates the issue of rater variation and the fact that individual raters seem to value or downgrade different features of writing when judging responses. Although raised more than two decades ago, our work in CAF in this chapter reiterates that these issues are still pertinent to teachers now in their early and continuous training.

Shaw, S.D. (2001). Issues in the assessment of second language writing (pp. 2-6). *Cambridge Research Notes, 6.* https://www.cambridgeenglish.org/Images/23117-research-notes-06.pdf

The last two research notes contain many individual contributions within each issue that are worth reading:

Barker, F., Kurteš, S., Sylvester, K., McKenna, S., & Lewis, C. (2008) (Eds.), *Cambridge Research Notes, 33.* https://www.cambridgeenglish.org/Images/23152-research-notes-33.pdf

Khalifa, H., & Barker, F. (2012) (Eds.), *Cambridge Research Notes, 49.* https://www.cambridgeenglish.org/Images/23166-research-notes-49.pdf

Barker et al. (2008) present work falling under the umbrella of the English Profile. This work focuses on the issue of criterial features and how these features appear or are indicative of certain proficiency ratings. The readings in this Research Note provide important background understanding to the work later carried out by scholars such as O'Keefe and Mark (2017). The readings also represent key reference points for teachers concerning what types of linguistic features might play a role in shaping understandings of particular CEFR proficiency levels.

Later, Khalifa, and Barker (2012) present their editorial which includes entries on writing scale validation and the management of raters in Cambridge English exam settings. Of note in these entries is again the issue of validation, rigour, and the trade-off between the individual nature of writing that takes place across different contexts and the fact that "good" writing seems to share a number of commonalities despite these contextual nuances.

Taken together, these five recommended readings serve as a reminder that early career L2 writing teachers are faced with working within these tensions and realities.

References

Abatayo, J.A. (2020). Enhancing assessment literacy through feedback and feedforward: A reflective practice in an EFL classroom. In S. Hidri (Ed.), *Perspectives on language assessment literacy* (pp. 69–83). Routledge.

Cambridge English (2021). *Write and Improve*. https://writeandimprove.com/

Cambridge Assessment English (2021). Cambridge Proficiency in English (CPE) Teachers' Handbook https://www.cambridgeenglish.org/Images/168194-c2-proficiency-teachers-handbook.pdf

Capel, A. (2010). A1–B2 vocabulary: Insights and issues arising from the English Profile Wordlists project. *English Profile Journal, 1*, E3. https://doi.org/10.1017/S2041536210000048

Curry, N., & Clark, T. (2020). Spelling errors in the preliminary English B1 exam: Corpus-informed evaluation of examination criteria for MENA contexts. In L. McCallum., & C. Coombe (Eds.), *The assessment of L2 written English across the MENA region* (pp. 359–392). Palgrave Macmillan.

Curry, N., & Riordan, E. (2021). Intelligent CALL systems for writing development: Investigating the use of Write & Improve for developing written language and writing skills. In K. Kelch., P. Byun., S. Safavi., & S. Cervantes (Eds.), *CALL theory applications for online TESOL education* (pp. 252–273). IGI Global.

Datchuk, S. M., Rodgers, D. B., Wagner, K., Hier, B. O., & Moore, C. T. (2021). Effects of writing interventions on the level and trend of total words written: A meta-analysis. *Exceptional Children, 88*(2), 145–162. https://doi.org/10.1177/00144029211027537

Divya, J. (2019). "Free writing" versus "writing fluency." *Journal of Asia TEFL, 16*(1), 369–376.

Durrant, P., Brenchley, M., & McCallum, L. (2021). *Understanding development and proficiency in writing: Quantitative corpus linguistics approaches*. Cambridge University Press. https://doi.org/10.1017/9781108770101

Ellis, R., & Barkhuizen, G. (2005). *Analyzing learner language*. Oxford University Press.

Fellner, T., & Apple, M. (2006). Developing writing fluency and lexical complexity with blogs. *THE JALT CALL Journal, 2*(1), 15-26. https://doi.org/10.29140/jaltcall.v2n1.19

Glaser, R. (1963). Instructional technology and the measurement of learning outcomes: Some questions. *American Psychologist, 18*(8), 519–521.

Green, A. (2012). *Exploring language assessment and testing: Language in action*. Routledge.

Harrison, J., & Barker, F. (Eds.). (2015). *English profile in practice* (Vol. 5). Cambridge University Press.

Housen, A., & Kuiken, F. (2009). Complexity, accuracy and fluency in second language acquisition. *Applied Linguistics, 30*(4), 461–473.

Housen, A., Kuiken, F., & Vedder, I. (2012). Complexity, accuracy and fluency: Definitions, measurement and research, In A. Housen., F. Kuiken., & I. Vedder (Eds,). *Dimensions of L2 performance and proficiency: Complexity, accuracy and fluency in Second Language Acquisition.* (pp. 1–20). John Benjamins Publishing Company.

Hulstijn, J. H. (1995). Not all grammar rules are equal: Giving grammar instruction its proper place in foreign language teaching. In R. Schmidt (Ed.), *Attention and awareness in foreign language learning* (pp. 359–386). Second Language Teaching & Curriculum Center, University of Hawaii at Manoa.

Hulstijn, J. H. (2011). Language proficiency in native and non-native speakers: An agenda for research and suggestions for second language assessment. *Language Assessment Quarterly, 8,* 229–249.

Jin, Y., Wu, Z., Alderson, C., & Song, W. (2017). Developing the China Standards of English: Challenges at macropolitical and micropolitical levels. *Language Testing in Asia, 7,*1, https://doi.org/10.1186/s40468-017-0032-5

Johns, T. F. (1994). From printout to handout: Grammar and vocabulary teaching in the context of data-driven learning. In T. Odlin (Ed.), *Perspectives on pedagogical grammar* (pp. 293–313). Cambridge University Press.

Larsen-Freeman, D. (2006). The emergence of complexity, fluency, and accuracy in the oral and written production of five Chinese learners of English. *Applied Linguistics, 27*(4), 590–619.

Leclercq, P., & Edmonds, A. (2014). How to assess L2 proficiency? An overview of proficiency assessment research. In P. Leclercq., A. Edmonds., & H. Hilton (Eds.), *Measuring L2 proficiency: Perspectives from second language acquisition* (pp. 9–34). Multilingual Matters.

McCallum, L. (2020). Relationships between measures of phraseological complexity and writing quality in a CEFR assessment context. *The Arab Journal of Applied Linguistics, 5*(1), 63–99.

Najeeb, S. S. (2013). Learner autonomy in language learning. *Procedia-Social and Behavioral Sciences, 70,* 1238–1242.

Negishi, M., & Tono, Y. (2014). An update on the CEFR-J project and its impact on English language education in Japan. ALTE.

O'Keefe, A., & Mark, G. (2017). The English Grammar Profile of learner competence: Methodology and key findings. *International Journal of Corpus Linguistics, 22*(4), 457–489.

Pallotti, G. (2009). Complexity, accuracy, and fluency: Defining, refining and differentiating constructs. *Applied Linguistics, 30*(4), 590–601.

Skehan, P. (2009). Modelling second language performance: Integrating complexity, accuracy, fluency and lexis. *Applied Linguistics, 30*(4), 510–532.

The Association of Language Testers in Europe (ALTE). ALTE Can Do statements. https://www.alte.org/resources/Documents/All%20Can%20Do%20English.pdf

The American Council on the Teaching of Foreign Languages (ACTFL) (2021). https://www.actfl.org/

The Council of Europe (2018). The Common European Framework of Reference for languages: learning, teaching and assessment. Companion volume with new descriptors. http://www.coe.int/lang-cefr

Vincent, B., & Nesi, H. (2021). Exploiting corpora to provide guidance for academic writing: the BAWE Quicklinks project. In M. Charles, & A. Frankenberg-Garcia (Eds.), *Corpora in ESP/EAP writing instruction: Preparation, exploitation, analysis* (pp. 13–30). Routledge.

Wolfe-Quintero, K., Inagaki, S., & Kim, H.Y. (1998). *Second language development in writing: Measures of fluency, accuracy and complexity*. University of Hawaii Press.

4
Writing teachers' pedagogical knowledge and assessment literacy

Deborah Crusan
Ali Panahi
Hassan Mohebbi

Introduction and theoretical framework

The topics of assessment literacy and the formation of a pedagogical knowledge base for L2 writing teachers have been gaining considerable research-based and practice-driven prominence and influence over the course of decades. Due to the substantial significance of teachers' application and implementation of assessment knowledge to assessing their students' writing (Coombe & Davidson, 2022; Crusan, 2022; Coombe, Vafadar, & Mohebbi, 2020), the focus has been on training and raising the awareness of second language writing teachers regarding assessment practices, purposes, and valuing and retaining teacher cognition of their beliefs, practices, and pedagogical and assessment knowledge base.

In the past, teachers appeared unfamiliar with the notion of reflection on their beliefs, values, knowledge base, and assessment literacy. Freeman (2002) reminds us that the 1970s was the decade of dramatic changes in which teachers began realizing their own and their students' writing processes, which in turn affected their pedagogical knowledge and practices; these changes have dominated whole facets of language education. Accordingly, researchers (e.g., Ball, Thames, & Phelps, 2008; Dorothy, 2019) define pedagogical content knowledge as knowledge of content, knowledge of students' needs, and knowledge of teaching. As they point out, language teachers' assessment literacy is an integral part of language teachers' competence. This knowledge should be a part of second language teachers' personal and professional frameworks of pedagogical knowledge, assessment literacy, and their beliefs and values. Scholars (Crusan, Plakans, & Gebril, 2016; Karimi & Norouzi, 2017; Scarino,

2013; Taylor, 2009, 2013) agree that teachers' and practitioners' knowledge base should contain components such as knowledge of language assessment and assessment paradigms, language pedagogy, sociocultural values, local practices, technical concepts, contents, skills and practices, personal purposes and individual attitudes, scores and decision-making, judgements, context-based-validations, and theories of language learning and language teaching. These components demonstrate that assessment is inseparable from learning and teaching. Teachers armed with this realization have drifted from more product-oriented activities and test-driven curricula for second language writing and instead have substituted a more product and process-oriented practice.

Gipps (1994) cited a main paradigm shift in the field of language education moving from quantification/testing to qualification/assessment. Testing leads to a single score-based report offering little data about second language learners' achievements and improvement while assessment supports the teaching and learning process and decision making. Shepard (2000) indicates some divisions in the move from behaviorist to a more cognitive social-constructivist model; the divisions are between psychometric testing settings (e.g., high stake-tests and a testing culture) and contemporary language learning contexts associated with Vygotskian theories (e.g., learning/assessment cultures). The growing impact of sociocultural theories of learning on assessment practices in second language education requires teacher-assessors to develop and expand the range, level, and quality of their knowledge base (Scarino, 2013). Motivated by the language assessment paradigm, socio-cultural perspectives, and their support of learning and teaching (Gipps, 1994, 1999), the field of second language education has begun recognizing the importance of teacher's assessment knowledge and skills and their application of assessment to the domain of learning and teaching to boost student achievement. Teachers' language assessment literacy, then, has been brought to the forefront.

Scarino (2013) maintains that teachers' language assessment literacy (LAL) has gained momentum following sociocultural perspectives. Classroom potential, classroom practice, teaching and learning activities, and students' achievement are all supported by teachers' LAL. At this time, however, no global or standard definition exists for the concept of assessment literacy (AL) although numerous definitions have been advanced. Stiggins (1999) points out that assessment literate teachers use assessment to contribute value and enhance learning. LAL can refer to the knowledge, skills, and principles needed by stakeholders in order to carry out effective assessment practices (Inbar-Lourie, 2017). Taylor (2009) stresses that assessment literacy training is crucially needed, and

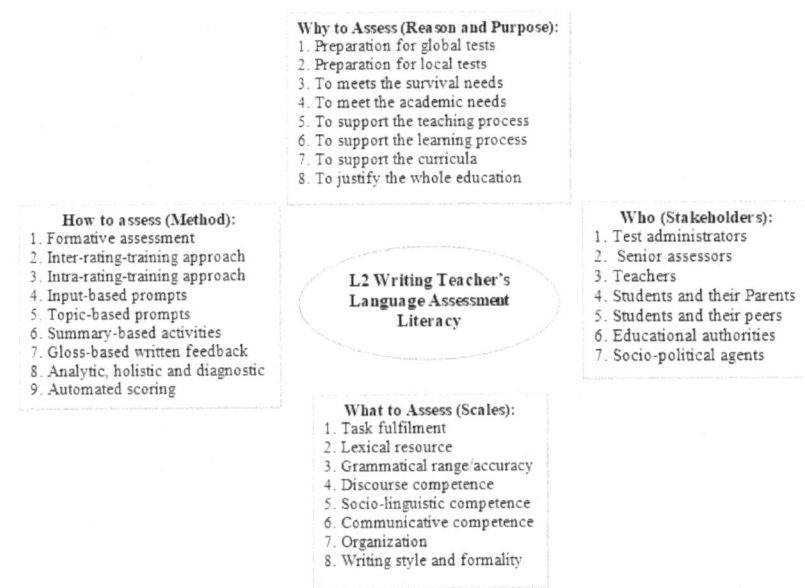

Figure 4.1 *Specific assessment literacy components for L2 writing teachers*

the field of language education has recognized, finally, the dearth of and the necessity for assessment training for prospective and practicing language teachers (Coombe, Vafadar, & Mohebbi, 2020; Crusan & Ruecker, 2022; Levi & Inbar-Lourie, 2019) listing theoretical knowledge, technical know-how, practical skills, understanding literacy level principles and contextual variables as important competencies.

Teachers need to understand general principles, practices, and concepts from a range of assessment paradigms to develop, use, and analyze global assessment techniques and locally apply them to the context in which they assess their learners' writing. Brown and Bailey (2008) suggest inclusion of information in second language writing assessment courses such as the purposes for assessment, norm-referenced and criterion-referenced measurement, washback, and practical skills including item writing, test revision, test analysis, and test scoring. Other important context-relevant assessment competencies include classroom assessment tool development, test administration, writing assessment and scoring, using test results to support teaching decisions, defining and describing proficiency (as a core unit), reporting results to numerous stakeholders (e.g. teachers, students, parents), the social context of assessment and testing (as a core unit), the relationship between assessment and curricula, and putting assessment into practice (Brindley, 2001; Gebril, Boraie, & Arrigoni, 2018; Inbar-Lourie, 2008; Scarino, 2013). Taken together,

Gippsian and Vygotskian frameworks can shed light on the way second language writing assessment supports students' achievement and improves the teaching and learning process.

In support of training of teachers in general assessment literacy components, principles, concepts, and practices, Figure 4.1 outlines what we view as specific and necessary components of L2 writing assessment literacy of both early career and more experienced teachers.

The inclusion of formative assessment in the list of specific components in Figure 4.1 indicates the methods of writing assessment, the performance descriptors of writing assessment (i.e., content of the writing), the stakeholders, and the logic behind writing assessment. Since we believe that implementation and knowledge of assessment for learning are critical L2 writing teacher responsibilities, we have included formative assessment serving as an umbrella term affecting all specific components. The figure, supported by formative assessment, is potentially backed up by scholars (Black & William, 1998; Gipps,1999; Poehner, 2010) who stressed that dynamic assessment contributes to both formative (assessment for learning) and summative assessment (assessment of learning), forming or shaping the outcome and process of learning and valuing both the product and process of learning. Therefore, we have included formative assessment of writing as a component of assessment literacy in teaching and assessing L2 writing, on which more focus must be placed, as it concentrates on the process of writing activities.

Other components of Figure 4.1 are equally important. When the teachers understand the principles and practices associated with interrating and intra-rating methods for L2 writing correction and feedback, this integrates both the summative and formative aspects of L2 writing development and assessment. The logic for the inclusion of input-based prompt is two-fold; on the one hand, ready-made writing input for analysis and awareness-raising of and modelling the upcoming writing assignment from the perspectives of assessment literacy and teachers' pedagogical knowledge base are crucial, specifically at much lower levels. On the other hand, when the prompt is presented, the conduct of prompt analysis, mind-mapping concerns, consideration of various paragraphs, instruction, and assessment should be viewed from the perspectives of the tripartite cycle of assessment, teaching, and learning.

The What to Assess portion of Figure 4.1 includes International English Language Testing System (IELTS) writing-related performance descriptors as an example. The competencies including communicative, socio-linguistic and discourse competence all should be regarded. In light of the mentioned paradigm shift adding more to the assessment literacy of second language writing teachers, a move from a single score-based report to a more assessment-based and process-triggered decision making is what should be expected on IELTS. Therefore, when teachers teach IELTS preparation courses, at various levels of teaching writing, they can apply quality-based knowledge to their assessment-based practice. All other specific components in Figure 4.1 are left to the interpretation and investigation of the reader.

Review of the literature

Investigation into L2 writing teachers' language assessment literacy (Coombe, Vafadar, & Mohebbi, 2020), critical language assessment literacy (Tajeddin, Khatib, & Mahdavi, 2022) and the effectiveness of pedagogical knowledge are scholastically and practically justified by what McNamara (2003) calls a paradigm war which accounts for the professional repertoire of the teachers and vividly illustrates the tension between alternative assessment (i.e., sociocultural view learning) and traditional assessment and psychometric testing (i.e.. cognitive view of learning). The move from cognitive to socio-cultural perspectives and practical implementation arising from socio-cultural views is important; it can be a starting point for appreciating the intellectual framework of a rich body of research on language assessment and language assessment literacy including ways in which language teachers develop, design, evaluate, implement, and exploit assessment in the context of language skills and subskills (Jiang, 2017; Vogt, Tsagari, & Spanoudis, 2020). We review here language assessment literacy training, assessment-related textbooks and topics, writing and assessment literacy, writing and formative assessment, and teacher's perceptions of assessment literacy.

Research conducted in the context of language assessment literacy training has indicated the effectiveness of training assessment to the teachers. Işik and Sari (2021) investigated the pre-service education background of 180 English Language teachers (ELTs) employing a mixed-methods research design through a questionnaire and follow-up interviews. Findings indicated that pre-service education background has a dramatic impact on teachers' assessment literacy. Worden (2019) examined the development of teachers' pedagogical knowledge looking at the effect of a project designed to boost L2 writing teachers' pedagogical content knowledge of genre. Data were collected from various drafts of each teacher's project, obtaining feedback from their trainers and peers, from their written reflections, and from their interviews; results revealed that in spite of challenges, teachers improved and developed their pedagogical and specialized knowledge.

Studies regarding the topics for training in language assessment literacy and the usefulness of language assessment-related textbooks revealed miscellaneous outcomes. Jeong (2013) used a mixed-methods approach and explored the topics in language assessment courses (LACs) in various countries. 140 LAC teachers participated in the survey; all 140 teachers preferred the same five topics: classroom assessment, alternative assessment, test specifications, test theory, and rubric development. Jeong

(2013) also indicated that present available textbooks concerning language assessment courses were considered challenging, unhelpful, and not user-friendly to teacher candidates. For example, one of the teachers commented that at first every new textbook excited her, but when she glanced at the content, she swiftly closed the book, quickly realizing that the book was aimed at large-scale assessment and are not directly related to classroom language teachers' needs. Overall, teachers reported that textbooks covered more test-oriented topics such as test specifications, ethics, and standardized assessment than on necessary classroom assessment topics. Along the same line, Brown and Bailey (2008) point out that the language assessment textbooks should represent a collection of theoretical aspects of testing and practical skills (i.e., a focus on test-construction skills). Further, Vogt and Tsagari (2014) discovered that undergraduate programs generally do not help teachers master fundamental concepts of assessment and practical skills. Even though we recognize the need for training, if it exists at all, that training is incomplete at best, at least in classroom assessment knowledge.

Vogt, Tsagari, and Csépes (2020) examined 1788 learners of English in Cyprus, Germany, Greece and Hungary about their experiences of assessment. They also investigated teachers' writing assessment literacy using questionnaire data from their 658 teachers. In general, both teachers and learners reported various areas and skills to be assessed in the EFL classroom with writing. Surprisingly, teachers and students preferred traditional approaches with more focus on discrete-point tests and extended writing and translation, as they saw these assessment methods as supportive of their learning. In a mixed-methods study, Burner (2015) examined formative assessment; respondents included four teachers and 100 students in a Norwegian English as a foreign language (EFL) writing class. The findings yielded contradictory results regarding teachers' and students' practices and perceptions of formative assessment of writing. As Burner recommends, contradictions uncover the need for raising teachers' and learners' consciousness regarding formative assessment to render it more efficient and helpful.

DeLucaa and Klingerb (2010) considered the standards-based movement in education and found that there is an urgent need for teachers' competency when assessing students. Administering a questionnaire to 228 teacher candidates, they investigated one pre-service teacher education program in Ontario, Canada; the study tackled teachers' assessment theory, practice, and philosophy; the student teachers' views towards assessment topics in a pre-service course were also explored. Overall, findings recommend the instruction of assessment-literacy-based topics such as creating a philosophy of assessment, modifying assessments, reporting achievement, item reliability, validity, and developing constructed-response items.

Another important issue concerns teachers' perception of language assessment literacy and their practice with it. Lam (2019) used a questionnaire, telephone interviews, and classroom observations and qualitatively examined perspectives of teacher assessment literacy from teachers' perspectives; findings revealed that some respondents had positive conceptions of alternative writing assessments; despite this, observation data showed that respondents possessed only a partial perception of the differentiation between assessment of learning and assessment for learning.

Practical implications and suggestions for early-career teachers

Assessment literacy is critically important for English language teachers. All stakeholders and all issues relevant to language assessment should be taken into account so that teachers fully comprehend and appropriately practice integrated elements affecting the cycle of teaching, learning, and assessment. Gebril, Boraie, and Arrigoni (2018) recommend assessment literacy for all teachers, trainers, teacher candidates, and novice teachers; they claim that assessment should be considered as an integral part of teacher education and teacher training courses. Others (Crusan, 2010, 2015; Weigle, 2007) support this claim. Therefore, language assessment should be a separate course for pre-service language teachers both practically and theoretically minus a one-size-fits-all approach to teaching assessment. Although many teachers and teacher candidates might believe that assessment is not their domain, the acquisition of assessment literacy in pre-service teacher training programs is vital. Even more important is changing the attitude of teachers who believe that assessment is something best left to others. To remedy that situation, teacher training courses should be established in any program training L2 writing (or any other modality) teachers with a focus on classroom assessment needs of students. One important part of that training should be that teachers develop an assessment philosophy undergirding their assessment theory and practice (Crusan & Ruecker, 2022).

It is crucial to remember that assessment and curriculum are intertwined (Crusan, 2010; Crusan & Ruecker, 2022). Because many teachers are not well-equipped with required pedagogical knowledge and assessment literacy, they might move forward in their practice without any clear perception of the realities and complexities of classroom assessment and decision making. With training, they might adopt a student-centered pedagogy which can shape interactions in the classroom, facilitating the learning process through assessment.

Conclusion

L2 writing assessment issues such as test specifications, test blueprints, rubrics, and design related to inter-rating and intra-rating are all more technical and therefore seem to be uniquely the province of language testers. However, language teachers need also to be assessment literate in order for them to be more effectively prepared to effectively and ethically assess the writing their students produce. Programs worldwide need to stress the importance of teacher writing assessment literacy, for it is assessment that will guide their philosophies, their pedagogies, and their responses to their students.

Further reading

Lee, J., & Butler, Y.G. (2020). Reconceptualizing language assessment literacy: Where are language learners. *TESOL Quarterly, 54 (4)*, 1085–1098. https://doi.org/10.1002/tesq.576

The article reports that the learner-centered approach in language teaching is one of the major paradigm-shifts in the past century. Therefore, it deals with the wide ranges of assessments implemented to collect information about learners and to facilitate their constructive learning. The authors argue that it is critical to incorporate the perspectives of learners in our understanding of language assessment literacy.

Maclellan, E. (2008). Pedagogical literacy: What it means and what it allows. *Teaching and Teacher Education, 24*(8), 1986–1992. https://doi.org/doi:10.1016/j.tate.2008.05.009

This article argues that pedagogical literacy is an important cognitive tool for understanding pedagogical content knowledge and pedagogical literacy, being an integral feature of a professional teacher. Therefore, reading and writing about pedagogical content knowledge is the essential means through which the teacher's pedagogical reasoning burgeons.

Akbari, R., & Dadvand, B. (2014). Pedagogical knowledge base: A conceptual framework for teacher admission. *System, 42*(2), 12–22. https://doi.org/10.1016/j.system.2013.11.001

The present study aims at reducing a part of the existing gap in the application of research findings on teacher cognition to L2 teacher selection/recruitment. Also, it elaborates on a significant degree of construct under-representation and construct irrelevance implicit in the exams, as many of them fail to assess relevant aspects of the pedagogical knowledge base of EFL teachers.

DeLuca, C., LaPointe-McEwan, D., & Luhanga, U. (2016) Approaches to classroom assessment inventory: A new instrument to support teacher assessment literacy. *Educational Assessment,*

21(4), 248-266. https://doi.org/doi:10.1080/10627197.2016.1236677
The article argues that according to recent research, current assessment literacy instruments do not fully reflect current transformations in the assessment landscape. Therefore, the article constructs a reliable instrument through construct validation and reliability testing with more than 400 teachers. The results of this article can support teacher assessment literacy.

References

Ball, D. L., Thames, M. H., & Phelps, G. (2008). Content knowledge for teaching: What makes it special? *Journal of Teacher Education, 59*, 389–407. https://doi.org/10.1177/0022487108324554

Black, P., & Wiliam, D. (1998). Assessment and classroom learning. *Assessment in Education: Principles, Policy & Practice*, 5(1), 7–74. http://dx.doi.org/ 10.1080/0969595980050102

Brindley, G. (2001). Language assessment and professional development. In C. Elder, A. Brown, K. Hill, N. Iwashita, T. Lumley, T. McNamara, & K. O'Loughlin (Eds.), Experimenting with uncertainty: Essays in honour of Alan Davies (pp. 126–136). Cambridge University Press.

Brown, J. D., & Bailey, K. M. (2008). Language testing courses: What are they in 2007? *Language Testing, 25*, 349–383. http://dx.doi.org/10.1177/0265532208090157

Burner, T. (2015). Formative assessment of writing in English as a foreign language, *Scandinavian Journal of Educational Research*, 1–23. https://doi.org/10.1080/00313831.2015.1066430

Coombe, C., & Davidson, P. (2022). Language assessment literacy 61. In Mohebbi, H., & Coombe, C. (Eds.), *Research Questions in Language Education and Applied Linguistics* (pp. 343–348). Springer.

Coombe, C., Vafadar, H., & Mohebbi, H. (2020). Language assessment literacy: What do we need to learn, unlearn, and relearn? *Language Testing in Asia, 10*(1), 1–16. https://doi.org/10.1186/s40468- 020-00101-6

Crusan, D. (2010). *Assessment in the second language writing classroom*. University of Michigan Press.

Crusan, D. (2015). Dance, ten; looks, three: Why rubrics matter. *Assessing Writing,26*,1–4. https://doi.org/10.1016/j.asw.2015.08.002

Crusan, D. (2022). Writing Assessment Literacy 77. In Mohebbi, H., & Coombe, C. (Eds.), *Research Questions in Language Education and Applied Linguistics: A reference Guide* (pp. 431–435). Springer.

Crusan, D., Plakans, L., & Gebril, A. (2016). Writing assessment literacy: Surveying second language teachers' knowledge, beliefs, and practices. *Assessing Writing, 28*, 43-56. https://doi.org/10.1016/j.asw.2016.03.001

Crusan, D., & Ruecker, T. (2022). *Linking assignments to assessments: A guide for teachers*. University of Michigan Press.

DeLucaa, C., & Klingerb, D. A. (2010). Assessment literacy development: identifying gaps in teacher candidates' learning. *Assessment in Education: Principles, Policy & Practice, 17(4)*. https://doi.org/10.1080/0969594X.2010.516643

Dorothy, W. (2019). Developing L2 writing teachers' pedagogical content knowledge of genre through the unfamiliar genre project. *Journal of Second Language Writing, 46*(3), https://doi.org/10.1016/j.jslw.2019.100667

Freeman, D. (2002). The hidden side of the work: teacher knowledge and learning to teach. *Language Teaching, 35*(1), 1e13. https://doi.org/10.1017/S0261444801001720

Gebril, A., Boraie, D., & Arrigoni, E. (2018). Assessment Literacy. In J., Liontas (Ed.) *The TESOL Encyclopedia of English Language Teaching*. (pp. 1–7). Wiley-Blackwell. https://doi.org/10.1002/9781118784235.eelt0342

Gipps, C. (1994). *Beyond testing: Towards a theory of educational assessment*. London: Falmer Press.Gipps, C. V. (1999). Sociocultural aspects of assessment. *Review of Research in Education, 24*, 355–392. https://doi.org/10.2307/1167274

Inbar-Lourie, O. (2008). Constructing a language assessment knowledge base: A focus on language assessment courses. *Language Testing, 25*(3), 385–402. https://doi.org/10.1177/0265532208090158

Inbar-Lourie, O. (2017). *Language assessment literacy*. In E. Shohamy, I. G. Or, & S. May (Eds.), *Language Testing and Assessment* (3rd ed.) (pp. 257–270). Springer.

Işik, A., & Sari, R. (2021). Are English language teachers assessment literate? *Çukurova Üniversitesi Eğitim Fakültesi Dergisi, 50*(2), 907–928. https://doi.org/10.14812/cufej.877706

Jeong, H. (2013). Defining assessment literacy: Is it different for language testers and non language testers? *Language Testing, 30*(3), 345–362. https://doi.org/10.1177/0265532213480334

Jiang, J. (2017). Language assessment: Critical issues—an interview with Antony John Kunnan. *Language Assessment Quarterly, 14(1)*, 75–88. http://dx.doi.org/10.1080/15434303.2016.1269770

Karimi, M.N., & Norouzi, M. (2017). Scaffolding teacher cognition: Changes in novice L2 teachers' pedagogical knowledge base through expert mentoring initiatives. *System, 65*(1), 38–48. https://doi.org/10.1016/j.system.2016.12.015

Lam, R. (2019). Teacher assessment literacy: Surveying knowledge, conceptions and practices of classroom-based writing assessment in Hong Kong. *System, 81(2)*, 78–89. https://doi.org/10.1016/j.system.2019.01.006

Levi, T., & Inbar-Lourie, O. (2019). Assessment literacy or language assessment literacy: Learning from the teachers. *Language Assessment Quarterly, 17*(2), 168–182. http://dx.doi.org/10.1080/15434303.2019.1692347

McNamara, T. (2003). Tearing us apart again. The paradigm war and the search for validity. *EUROSLA Yearbook, 3*, 229–238. https://doi.org/10.1075/eurosla.3.13mcn

Poehner, M. E. (2010). *Dynamic assessment: A Vygotskian approach to understanding and promoting L2 development.* Springer

Scarino, A. (2013). Language assessment literacy as self-awareness: Understanding the role of interpretation in assessment and in teacher learning. *Language Testing 30*(3), 309–327. https://doi.org/10.1177/0265532213480128

Shepard, L. A. (2000). The role of assessment in a learning culture. *Educational Researcher, 29*(7), 4–14. http://doi.org/10.3102/0013189X029007004

Stiggins, R. J. (1999). Assessment, student confidence, and school success. *Phi Delta Kappan, 81*(3), 191–198. https://doi.org/20439619

Tajeddin, Z., Khatib, M., & Mahdavi, M. (2022). Critical language assessment literacy of EFL teachers: Scale construction and validation. *Language Testing,* https://doi.org/10.1177/02655322211057040

Taylor, L. (2009). Developing assessment literacy. *Annual Review of Applied Linguistics, 29*, 21–36. https://doi.org/10.1017/S0267190509090035

Taylor, L. (2013). Communicating the theory, practice and principles of language testing to test stakeholders: Some reflections. *Language Testing, 30*(3), 403–412. https://doi.org/10.1177/0265532213480338

Vogt, K., & Tsagari, D. (2014). Assessment literacy of foreign language teachers: Findings of a European study. *Language Assessment Quarterly, 11*(4), 374–402. https://doi.org/10.1080/15434303.2014.960046

Vogt, K., Tsagari, D., & Spanoudis, G. (2020). What do teachers think they want? A comparative study of in-service language teachers' beliefs on LAL training needs. *Language Assessment Quarterly, 17*(4), 386–409. https://doi.org/10.1080/15434303.2020.1781128

Vogt, K., Tsagari, D., & Csépes, I. (2020). Linking learners' perspectives on language assessment practices to teachers' assessment literacy enhancement (TALE): Insights from four European countries. *Language Assessment Quarterly, 17*(4), 410–433. https://doi.org/10.1080/15434303.2020.1776714

Weigle, S. C. (2007). Teaching writing teachers about assessment. *Journal of Second Language Writing, 16*, 194–209. https://doi.org/10.1016/j.jslw.2007.07.004

Worden, D. (2019). Developing L2 writing teachers' pedagogical content knowledge of genre through the unfamiliar genre project. *Journal of Second Language Writing, 46*(2). https://doi.org/10.1016/j.jslw.2019.100667

5
Testing issues in writing

Chengyuan Yu

Introduction

The relationship between learning and assessment has been a heatedly discussed topic in the field of English language education in general and language testing and assessment in specific in recent years. Various terms have been proposed to refer to the practices denoting different relationships between the two concepts, including assessment of learning (AoL), assessment for learning (AfL), and assessment as learning (AaL). AoL usually takes the form of traditional testing that mainly serves "reporting and administrative purposes" (Lee, 2017, p. 10). AfL highlights using alternative assessment types, for example, teacher-mediated classroom assessment, peer assessment, and self-assessment, to improve learning and teaching (Black et al., 2004). AaL or learning-oriented assessment further extends AfL and incorporates assessment as part of learning (Dann, 2002). In practice, the juxtaposition of AoL, AfL and AaL and specific assessment types (e.g., traditional standardized testing and classroom assessment) may have led to a misunderstanding of standardized tests (*Testing* is distinguished from *assessment* regarding the degree of *standardization*, with testing being more standardized, cf. American Educational Research Association (AERA), American Psychological Association (APA), & National Council on Measurement in Education (NCME), 2014). Many practicing teachers, both experienced and early-career, think it difficult, if not impossible, to use standardized tests (*standardized* is used to highlight the standardized characteristic of testing) to enhance learning, and often overlook that certain components of standardized tests can be of important pedagogical value, including sample questions and responses, scoring rubrics (Baker et al., 2020), and the provision of criterion-referenced interpretation (Jones & Saville, 2016). This is especially true for the testing of productive skills, that is, writing and speaking, of which test takers' performance should be elicited through tasks and evaluated with rubrics. Of the two productive skills, the learning-oriented assessment of writing has attracted more scholarly attention in recent years, as evidenced by volumes dedicated to this topic (e.g., Lee, 2017). This is not unexpected as writing is important for both language learning and academic study in general. For second language (L2) learners, writing not only constitutes a worthwhile enterprise itself, but also facilitates the learning of grammar, vocabulary, and speaking (Weigle, 2002). For students at different stages of education (primary, secondary, and tertiary), the learning of content knowledge can be achieved and demonstrated through writing (Graham et al., 2013). Therefore, this chapter intends to draw on Carless's (2015) model of learning-oriented assessment and Jones and Saville's (2016) systemic approach to learning-oriented assessment to provide practical guidance for early-career and practicing teachers on the use of standardized writing tests for learning-oriented purposes.

Literature review

The standardized testing (used interchangeably with testing in the present paper) of writing has roughly undergone three historical periods: (1) pre-scientific direct essay tests, (2) psychometric-structuralist indirect tests, and (3) integrative-sociolinguistic direct writing tests (Cumming, 2009; Hamp-Lyons, 2001). The testing of writing has a long history of direct testing, which requires test takers to write essays that are assessed according to a pre-designed scoring guide emphasizing the mechanical errors and linguistic correctness (Shaw & Weir, 2007). According to Elliot (2005), direct essay tests started as early as the early twentieth century. During World War I, however, under the influence of psychometric-structuralist theories, multiple-choice indirect testing of writing was widely used to assign a substantial number of soldiers to different jobs. Compared with direct testing in the first period, multiple-choice formats made scoring easier and more economical. The indirect testing occupied the second period until writing scholars began to highlight writing as a process in the 1960s and 1970s (Crusan, 2014). Such a theoretical understanding of writing impacted the testing of writing, which experienced a come-back of the use of authentic tasks. The use of rubrics was introduced by the Educational Testing Service (ETS) which developed a holistic-scoring five-point rubric. Different from the direct testing in the first period, the third period displaced the single focus on linguistic correctness and delved into the overall quality of writing.

Nowadays, prompt-based writing tasks using a scoring rubric to evaluate actual writing are still widely adopted by influential international English language tests, for example, the International English Language Testing System (IELTS), the Test of English as a Foreign Language (TOEFL), and the Pearson English Test (PET). The holistic scoring rubric, by which only one single score is collected (Harsch & Martin, 2013), has now been replaced by more fine-grained analytical scoring rubrics, which evaluate the writing performance in multiple dimensions and elicit several scores for different performance criteria (Barkaoui, 2010). While it has been found that a holistic scoring rubric may lead to higher inter-rater reliability (e.g., Barkaoui, 2011), raters can still have different understandings of the criteria, which poses threats to validity (Weigle, 2002). In comparison, analytic methods can limit rating criteria to relevant constructs, making it operational to calibrate rater training as well as to generate diagnostic feedback to students on several aspects of writing quality (e.g., East, 2009; Knoch, 2009). Given the abovementioned strengths, analytic scoring rubrics have been adopted by IELTS, TOEFL, and many other international standardized writing tests. For example, the second writing task of the IELTS academic test not only focuses on the three linguistic dimensions in the scoring rubric (i.e., coherence and cohesion, lexical resource, and grammatical range and accuracy), but also highlights the social dimension of writing through the sub-scale of task response that evaluates writers' own position. In addition to the scoring rubric and sample test papers, testing companies also provide sample essays with a verified score from experienced raters, which can facilitate stakeholders' understanding of the scoring criteria.

Despite the efforts from testing companies, many classroom teachers still feel hesitant to learn about standardized writing tests due to the purportedly intimidating use of advanced statistics in testing (Weigle, 2007). Paradoxically, classroom teachers often need to prepare their students for standardized writing tests. The failure to understand the scoring of standardized writing tests and their relevance to writing skills prescribed in the curriculum negatively influences the effectiveness of teaching (Weigle, 2007). Therefore, it is necessary to integrate the knowledge of standardized writing tests into English language teacher education. In addition, using standardized writing tests also has the potential to benefit classroom teaching, as "[t]he processes of working towards well-designed summative assessment can also afford opportunities for formative assessment strategies, such as peer feedback, student self-evaluation and related teacher feedback" (Carless, 2015, p. 964). Specifically, the rubrics, scoring criteria, criterion-referenced interpretation, and exemplar responses can improve students' evaluative expertise (Baker et al., 2020; Crusan, 2021; Carless, 2015; Jones & Saville, 2016; Liu & Yu, 2022; Yu & Liu, 2021) that is crucial for students to monitor, evaluate, and improve their learning (Sadler, 1989). Furthermore, standardized testing usually "focuses on proficiency, relating what is learned to ability in a 'real world'," and uses a "measurement model ensuring comparable and interpretable measures" (Jones & Saville, 2016, p. 11). Given the abovementioned, this paper, drawing on major learning-oriented assessment models, explores the possibility of using standardized writing tests for learning-oriented purposes and attempts to provide guidance for writing teachers on how to use such tests to facilitate students' development of writing ability.

Theoretical framework

Based on a synthesis of theories of assessment for learning (e.g., Boud &

Falchikov, 2007; Gibbs, 2006; Sadler, 2010; Sambell et al., 2013), Carless (2015) proposed a learning-oriented assessment approach incorporating three inter-related core elements and visualized them as a triangle. At the apex of this model is the *learning-oriented assessment tasks* that can drive students' efforts and learning. Such assessment tasks should be authentic problems that students will encounter in their real-life situations. The design of learning-oriented assessment tasks is supported by the other two core components: *developing evaluative expertise* and *student engagement with feedback*, which are positioned at the other two angles of the triangle. *Developing evaluative expertise* refers to students' evolving ability to engage with quality criteria, develop evaluative capacities, and make judgments about both their own and others' work. Evaluative expertise is metacognitive in nature, being critical for students' self-regulative learning. Specifically, students need to know the criteria of quality performance and use such criteria to monitor, evaluate, and improve their learning (Sadler, 1989). *Developing evaluative judgment* is also crucial for supporting student engagement with feedback, the third component of Carless's model. The evolving evaluative expertise can facilitate the understanding and use of different feedback information, including teacher feedback, peer feedback, and self-feedback (Boud & Molloy, 2013; Nicol, 2010). In return, student engagement with feedback can support the development of evaluative expertise. In a learning-oriented assessment task, teachers should assist students in developing evaluative expertise and meanwhile coordinate feedback activities. This model demonstrates how teachers can use assessment tasks to enhance student learning, making it useful for guiding classroom teachers to implement and benefit from assessment tasks.

Although Carless's (2015) model delineates how an assessment task can be learning-oriented by highlighting the role of evaluative expertise and engagement with feedback, this model seems confined to classroom teaching. With an awareness of a larger language learning ecosystem that includes classroom learning, classroom-based assessment, and external examinations, Jones and Saville (2016) argued that standardized testing can and should also be learning-oriented, in that it has significant strength to facilitate learning through focusing on proficiency, relating itself to real-world abilities, and drawing on measurement models thus making scores comparable and interpretable. Jones and Saville's (2016) model also places tasks at the center of language assessment, linking learning, teaching, and assessment. Specifically, a learning-oriented task provides opportunities for teacher-student and student-student interaction, which can be observed by teachers who facilitate interaction by providing feedback to consolidate the learning goal of the task. Jones and Saville's (2016) model of systemic learning-oriented assessment recognizes the learning-oriented value of standardized testing and alludes to the power of scoring criteria that can be explained with authentic language use in a real-world context. The ideas from Jones and Saville (2016) have

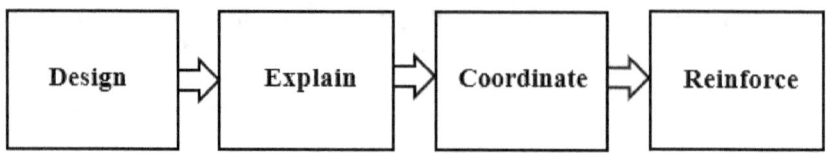

Figure 5.1 *A four-step guide to using standardized writing tests in classrooms*

the potential to extend the use of assessment tasks to standardized tests. Therefore, the following section of this chapter discusses how standardized testing can be leveraged by classroom teachers to support learning and specifically exploit the usefulness of sample questions and exemplar responses (Carless & Chan, 2017), scoring rubrics (Baker et al., 2020), and the provision of criterion-referenced interpretation (Jones & Saville, 2016) of standardized language tests in designing and implementing learning-oriented assessment tasks.

Practical implications and suggestions for classroom teachers

The proposed guide comprises four sequential steps: (1) design, (2) explain, (3) coordinate, and (4) reinforce (see Figure 5.1). Each step consists of several principles and recommended practices that teachers can adopt in their classroom teaching.

Design

The first step for classroom teachers is to design a learning-oriented assessment task. Teachers need to consider the needs and proficiency level of their students, the local syllabus, and the potential standardized writing tests that can be used in classrooms, and design classroom activities. To achieve the local learning outcome, teachers are recommended to consider the following three principles when using standardized writing tests to design learning-oriented assessment tasks.

Principles

Principle 1: The writing test should suit the teaching objective. Different writing tests are designed to test different and specific focal constructs. For example, writing tests that are designed for high school exit examinations for native English speakers differ from those for international non-native speakers who plan to study in graduate programs at English-medium-instruction universities in terms of, for example, genre, register and style, expected length, and target audience. Therefore, the writing test should suit the teaching objective. Specifically, if teachers are teaching native English high school students, it may be more suitable to choose the high school exit examinations for native English speakers, instead of admissions English tests for international graduate students.

Principle 2: The test task, rubric, official exemplar, and criterion-referenced interpretation and feedback should be carefully considered. Specific components of standardized writing tests can be of potential use for designing learning-oriented assessment tasks, including sample questions and responses, scoring rubrics (Baker et al., 2020), and criterion-referenced interpretation (Jones & Saville, 2016). These materials containing detailed criteria and concrete writing samples can show students what good writing can be like, and more importantly, break the abstract concept of good writing into several accessible dimensions, which can facilitate students' development of evaluative expertise to fully engage themselves in feedback-related activities (Carless, 2015). Therefore, these components of standardized writing tests should be carefully considered in the design stage.

Principle 3: The test materials should be revised if necessary. Although the chosen tests can reflect students' learning objectives, standardized tests often target long-term learning goals that cannot be fully covered in one teaching unit or one semester. It is important to select a focal part of the scoring rubrics in the classes, and to direct students' attention to specific aspects of the sample responses or criterion-referenced interpretation. In addition, local teaching syllabi and external examinations are not designed per the same construct, and the writing expectations can likely be different. Therefore, teachers may need to tailor the test materials to meet local needs. Teachers can add more details to sub-dimensions, or lower the requirement of some aspects.

Practice

A five-step practical guide for using standardized writing tests to design a learning-oriented assessment task is proposed to reflect the abovementioned three principles and highlight the teacher's role, step-wise implementation, collaboration, and interaction.

Recommendation 1: Select a suitable test, analyze, revise, and integrate. Before classroom teaching, teachers need to select a suitable test, analyze the task setting, prompt, scoring rubrics, exemplars, and criterion-referenced interpretation of the writings, and consider how to integrate the test into their teaching of writing. Teachers are recommended to explore the official websites, test preparation materials, sample papers, and test syllabus to make sense of the test, and to tell if the writing task in the test is consistent with the genre, register and style, expected length, and target audience of the writing that they are teaching. If so, teachers can consider revising the test to narrow the discrepancy between the purpose of the test and their teaching objective.

Recommendation 2: Individual study and writing. When the revision is completed, teachers can ask students to do a pre-class study of all the revised test materials and write on the test task. According to Carless and Chan (2017), reading test materials and individual writing can be time-consuming. It is better to "derive individual insights" before class and "preserve time for classroom dialogue" (p. 939). Writing after studying the test materials can provoke students' judgment on their own writing as well as transfer insights to their own work (Carless & Chan, 2017). However, teachers should also consider local students' motivation and the duration of their classes. If students are not motivated and time is allowed, teachers can have students do pre-instruction self-study in class.

Recommendation 3: Group discussion on the rubric, official exemplar, and criterion-referenced interpretation and feedback. Group work enables students to share different ways of resolving a problem (Van Berkel & Schmidt, 2000), promotes self-awareness of knowledge acquisition (Seethamraju & Borman, 2009), and enhances learning outcomes. Therefore, teachers are advised to use group discussion in their assessment tasks to facilitate students' understanding of the rubric, exemplar, and criterion-referenced interpretation and feedback, through which students can train their own evaluative judgment. The teacher may need to consider students' intercultural communication competence to encourage discussion among students from diverse cultures (if this is the case). Alternatively, ice-breaking activities can be arranged.

Recommendation 4: Self-assessment and peer-assessment with scores, interpretation, and feedback. After group discussion, students are expected to gain an understanding of what quality writing is like, and it is time for them to practice such conceptual knowledge. It is recommended that students work independently and use their developing evaluative expertise to evaluate their own writing and their peers' writing, to assign scores, to provide interpretation on the scores, and to offer feedback for improvement, because the use of self-assessment and peer-assessment can promote metacognitive awareness of writing and feedback-giving as well as self-regulation of learning (Dann, 2002; Topping, 2009). However, it is necessary to provide guidance during self-assessment and peer-assessment as assessing productive skills can be a challenging task.

Recommendation 5: Group discussion on the results of self-assessment and peer-assessment. To review the results of self-assessment and peer-assessment, it is recommended to organize another round of group discussion. Students can be instructed to compare different scoring results and feedback on the same written response, during which they can gain a deeper understanding of the quality of writing. Steps 4&5 can also link students' development of evaluative judgment and engagement with feedback (Carless, 2015), since feedback, as well as self- and peer-assessment, provide a venue for practicing evaluative judgment which can in return be used in giving and understanding feedback and assessment activities.

Explain

For students, assessing their own writing and peers' writing can be a challenging task, as in many contexts they will seldom have relevant experience. Therefore, it is necessary for teachers to scaffold, including providing clear directions, clarifying the learning goals, and addressing the test components that students may have difficulty understanding. It is by scaffolding that students learn new knowledge and skills that are slightly beyond their reach (Vygotsky, 1978).

Principles

Principle 1: The writing test task should be related to the learning objective. Best learning outcomes can be achieved if the assessment we have can be aligned with the learning objective for students' long-term (at least at the course level) development (Boud & Falchikov, 2006). This can make students believe what they do is meaningful so that they engage themselves in the task. Therefore, teachers need to relate the use of standardized writing tests to the learning objective, for example, explaining the importance of certain dimensions in the scoring rubric.
Principle 2: The test components that students may have difficulty understanding should be paid attention to. Scaffolding is an effective way of supporting learning and narrowing the gap between what they have already known and what they are supposed to know. As students need to use a variety of test components in the learning-oriented assessment tasks, teachers need to explain to students the components that they may have difficulty understanding, for example, analytic scoring and the multidimensionality of writing.

Practice

Recommendation 1: Introduce the concept of analytic scoring. Scoring is a challenging task for students as even two experienced raters can still diverge on one writing sample. While the purpose of having students rate their own and peers' writing is not to train reliable professional raters, it is important to create space for students to practice and improve the accuracy of their evaluative judgment or to direct them to the standard of good writing. As analytic scoring is widely used in existing writing tests and students may not understand the multidimensionality of writing and analytic scoring, it is necessary to introduce the concept of analytic scoring to them.
Recommendation 2: Direct students towards different aspects of their writing. By using analytic scoring in self-assessment and peer-assessment, teachers are able to cultivate relatively sophisticated and multidimensional judgment expertise that is relevant to the assessed construct (East, 2009; Knoch, 2009). Teachers can juxtapose the scoring rubric with the official exemplars and the diagnostic interpretation and feedback, to ex-

plain how the final scores are made, how the scores can be interpreted in the sample responses, and how certain actions can be taken to improve. By so doing, teachers can metacognitively direct students toward the different aspects of their writing.

Recommendation 3: Highlight the value of group discussion, self-assessment, and peer-assessment. Research shows that students can understand peer feedback better than teacher feedback, but they may fail to understand the value of peer feedback and use much fewer peer suggestions in revising their writing (Zhao, 2010). One useful measure to enhance students' understanding is to organize group discussions on peer-feedback (Zhao, 2010) as well as self-feedback. Teachers may need to explain the value of these assessment activities so that students can have more engagement. The teacher needs to keep their students' characteristics in mind and adjust the operationalization of the self- and peer assessment activities.

Coordinate

As self-assessment and peer-assessment are used in the classrooms of learning-oriented assessment, teachers are no longer the center of the class, but facilitators and coordinators to guide the student-centered class.

Principle

Principle 1: Interaction and communication should be encouraged. According to sociocultural theories, social interaction lays the foundation of learning which is an internalization process transforming the social into the cognitive (Vygotsky, 1978). Oftentimes, some students may have a better understanding of something than others. Through interaction and communication, students who know less can learn from those who already know and students who know better can also consolidate their knowledge. This is also true for the interaction between teachers and students. In addition, discussion on feedback and other assessment products can enhance student engagement with these learning resources and thus support their development of evaluative judgment (Carless, 2015).

Principle 2: The gap between teaching objectives and students' current states should be evaluated. Learning occurs when something that is not known previously is now understood (Vygotsky, 1978). It is very likely that students may still not understand some contents after the teacher's instruction. To engage students in the assessment tasks, teachers need to provide timely instruction, feedback, and explanation, and to observe the gap between the teaching objective and students' current status.

Principle 3: Students' cognitive, affective, and emotional states should be monitored and cared about. Engagement with feedback is not only cognitive, but also affective and emotional (Liu & Yu, 2021), especially in receiving and responding to critical or encouraging feedback, and all these aspects can be relevant to students' learning (Yang & Carless, 2013). Therefore, teachers are advised to monitor and make a response to all the above aspects when coordinating the assessment activities.

Practice

Recommendation 1: Guide students to compare exemplars with their own task responses. Testing companies often provide exemplar writing samples, which students can compare with their own writing. As these exemplars are usually assigned an official score, students can also take into consideration the scores in the comparison. Analyzing the writing and scores of their own and the sample writing, they can reflect on their use of the scoring rubric. Such a metacognitive process can be an excellent opportunity for them to practice their evaluative expertise.

Recommendation 2: Observe students' interaction. As students may not perform as expected or encounter problems or challenges in the assessment activities, teachers are advised to observe students' interactions. For example, if students take the feedback personally, teachers can intervene by pointing out the good points in their writing and reminding them that critical feedback can help them.

Recommendation 3: Pay attention to students' self-assessment and peer-assessment. Students' self-assessment and peer-assessment can suggest their evaluative expertise, which is important for their understanding of writing and the development of their writing ability (Black et al., 2004; Carless, 2015). Attention to students' interaction during these assessment activities cannot only help teachers understand students' development of evaluative expertise, but also monitor their engagement with different feedback.

Recommendation 4: Provide instantaneous feedback when necessary. When teachers observe students' interaction and notice problems in the giving and receiving of feedback, it can be advisable to provide instantaneous feedback or comments. However, teachers should tell if it is more appropriate not to interrupt their discussion but to summarize major problems after the activities.

Recommendation 5: Create a friendly atmosphere. As critical feedback is foreseeable and expected in the process, it is important to encourage interaction, keep students from negative emotions, and maximize their engagement with feedback. Teachers are advised to create a friendly atmosphere to bring about students' positive attitudes toward learning-oriented assessment activities.

Reinforce

This step helps teachers to recap the problems identified in student-oriented assessment tasks and review the key points of the learning objective.

Principle

Principle 1: Problems identified in the learning-oriented assessment tasks should be addressed. As it may not be appropriate to interrupt students' discussion or some problems are not restricted to the observed students, teachers need to address the problems identified during the learning-oriented assessment.

Principle 2: Reflections on the learning-oriented assessment tasks should be elicited. Students are encouraged to reflect on their thinking and feeling during the assessment tasks, which can be another opportunity for teachers to identify potential problems. Reflection can be an effective metacognitive activity where students can think about their learning.

Practice

Recommendation 1: Invite students to share their experiences. One effective way to reflect is to invite students to journal or share their experiences during giving and dealing with group discussion, scoring, and feedback. Teachers can ask students to report on the good practices according to their understanding and difficulties encountered, which provides opportunities for intervention.

Recommendation 2: Summarize problems of students' self- and peer-assessment. The reflection stage can be a good time point for summarizing problems, which can also prepare students for better practice in the future.

Recommendation 3: Reinstate the criteria of the writing. Teachers can end the class by reinstating the criteria of good writing to strengthen students' understanding, which is also the core of evaluative expertise.

Suggestions for action research or case study

This guide is merely a prototype of using standardized writing tests in classrooms for learning-oriented purposes. As no intervention study using this guide has been conducted at the time of writing, the empirical endeavor is encouraged in different local contexts. Teachers can adjust any part of this guide in their actual teaching or conduct action research to experiment with the recommended practice by considering their local contextual factors.

Further reading

Carless, D. (2015). Exploring learning-oriented assessment processes. *Higher Education, 69*(6), 963–976. https://doi.org/10.1007/s10734-014-9816-z

This journal article believes that summative assessment which includes standardized assessment can be learning-oriented if deep approaches to learning can be encouraged, for example, the activation of high-level cognitive engagement. Based on this assumption, it presents a model to capture the three core elements of learning-oriented assessment: (1) the assessment tasks in which students are involved, (2) students' development of self-evaluative capabilities, and (3) student engagement with feedback. The *assessment tasks* should assess the real-life problem to be able to drive the students' efforts and learning. *Evaluative expertise* can be metacognitive and important for students to monitor and improve their learning. It can be developed through *engagement with feedback* in *learning-oriented assessment tasks* and *student engagement with feedback* can in return facilitate the *development of evaluative expertise.* The core elements in this model can help teachers design their own learning-oriented assessment tasks.

Carless, D., & Chan, K. K. H. (2017). Managing dialogic use of exemplars. *Assessment & Evaluation in Higher Education, 42*(6), 930–941. https://doi.org/10.1080/02602938.2016. 1211246

This journal article reports an in-depth analysis of multiple sources of qualitative data to investigate the role of the dialogic use of exemplars in promoting students' understanding of standards and criteria of quality work. This study shows that guiding students to analyze exemplars and academic standards can support their development of evaluative judgment, a metacognitive competence important for learning in assessment tasks. To achieve this goal, teachers may need to first withhold their own evaluative judgment to prioritize student engagement in assessment tasks and to encourage dialogues about exemplars. The assessment tasks thus should start with student-led dialogues, taking in the form of peer assessment. After that, teachers need to lead the dialogues around the exemplars to provide opportunities for their tacit knowledge about standards and criteria understood by students. This study illustrates how teachers can manage learning-oriented assessment through the dialogic use of exemplars, which can be a demonstration for novice teachers.

Jones, N., & Saville, N. (2016). *Learning oriented assessment: A systemic approach.* **Cambridge University Press.**

This volume presents a systemic approach to learning-oriented assessment that aligns standardized assessment and classroom assessment at both the micro and macro level and highlights the linking of evidence from all levels into a coherent and coordinated system to develop nation-wide standards and higher-order learning outcomes. This aligning approach regards classroom assessment and standardized assessment as learning-oriented and complementary to each other. Standardized assessment defines learning goals and evaluates learning outcomes, while classroom assessment activities provide a variety of observable performance and informal records as complimentary evidence to support further learning. Novice writing teachers are encouraged to read this volume to develop an ecological understanding of various assessment types so that they can better guide students to meet external criteria through their use of classroom assessment activities.

White, E. (2019). (Re)visiting twenty-five years of writing assessment. *Assessing Writing*, 42, 100419. https://doi.org/10.1016/j.asw. 2019.100419

This paper is a reflective essay that provides the author's perceptions of writing assessment in the United States over a period of twenty-five years. It is an update of the article that the author wrote for the inaugural issue of *Assessing Writing* in 1994. This article reports the historical development of writing from 1994 to 2019, reminding four groups of stakeholders: teachers, researchers, testing organizations, and students, that the issues he raised in 1994 still exist and informing them of how recent development of writing assessment may change and benefit their beliefs and practices. This article is structured into four main parts as regards the four stakeholder groups and discusses concerns and important issues for each group. Therefore, writing teachers are encouraged to read this paper to make sense of the needs and motivation of other stakeholders to facilitate their own teaching and assessment practice in the classrooms.

References

AERA, APA, & NCME. (2014). *Standards for educational and psychological testing*. American Educational Research Association.

Baker, B. A., Homayounzadeh, M., & Arias, A. (2020). Development of a test taker-oriented rubric: Exploring its usefulness for test preparation and writing development. *Journal of Second Language Writing*, 50, 100771. https://doi.org/10.1016/j.jslw.2020.100771

Barkaoui, K. (2010). Explaining ESL essay holistic scores: A multilevel modeling approach. *Language Testing*, 27(4), 515–535. https://doi.org/10.1177/0265532210368717

Barkaoui, K. (2011). Effects of marking method and rater experience on ESL essay scores and rater performance. *Assessment in Education: Principles, Policy & Practice*, 18(3), 279–293. https://doi.org/10.1080/0969594x.2010.526585

Black, P., Harrison, C., Lee, C., Marshall, B., & Wiliam, D. (2004). Inside the black box: Raising standards through classroom assessment. *Phi Delta Kappan*, 86(1), 8–24.

Boud, D., & Falchikov, N. (2006). Aligning assessment with long-term learning. *Assessment & Evaluation in Higher Education*, 31(4), 399–413. https://doi.org/10.1080/02602930600679050

Boud, D., & Falchikov, N. (2007). Developing assessment for informing judgment. In D. Boud & N. Falchikov (Eds.), *Rethinking assessment in*

higher education (pp. 181–197). Routledge.
Boud, D., & Molloy, E. (2013). Rethinking models of feedback for learning: The challenge of design. *Assessment and Evaluation in Higher Education, 38*(6), 698–712.
Carless, D. (2015). Exploring learning-oriented assessment processes. *Higher Education, 69*(6), 963–976. https://doi.org/10.1007/s10734-014-9816-z
Carless, D., & Chan, K. K. H. (2017). Managing dialogic use of exemplars. *Assessment & Evaluation in Higher Education, 42*(6), 930–941. https://doi.org/10.1080/02602938.2016.1211246
Crusan, D. (2014). Assessing writing. In A. J. Kunnan (Ed.), *The companion to language assessment* (pp. 201–205). Wiley Blackwell.
Crusan, D. (2021). Writing assessment literacy. In H. Mohebbi, & C. Coombe (Eds.). *Research questions in language education and applied linguistics* (pp. 431–435). Springer.
Cumming, A. (2009). Assessing academic writing in foreign and second languages: Research timeline. *Language Teaching, 42*(1), 95–107.
Dann, R. (2002). *Promoting assessment as learning: Improving the learning process.* Routledge/Falmer.
East, M. (2009). Evaluating the reliability of a detailed analytic scoring rubric for foreign language writing. *Assessing Writing, 14*(2), 88–115. https://doi.org/10.1016/j.asw.2009.04.001
Elliot, N. (2005). *On a scale: A social history of writing assessment.* Peter Lang.
Gibbs, G. (2006). How assessment frames student learning. In C. Bryan & K. Clegg (Eds.), *Innovative assessment in higher education* (pp. 23–36). Routledge.
Graham, S., Gillespie, A., & McKeown, D. (2012). Writing: importance, development, and instruction. *Reading and Writing, 26*(1), 1–15. https://doi.org/10.1007/s11145-012-9395-2
Hamp-Lyons, L. (2001). Fourth generation writing assessment. In T. Silva & P. K. Matsuda (Eds.), *On second language writing* (pp. 117–125). Laurence Erlbaum Associates.
Harsch, C., & Martin, G. (2013). Comparing holistic and analytic scoring methods: issues of validity and reliability. *Assessment in Education: Principles, Policy & Practice, 20*(3), 281–307. https://doi.org/10.1080/0969594x.2012.742422
Jones, N., & Saville, N. (2016). *Learning oriented assessment: A systemic approach.* Cambridge University Press.
Knoch, U. (2009). Diagnostic assessment of writing: A comparison of two rating scales. *Language Testing, 26*(2), 275–304. https://doi.org/10.1177/0265532208101008
Lee, I. (2017). *Classroom writing assessment and feedback in L2 school contexts.* Springer.
Liu, C., & Yu, S. (2022). Reconceptualizing the impact of feedback in second language writing: A multidimensional perspective. *Assessing*

Writing, 53, 100630. https://doi.org/10.1016/j.asw.2022.100630

Nicol, D. (2010). From monologue to dialogue: Improving written feedback processes in mass higher education. *Assessment and Evaluation in Higher Education, 35*(5), 501–517.

Sadler, D. R. (1989). Formative assessment and the design of instructional systems. *Instructional Science, 18*, 119–144.

Sadler, D. R. (2010). Beyond feedback: Developing student capability in complex appraisal. *Assessment and Evaluation in Higher Education, 35*(5), 535–550.

Sambell, K., McDowell, L., & Montgomery, C. (2013). *Assessment for learning in higher education*. Routledge.

Seethamraju, R., & Borman, M. (2009). Influence of group formation choices on academic performance. *Assessment & Evaluation in Higher Education, 34*(1), 31–40. https://doi.org/10.1080/02602930801895679

Shaw, S. D., & Weir, C. J. (2007). *Examining writing: Research and practice in assessing second language writing*. Cambridge University Press.

Topping, K. J. (2009). Peer assessment. *Theory into Practice, 48*(1), 20–27. https://doi.org/10.1080/00405840802577569

Van Berkel, H. J. M., & Schmidt H. G. (2000). Motivation to commit oneself as a determinant of achievement in problem-based learning. *Higher Education, 40*, 231–242.

Vygotsky L. S. (1978). *Mind and society: The development of higher mental processes*. Harvard University Press.

Weigle, S. C. (2002). *Assessing writing*. Cambridge University Press.

Weigle, S. C. (2007). Teaching writing teachers about assessment. *Journal of Second Language Writing, 16*(3), 194–209. https://doi.org/10.1016/j.jslw.2007.07.004

Yang, M., & Carless, D. (2013). The feedback triangle and the enhancement of dialogic feedback processes. *Teaching in Higher Education, 18*(3), 285–297. https://doi.org/10.1080/13562517.2012.719154

Yu, S., & Liu, C. (2021). Improving student feedback literacy in academic writing: An evidence-based framework. *Assessing Writing, 48*, 100525. https://doi.org/10.1016/j.asw.2021.100525

Zhao, H. (2010). Investigating learners' use and understanding of peer and teacher feedback on writing: A comparative study in a Chinese English writing classroom. *Assessing Writing, 15*(1), 3–17. https://doi.org/10.1016/j.asw.2010.01.002

6
Teacher cognition, pedagogical practice, and meeting student needs in L2 writing

K. James Hartshorn

Introduction

This chapter includes a general description of teacher cognition, a discussion of relevant theory, and practical applications within second language (L2) writing. At the outset, it is necessary to understand what is meant by teacher cognition; the English word *cognition* comes from Latin and refers to mental activity such as thinking and reasoning. Teacher cognition more specifically denotes a variety of psychological constructs related to features of a teacher's work. This includes the "unobservable cognitive dimension of teaching—what teachers know, believe, and think," as well as the ways in which these constructs inform "what teachers do in the language teaching classroom" (Borg, 2003, p. 81). Thus, the term teacher cognition functions as a hypernym for an array of related elements.

The fact that there are millions of resources[1] on teacher cognition suggests its prominence as a support for effective teaching and learning. Li (2017, p. 13) underscored the importance of studying teacher cognition because it "heavily influences the way teachers plan their lessons, the decisions they make in the teaching process and what kind of learning they promote in the classroom." Nevertheless, teacher cognition is a large area of inquiry and not all scholars are aligned in terms of theoretical perspectives, research priorities, and their implications for the classroom. As with many phenomena, teacher cognition can be viewed through different theoretical lenses.

Theoretical frameworks

Traditional perspectives for teacher cognition

Historically, the predominant theoretical position for teacher cognition research has been the cognitive perspective. This view suggests that teacher beliefs are the primary impetus for teacher behavior in the classroom. Through this lens, we examine teacher beliefs and how they shape classroom decisions. Li (2020, p. 25) describes this perspective as viewing teacher cognition as "fixed" and "constant across situations." Though substantial evidence suggests that teacher knowledge and beliefs strongly impact classroom behavior (e.g., Richards & Lockhart, 1994; Woods,1996), many scholars assert that using a cognitive perspective to examine teacher cognition may not account for other complex contextual factors that may also shape teacher behavior. Accordingly, Borg (2003, p. 106) has warned that a study of teacher cognition that neglects context will likely be "flawed."

Moreover, a growing body of research highlights cases where teacher classroom behavior appears inconsistent with teacher beliefs (e.g., Junqueira & Payant, 2015; Lee, 1998, 2003, 2011; Tsui, 1996, 2003). Thus, some scholars have adopted an interactionist perspective where apparent discrepancies between teacher beliefs and behaviors can be viewed as outcomes of teacher-student interactions (Skott, 2001, as cited in Li, 2020). Other scholars have also expressed the need for perspectives that account for the larger sociocultural contexts in which teacher beliefs and knowledge are established and developed (e.g., Burns et al., 2015; Kubanyiova & Feryok, 2015).

Newer perspectives for teacher cognition

In response to the limitations that have been pointed out regarding traditional views, some scholars have advocated a Vygotskian sociocultural perspective with which to view teacher cognition. For example, building on discursive psychology which makes no distinction between beliefs and behaviors, Li (2020) has argued that sociocultural theory provides necessary social and discursive elements that can appropriately account for context and interaction within the development of teacher cognition. Sociocultural theory grows from the seminal work of Vygotsky (1978, 1986) with refinements from many others. Lantolf and Thorne (2006, p. 1), for example, describe a sociocultural perspective as "a framework through which cognition can be systematically investigated without isolating it from social context." Within this perspective, teaching is viewed as a social activity and interaction is seen as critical to teaching and learning. Thus, teacher cognition is seen as socially mediated and dynamic, developing integrally within social and professional contexts (Li, 2020, p. 44).

While lauding the benefits of alternate perspectives, some scholars have warned against "overly intellectualized" theory or criticisms that could sever teacher cognition from its historical roots and make it less accessible or relevant to teaching practice (Borg, 2019, p. 1167). At the same time, Burns et al. (2015) have questioned the term "cognition" itself, and whether it is still the best term to describe this field of inquiry. Extensive refinement in understanding of psychology, teaching, and learning over the past several decades might justify new labels that move beyond the narrow meaning of "cognition." Borg (2019, p. 1152) has also questioned the appropriateness of including "nonbehavioral" elements under the teacher cognition umbrella such as "motivation," "commitment," "resilience," and "identity." Other areas of concern include debate over the appropriateness of research methods. For example, some question whether qualitative methods should be preferred or whether there is an appropriate place in the study of teacher cognition for quantitative and mixed methods research (Borg, 2019).

Though an attempt to resolve such issues still in debate is beyond the scope of this chapter, we are likely to see these and many other topics about teacher cognition continue to be addressed in academic conferences and forthcoming publications. For our purposes here, I adopt an eclectic perspective that simply seeks to highlight relevant literature from its own frame of reference. For the foreseeable future, we are likely to see and perhaps benefit from theoretical and methodological pluralism in the world of teacher cognition research.

Literature review

With this theoretical introduction to teacher cognition in mind, we now consider some key literature. Borg (2003, p. 81) has described three interrelated areas that tend to shape teacher cognition in language teaching and learning contexts. These include prior language learning experience, teacher education, and classroom practice.

Prior language learning experience

One salient finding to emerge from teacher cognition research is that often teachers' own previous language learning experiences have a powerful influence on their beliefs about teaching and learning. Noting the thousands of hours students spend "in direct contact with classroom teachers," Lortie (1975, p. 61) has described this phenomenon as a practitioner's "apprenticeship of observation." To underscore the bidirectional impact of such experiences, Moodie (2016) has added what he calls the "anti-apprenticeship of observation," suggesting that classroom experience can shape both effective and less effective views of teaching. The truth is that for many practitioners, the language teaching philosophies forged in their own learning experiences may be, at least initially, their primary source of guidance for the classroom and may be resistant to change (e.g., Bailey et al. 1996; Numrich, 1996).

Teacher education

Studies have shown that teacher education can be rather effective in helping teachers refine skills and overcome uninformed or underdeveloped assumptions. However, the research also suggests that not all student-teachers benefit equally from their formal training as some continue to be strongly influenced by philosophies developed prior to their teacher preparation courses (e.g., MacDonald et al., 2001; Peacock, 2001; Richards et al. 1996). Moreover, this literature also suggests that appropriate behavioral changes may not always be associated with actual changed beliefs. For example, some behaviors may be the result of a student-teacher attempting to meet specified expectations—such practices may be discarded when external pressures are removed. Nor are actual changes in belief always a guarantee of changed behavior in classroom practice. Continued research may help us better understand the nuanced effects of teacher education.

Classroom practice

Extensive research also suggests that classroom behavior of second language practitioners is "shaped by a wide range of interacting and often conflicting factors" that may often but not always "reflect teachers' stated beliefs, personal theories, and pedagogical principles" (Borg, 2003, p. 91). These departures could arise from higher-level needs or pragmatic concerns. They might include efforts to address affective issues and classroom management (Breen, 1991), attempts to accommodate different student learning styles (Bailey, 1996), endeavoring to empower students with more control in the classroom (Richards, 1996), the effects of institutional expectations (Burns, 1996; Tsui, 1996), and a variety of practical constraints (Junqueira & Payant, 2015). Nevertheless, just as some classroom behavior is a direct reflection of teacher beliefs, some beliefs are forged by the teacher in the classroom precisely because of the unique experiences the practitioner has while teaching.

Teacher cognition in L2 writing

Some early studies in L2 writing identified factors that tend to influence pedagogical practices (Burns, 1992), consistency and change in teacher beliefs about L2 writing instruction over time (Shi & Cumming, 1995), and the disconnects between preferred pedagogical methods and expectations imposed by administrators and public assessments (Tsui, 1996). Lee (1998, 2003) also found discrepancies between stated beliefs and practice in the L2 writing classroom and has concluded that better training, research, and empowerment of teachers may help them refine their beliefs and allow them to become more effective L2 writing educators (Lee, 2010, 2011, 2013). Despite noted discrepancies between beliefs and behaviors, however, other scholars have observed fairly high levels of consistency underscoring the importance of context in conducting and interpreting such research (e.g., Ferris, 2014; Min, 2013).

Other research suggests the complexity associated with teaching cognition in L2 writing. For example, Yigitoglu and Belcher (2014) observed that the impact on beliefs about teaching and learning in L2 writing is not limited to L2 experiences. They found that experiences with literacy and writing development in the L1 can also influence pedagogical decisions in the L2 writing classroom. Furthermore, Wei and Cao (2020) noticed differential behaviors in providing feedback and concluded that more demanding feedback strategies were associated with professional training while less demanding feedback strategies were associated with direct classroom experience as a language learner or classroom teacher. Ngo (2018) observed that cognition regarding teaching and learning in L2 writing can change extensively over time in a dynamic fashion that is complex and that follows a non-linear trajectory (p. 79). She also noted that context can simultaneously expand and constrain teacher cognition about L2 writing (p. 87).

Other work in teacher cognition has focused on very practical issues such as determining how to help practitioners create a meaningful learning environment in the classroom and ensuring that teacher preparation and ongoing professional development help teachers make well informed pedagogical decisions (e.g., Kubanyiova, 2015; Kubanyiova & Feryok, 2015). Similarly, Crookes (2015) has posited that research and professional development with teacher cognition should help L2 writing practitioners in the refinement of their teaching philosophies in ways that enhance classroom practice. Though teacher cognition has been studied for many decades, scholars continue to emphasize the need for much more teacher cognition research, particularly in L2 writing (Nazari & Oghyanous, 2022; Sun & Zhang, 2021).

Based on this literature, we can make several general observations from this brief survey of teacher cognition research in L2 writing.

1. Studying teacher cognition is important for informing teacher preparation and helping teachers to develop professionally as L2 writing practitioners.
2. Relationships between beliefs and classroom practices in L2 writing can be extremely complex and may not always be easily understood.
3. There are multiple theoretical frameworks and research methods being used to study and understand teacher cognition.
4. While teacher behavior is often consistent with beliefs, this is not always the case and departures can occur for a wide array of reasons.
5. Teacher cognition can be greatly impacted by a practitioner's own language learning, teacher preparation, and experiences teaching in the L2 writing classroom.
6. Some instances of discrepancies between beliefs and practice may be best understood by carefully examining the sociocultural contexts in which the teaching and learning occur.
7. Additional research may help the field better understand many aspects of teacher cognition, particularly in L2 writing.

Practical implications

Building on this basic understanding of teacher cognition in L2 writing, the remainder of the chapter presents practical ways some of these principles may be applied in specific contexts to support your development as an L2 writing professional. Though it may be uncommon to reference metacognition in a discussion about teacher cognition, doing so may allow you to better identify, manage, and refine your teacher cognition—what you know, think, and believe about teaching and learning in L2 writing. The term "Metacognition" comes from the Latin word "cognition" with the addition of Greek prefix *meta* (meaning beyond or above). The resulting definition is an "awareness and understanding of one's own thought processes," especially in regard to "having a role in directing those processes" (Oxford English Dictionary, n.d.). In other words, metacognition is the process of thinking about your thoughts and beliefs, especially in ways that help you better understand your own teacher cognition and allow you to make it more transparent and explicit for yourself and others.

An essential first step in your metacognition could be to clearly articulate what you believe about teaching and learning in L2 writing. Though specifying your beliefs may seem unnecessary, many less experienced teachers may be uncertain about their beliefs about L2 writing. A few analogies may help underscore this point. Imagine you inherited something valuable that is in a lockbox, but you aren't sure what it is. It's likely that you would want to open the box and carefully examine the contents. Similarly, it can be helpful to take the time to reflect and then articulate your beliefs about L2 writing. Subsequently, imagine you now know what is in your lockbox, having opened it, but then you misplace your key. Thus, nothing new can be placed into the box and nothing in the box can be removed. Teacher cognition may be like this for some teachers in that it may be resistant to change. These lockbox analogies represent problematic scenarios that could undermine the robust understanding of teacher cognition needed to optimize your success as an L2 writing teacher.

A better analogy might be to think of your teacher cognition as a cell in a living organism. Unlike the lockbox, the cell wall is made of a permeable membrane. Ongoing metabolic processes regularly allow the cell to take in needed nutrients and to eliminate waste. Through such processes, the cell stays healthy and continues to grow and function as it should. In a similar way, we may benefit as the metaphorical wall around our teacher cognition stays permeable. This will ensure that we are open to new insights and that we are willing to discard poorly conceived ideas or behaviors that might hinder our efforts toward effective L2 writing pedagogy.

We can develop professionally by engaging in metacognitive practices

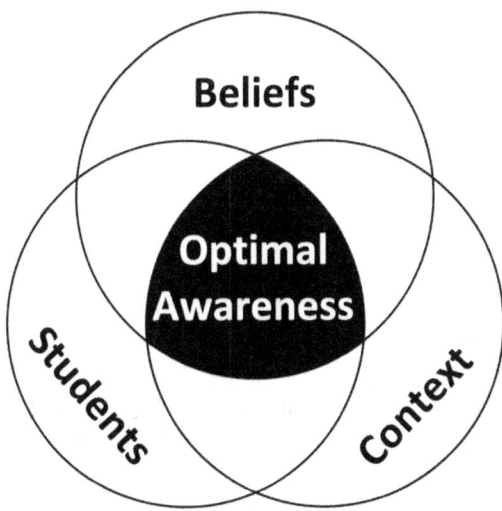

Figure 6.1 *Optimizing understanding of your beliefs, context, and students*

that include thoughtful reflection and introspection regarding our beliefs about the teaching and learning of L2 writing. Effective metacognition may help you to optimize your awareness and understanding in three key areas presented in Figure 6.1 including:

1. Understanding your beliefs about L2 writing
2. Understanding your teaching and learning context
3. Understanding the specific needs of your students

Your efficacy as an L2 writing teacher will most likely be optimized as you operate at the intersection of these three areas labeled "optimal awareness" in Figure 6.1. Each of these will be briefly examined below.

Understanding your beliefs

The literature examined previously presented examples of discrepancies between teacher beliefs about L2 writing and classroom practices. You will not be able to evaluate your classroom practice relative to your beliefs until you have a clear understanding of what you believe. Until you begin this journey of discovery, you may be prone to default toward pedagogical practices you have seen or experienced, regardless of whether they may be the most appropriate for your context.

To begin this process, you could sit down with a piece of paper divided into two columns (see Figure 6.2). In one column labeled "what," you could make a list of some of your most salient assumptions—what you know, think, or believe about L2 writing development. In a second column labeled "why," you could record the reasons for your beliefs. Is

What	Why
1.	
2.	
3.	
4.	

Figure 6.2 *Belief document: The what and why of your teacher cognition*

your thinking based on a particular body of research? Is it something a professor or colleague mentioned in a class or conversation? Does the belief come from personal experience, from your own learning or observations while teaching? It will be helpful to be as specific and explicit as possible in articulating your beliefs and providing support for each.

I recommend maintaining this belief document over the course of your career, so beliefs can be added or discarded as may be appropriate. Over time, this could become an extremely valuable resource you could use to evaluate your teaching practice. However, in order to optimize the value of this exercise, you will need to continue to engage in regular metacognition. You can do this as you actively seek, study, and evaluate new research, as you discuss what you learn from colleagues, and as you carefully reflect on new insights you glean from your classroom experiences. In addition to your belief document, I recommend keeping a journal or field notes about your classroom experiences. This record could help inform your belief document. I also encourage you to develop the habit of regularly challenging your beliefs. Eventually, only the most defensible items should remain in your belief document—those that have truly earned their place through robust rationale born from solid research or repeated experience.

Understanding the teaching and learning context

In addition to understanding your own beliefs, you need to understand the teaching and learning context in which you work. Hyland (2019) has presented several different L2 writing perspectives illustrated in Figure 6.3. Though certainly not mutually exclusive, they each provide distinct guidance for what teachers should do to facilitate L2 writing development. Hyland noted that these perspectives represent unique "curriculum options, each organizing L2 writing around a different focus" (p. 3). For example, in one context, a lower proficiency class might focus heavily on linguistic structure including grammar rules and vocabulary choices. In another class, the emphasis might be on creative expression. In such a class, you might help students develop their own voice as they relate

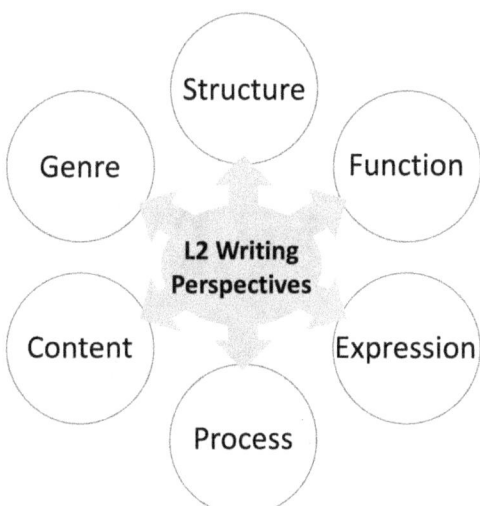

Figure 6.3 *Hyland's L2 writing perspectives*

opinions and personal experiences on their journey toward self-discovery.

In most cases, however, teachers may draw from several of these perspectives simultaneously though some may be more prominent than others in specific situations. For example, in an English for specific purposes context, an L2 writing teacher may draw heavily from the content, genre, and function perspectives along with some focus on structure and process. Effective writing teachers can look closely at their specific context and determine how much of these perspectives should be incorporated to meet student needs in relation to specific program or course objectives. While in some well-defined contexts the focus will be very straightforward, in other contexts it may be much more difficult to determine what kind of writing instruction and practice will be most beneficial. It may require conscientious decisions regarding which aspects of these L2 writing perspectives will be utilized, and to what extent.

Along with careful consideration of the right combination of L2 writing perspectives to include in a course, Figure 6.4 provides additional insight regarding the teaching and learning context. You could begin by asking detailed questions about why the course exists and what it is supposed to help the students learn. Then you need to understand who the students are and what needs they have that may have an impact on your ability to achieve the purposes of the course (student needs will be addressed in a little more detail in the next section). With a clear understanding of student needs, evaluating *where* and *when* of the instruction along with other relevant contextual constraints will help you determine *how* best to teach your students. Given *who* your students are, the *how* of

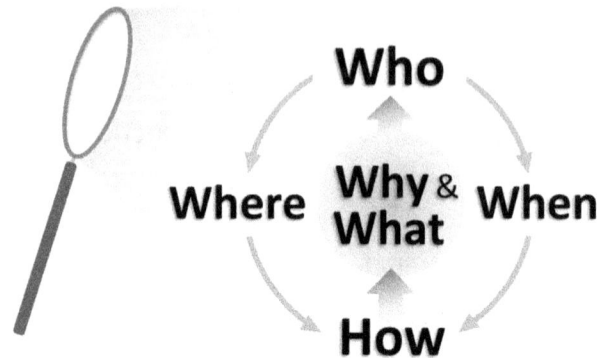

Figure 6.4 *Questions about your L2 students and the teaching and learning context*

your methods and pedagogical decisions will determine whether or not you achieve the *what* and fulfill the *why* of a given writing course.

Understanding your students

Building on the context described above, a clear awareness of your students and their needs may be the most important type of understanding essential to being an effective L2 writing teacher. Insights from teacher cognition research suggest the likelihood that some influences from our experience as a student or a teacher could obscure our ability to accurately perceive our students and their needs. Consider Figure 6.5, which depicts two types of teachers. The teacher on the left will be described as *reflexive*. This term includes two senses of the word reflexive. First, it refers to an inordinate preoccupation with personal preferences or assumptions. Second, it refers to the automatic or involuntary process of defaulting to pedagogical approaches that may neglect the greatest needs of the students. This scenario is represented by the teacher attempting to see her students by looking through a mirror, only to have her vision of her students obscured by an uninformative view of herself along with her biases and predispositions.

Conversely, the teacher on the right will be described as *perceptive*, meaning to understand, discern, or become aware of something that might not otherwise be obvious. Rather than use a mirror that both obscures her view of her students and misinforms her regarding student needs, the perceptive teacher on the right is represented by the use of a magnifying glass that enlarges her view of her students, providing needed details necessary to effectively help them develop their L2 writing. The perceptive teacher seeks to understand her students in ways that allows her to shape the L2 writing experience, so their writing develops in the

Figure 6.5 *Replacing reflexive teacher cognition with perceptive behaviors*

most important and relevant ways.

Building on an appreciation of the teaching and learning context, the perceptive teacher comes to understand more deeply who her students are, their educational backgrounds, their experiences with L1 and L2 writing, their writing weaknesses that need to be overcome, and their hopes, aspirations, and dreams for how they will use their writing skills in the future. The perceptive teacher doesn't teach writing; she teaches students how to write more effectively. She doesn't teach a class; she teaches individuals, each of whom may have unique needs that are carefully considered as she plans lessons and provides feedback. She is more concerned with producing better writers than simply helping her students to produce better writing. The key here is to work toward being less reflexive and more perceptive in our work with our L2 writing students.

Conclusion

This chapter has provided a basic description of teacher cognition, relevant theory, and practical ideas for professional development designed to help you identify, manage, and refine your beliefs about L2 writing. Rather than being content with the status quo, you have been invited to engage in meaningful metacognition, to learn from ongoing research and experience, and to be willing to perceptively identify and effectively meet student needs. Such efforts will certainly help you develop as an L2 writing professional as you support your students in achieving their full potential as L2 writers.

Suggestions for action research and professional development

1. Studying video recordings of our teaching can be an extremely powerful way to identify areas in which we can improve. After creating a belief document as described in this chapter, regularly record your teaching, and evaluate it against the principles outlined in your belief document.
2. Encourage colleagues in your community of practice to create a belief document. Then compare and discuss similarities and differences in your documents, including the evidence for the selected beliefs.
3. Identify what you believe to be the most important conditions needed to facilitate L2 writing development along with the most menacing threats that could undermine it?
4. Carefully study teacher cognition in your own L2 writing class or in the class of a colleague and identify ways in which a sociocultural perspective provides insights that may not be as apparent from a different theoretical perspective.

Further reading

Borg, S. (2019). Language teacher cognition: Perspectives and debates. In X. Gao (Ed.), *Second handbook of English language teaching*, (pp. 1149-1170). Springer International Publishing.

As an early researcher of teacher cognition in L2 contexts, Simon Borg provides valuable insights in this chapter regarding historical perspectives and recent developments. This work includes criticism of divergent theory and methodology in teacher cognition research and many of the core issues currently being debated in the field. He expresses concern that some newer perspectives may take the notion of teacher cognition too far from its historical roots, rendering it less practical and relevant to those who might otherwise benefit from it the most. This includes some criticism or cautions regarding several of the articles included in a special issue of the Modern Language Journal emphasizing teaching cognition in applied linguistics (the next entry in this list for further reading).

Kubanyiova, M. & Feryok, A. (Eds.). (2015). Language teacher cognition in applied linguistics research: Revisiting the territory, redrawing the boundaries, reclaiming the relevance [Special issue]. *Modern Language Journal*, 99(3), 435-636.

This special issue of the Modern Language Journal includes ten articles devoted to the notion of teacher cognition in L2 language contexts. Though the target of some criticism from Simon Borg (mentioned above), many of these articles choose to view teacher cognition from more recent viewpoints including sociocultural perspectives. The work acknowledges the useful insights that have grown out of earlier research on teacher cognition, but nevertheless claims that limited progress since that time, thus necessitating this body of work. These articles focus on a variety of topics such as how practitioners foster meaningful learning environments, how teacher preparation can support the creation of such learning environments, and how teacher cognition can be reinvigorated by reexamining its conceptual, epistemological, and ethical underpinnings.

Li, L. (2020). *Language teacher cognition: A sociocultural perspective.* **Palgrave Macmillan.**

Building on her previous work (Li, 2017), this book by Li Li uses discursive psychology to examine teacher cognition from a sociocultural perspective including the importance of context and social interaction in the development of a teacher's knowledge and beliefs. The work seeks to answer relevant questions about the role of sociocultural theory in understand teacher beliefs and behaviors, how conversation analysis might reveal important insights about cognitive development in the work of teachers, and whether discursive psychology and sociocultural theory can be appropriately brought together to account for observed phenomena.

References

Bailey, K. M. (1996). The best laid plans: teachers' in-class decisions to depart from their lesson plans. In K. M. Bailey & D. Nunan (Eds.), *Voices from the Language Classroom* (pp. 15–40). Cambridge University Press.

Borg, S. (2003). Teacher cognition in language teaching: A review of research on what language teachers think, know, believe, and do. *Language Teaching, 36*(2), 81–109.

Borg, S. (2019). Language teacher cognition: Perspectives and debates. In X. Gao (Ed.), *Second handbook of English language teaching* (pp. 1149–1170). Springer International Publishing.

Breen, M. P. (1991). Understanding the language teacher. In R. Phillipson, E. Kellerman, L. Selinker, M. Sharwood Smith & M. Swain (Eds.), *Foreign/Second Language Pedagogy Research* (pp. 213-233). Multilingual Matters.

Burns, A. (1992). Teacher beliefs and their influence on classroom practice. *Prospect, 7*(3), 56–66.

Burns, A. (1996). Starting all over again: From teaching adults to teaching beginners. In D. Freeman & J. C. Richards (Eds.), *Teacher Learning in Language Teaching* (pp. 154–177). Cambridge University Press.

Burns, A., Freeman, D., & Edwards, E. (2015). Theorizing and studying the language-teaching mind: Mapping research on language teacher cognition. *The Modern Language Journal, 99*(3), 585–601. https://doi.org/10.1111/modl.12245

Crookes, G. V. (2015). Redrawing the boundaries on theory, research, and practice concerning language teachers' philosophies and language teacher cognition: Toward a critical perspective. *The Modern Language Journal, 99*(3), 485–499.

Ferris, D. R. (2014). Responding to student writing: Teachers' philosophies and practices. *Assessing Writing, 19*, 6-23. https://doi.org/10.1016/j.asw.2013.09.004

Hyland, K. (2019). *Second language writing.* Cambridge University Press.

Junqueira, L., & Payant, C. (2015). "I just want to do it right, but it's so hard": A novice teacher's written feedback beliefs and practices. *Journal of Second Language Writing, 27,* 19–36. https://doi.org/10.1016/j.jslw.2014.11.001

Kubanyiova, M. (2015). The role of teachers' future self guides in creating L2 development opportunities in teacher-led classroom discourse: Reclaiming the relevance of language teacher cognition. *The Modern Language Journal, 99*(3), 565–584.

Kubanyiova, M., & Feryok, A. (2015). Language teacher cognition in applied linguistics research: Revisiting the territory, redrawing the boundaries, reclaiming the relevance. *The Modern Language Journal, 99*(3), 435–449. https://doi.org/10.1111/modl.12239

Lantolf, J. P., & Thorne, L. (2006). *Sociocultural theory and the genesis of second language development.* Oxford University Press.

Lee, I. (1998). Writing in the Hong Kong secondary classroom: teachers' beliefs and practices. *Hong Kong Journal of Applied Linguistics, 3*(1), 61–76.

Lee, I. (2003). L2 writing teachers' perspectives, practices and problems regarding error feedback. *Assessing Writing, 8*(3), 216–237. http://dx.doi.org/10.1016/j.asw.2003.08.002

Lee, I. (2010). Writing teacher education and teacher learning: testimonies of four EFL teachers. *Journal of Second Language Writing, 9*(3), 143–157. http://dx.doi.org/10.1016/j.jslw.2010.05.001

Lee, I. (2011). Feedback revolution: what gets in the way? *ELT Journal, 65*(1), 1–12. http://dx.doi.org/10.1093/elt/ccp028

Lee, I. (2013). Second language writing: perspectives of a teacher educator-researcher. *Journal of Second Language Writing, 22,* 435–437. http://dx.doi.org/10.1016/j.jslw.2013.08.005

Li, L. (2017). *Social interaction and teacher cognition.* Edinburgh University Press.

Li, L. (2020). *Language teacher cognition: A sociocultural perspective.* Palgrave Macmillan.

Lortie, D. (1975). *Schoolteacher: A sociological study.* University of Chicago Press.

MacDonald, M., Badger, R., & White, G. (2001). Changing values: What use are theories of language learning and teaching? *Teaching and Teacher Education, 17*(8), 949–963.

Min, H.-T. (2013). A case study of an EFL writing teacher's belief and practice about written feedback. *System, 41*(3), 625–638. https://doi.org/10.1016/j.system.2013.07.018.

Moodie, I. (2016). The anti-apprenticeship of observation: how negative prior language learning experience influences English language teachers' beliefs and practices. *System, 60*, 29–41. https://doi.org/10.1016/j.system.2016.05.011

Nazari, M., & Alizadeh Oghyanous, P. (2022). Contributions of a genre-based teacher education course to second language writing teachers' cognitions. *Innovation in Language Learning and Teaching*, 1–13.

Ngo, X. M. (2018). A sociocultural perspective on second language writing teacher cognition: A Vietnamese teacher's narrative. *System, 78*, 79–90.

Numrich, C. (1996). On becoming a language teacher: Insights from diary studies. *TESOL Quarterly, 30*(1), 131–153.

Peacock, M. (2001). Pre-service ESL teachers' beliefs about second language learning: A longitudinal study. *System, 29*, 177–195.

Richards, J. C. (1996). Teachers' maxims in language teaching. *TESOL Quarterly, 30* (2), 281–296.

Richards, J. C., & Lockhart, C. (1994). *Reflective teaching in second language classrooms*. Cambridge: Cambridge University Press.

Richards, J. C., Ho, B., & Giblin, K. (1996). Learning how to teach in the RSA Cert. In D. Freeman & J. C. Richards (Eds.), *Teacher learning in language teaching* (pp. 242–259). Cambridge University Press.

Shi, L., & Cumming, A. (1995). Teachers' conceptions of second language writing instruction: five case studies. *Journal of Second Language Writing, 4*(2), 87–111. https://doi.org./10.1016/1060-3743(95)90002-0

Sun, Q., & Zhang, L. J. (2021). A sociocultural perspective on English-as-a-foreign-language (EFL) teachers' cognitions about form-focused instruction. *Frontiers in Psychology, 12*.

Tsui, A. B. M. (1996). Learning how to teach ESL writing. In D. Freeman & J. C. Richards (Eds.), *Teacher learning in language teaching* (pp. 97–119). Cambridge University Press.

Tsui, A. B. M. (2003). *Understanding expertise in teaching*. Cambridge University Press.

Vygotsky, L. (1978). *Mind in society*. Harvard University Press.

Vygotsky, L. S. (1986). *Thought and language*. MIT Press.

Wei, W., & Cao, Y. (2020). Written corrective feedback strategies employed by university English lecturers: A teacher cognition perspective. *SAGE Open, 10*(3). https://doi.org/10.1177/2158244020934886

Woods, D. (1996). Teacher cognition in language teaching. Cambridge

University Press.

Yigitoglu, N., & Belcher, D. (2014). Exploring L2 writing teacher cognition from an experiential perspective: The role learning to write may play in professional beliefs and practices. *System, 47,* 116–124.

7
Individual differences and writing instruction

Olena Vasylets
Rosa M. Manchón

Introduction

Individual differences (IDs) refer to "dimensions of enduring personal characteristics that are assumed to apply to everybody and of which people differ by degree" (Dörnyei, 2006, p. 42). The study of IDs constitutes a major research interest in second language acquisition (SLA) studies (see Papi & Li, 2022, for an updated, comprehensive treatment). However, it is not until recently that a research interest in whether and how IDs may affect writing has been added to SLA research agendas. This is a welcome expansion of IDs research for theoretical and applied implications. For instance, regarding aptitude (of the most widely researched IDs), DeKeyser (2019) synthesizes global research findings in the domain of pedagogical relevance, one of which is precisely that "aptitude plays a big role during communicative practice, for monitoring output" and "for learning from producing 'comprehensible output'" (p. 326). The way in which producing written language (i.e. comprehensible written output) may lead to language learning is precisely the key question in current explorations of write as a site for language learning (see Leow & Manchón, Chapter 14 in this volume; Manchón & Vasylets, 2019). Therefore, a central concern in the body of work is to ascertain the effect of IDs in learning through writing. In the sections that follow we synthesize main research findings on the connection between IDs and writing and explore implications for writing instruction.

Theoretical framework

In ascertaining the role of IDS in writing we are concerned with both the act of writing itself and the engagement with and use of the feedback provided on one's own writing. SLA-oriented L2 writing research has theorized the important role that IDs may play in writing (Kormos, 2012) and feedback processing (Bitchener, 2019), and a body of empirical research (as reviewed in Ahmaddian & Vasylets, 2021; Papi, 2021) has investigated the mediation of learner-related variables (both cognitive and affective) on written texts before and after receiving feedback. In what follows we discuss the rationale for research in the domain.

Studying the role of IDs in writing is relevant theoretically, empirically, and pedagogically. **Theoretically and empirically**, writing and feedback processing offer an intriguing combination of input processing (for example, when processing input in the form of feedback and in writing-from sources tasks) and output production that has not been accounted for in current models of IDs in SLA. At the same time, writing entails the orchestration of a number of processes (planning, linguistic encoding, revision and monitoring) that may be influenced by IDs. Similarly, regarding feedback, Bitchener (2019) suggests that feedback processing entails paying attention to written corrective feedback (WCF) input, noticing the gap between one's own output and the WCF received, understanding WCF input, analysing/comparing WCF input and knowledge in long-term memory, and hypothesis formation and testing. He further elaborates on the role that cognitive and affective (especially motivation) IDs may play in the implementation of these processes, especially when writers try to understand and analyze the WCF and when they try to formulate and test hypotheses about the L2 on the basis of the feedback received. Additional empirical evidence on these predicted effects of IDs needs to be sought. From a different angle, certain assumptions in IDs research need to be further validated empirically. For instance, working memory may be differentially implicated in speaking and writing given the greater availability of time in the writing condition, which may free up cognitive resources to be devoted to linguistic encoding, for example (see Ahmaddian & Vasylets, 2021). Regarding aptitude, Li (2019) concludes that the "predictive research shows that overall aptitude is a strong predictor of learning success but seems less predictive of L2 writing" (p. 93), a claim that also needs to be further substantiated empirically.

Pedagogically, given that literacy practices are central and ever present in instructed SLA contexts (e.g., Harklau, 2002), and given also the widely accepted pedagogical relevance of matching instructional interventions to learners' abilities (e.g. Robinson, 2012), research on the effects of cognitive and affective IDs on the texts written by L2 users and in their processing of feedback is of the most relevance for the teaching of writing. Equally relevant from a pedagogical perspective would be to elucidate whether such effects are mediated by, at least, (i) pedagogically-relevant task-related factors (for instance, whether students are asked to write writing in paper-based or screen-based environments, or when writing more and less cognitively complex tasks); and (ii) the type of feedback provided by the teacher and/or the way in which students are encouraged to engage with and make use of the feedback.

In short, there are sound theoretical, empirical, and applied reasons to pursue a more nuanced understanding of the role of IDs in L2 writing.

Literature Review

We will now provide a synthesis of the main available research findings with respect to the IDs that have attracted more empirical attention. We focus our review primarily on the act of writing itself. Readers are referred to Ahmaddian and Vasylets (2021), Papi (2021) and Papi, Vasylets and Ahmaddian (2022) for a fuller analysis of research insights on the role of IDs in WCF use.

Language aptitude

Regarding writing, a positive relationship between language aptitude and the quality of L2 written production has been reported. For example, Yang et al.'s (2019) study with the university EFL learners in China found that the quality of L2 written texts was predicted by the students' ability to learn new vocabulary and by grammatical sensitivity. In Kormos and Trebits's (2012) study, secondary school learners in Hungary performed two writing tasks with different levels of complexity (given storyline vs. designing own plot). The authors found that learners with higher grammatical sensitivity (a component of language aptitude) produced longer clauses, but only in the task which was considered simple (the task with the given storyline). Vasylets et al. (2022) with Spanish EFL university students added a further piece of the puzzle by adding the variable of writing environments: They found that the role of aptitude varied in pen-and-paper vs. computer-based L2 writing. For instance, the role of grammatical sensitivity appeared to be more prominent in pen-and-paper writing as compared to writing on the computer.

Working memory

Studies on the role of working memory (WM) in L2 writing have produced mixed findings. Whereas some studies have reported absence of a connection between WM and L2 writing quality (Michel et al., 2019), others have shown that the effects of WM in L2 writing may be proficiency-dependent. For example, in the study with the secondary school learners in Hungary, Kormos and Safár (2008) found that phonological short-term memory was positively connected to the quality of L2 English writing for beginner learners, but not for intermediate learners. Similarly, Vasylets and Marín's (2021) study with Spanish EFL university students found that at low level of L2 proficiency, WM was positively connected to writing accuracy; however, for writers with higher proficiency, WM was positively linked to the lexical sophistication of the texts.

Motivation and L2 future selves

Several studies have explored the role of motivation from the perspective of future L2 selves (Dörnyei, 2009) in L2 writing. For example, in the study by Cho (2015), 112 ESL students from a major US university were assigned to four different scenarios: (1) *successful future* selves, (2) *unsuccessful future* selves, (3) *successful past* selves, and (4) *successful* future of *others*. The experimental task required to imagine the assigned scenario (e.g., imagine successful future) and then write a short essay and revise it. The analysis revealed that the successful past selves group was the one that persisted longer in the revision task. This finding suggests that the recall of successful past behaviors might benefit revision in L2 writing. Similarly, Jang and Lee (2019) conducted a study with Korean EFL university students to explore how ideal L2 self and ought-to L2 self might influence choice of writing strategies and L2 writing quality. The results showed that ideal L2 self positively contributed to writing quality and to the adoption of planning strategies. In the study with the EFL learners at a university in Iran, Tahmouresi, and Papi (2021) found that the ideal L2 writing self positively predicted L2 writing joy, motivation and achievement, while ought-to L2 writing self was associated with L2 writing anxiety.

Beliefs

Study of beliefs is still rare in L2 writing research. In a pioneering study, Manchón (2009) investigated the effects of instruction on the development of L2 writing beliefs. A self-report questionnaire tapping into 5 dimensions of beliefs about writing (person, task, strategy, teacher, and feedback) was administered at two points in a one-year EFL writing course to 15 Spanish university students. Other sources of data were retrospective questionnaire completed by the participants, a teacher written report and a teacher interview. The main findings were that the instruction received helped the participants to reinforce their self-efficacy beliefs, gain higher awareness of the multidimensional nature of L2 writing, and develop a more sophisticated understanding of the teacher role in the L2 writing classroom. The study by Han (2017) with Chinese EFL learners found that beliefs could influence their emotional reaction to and engagement with WCF. For example, learners who considered them to be under-achievers had a low degree of motivation to engage with WCF.

Self-efficacy

Writing self-efficacy has been associated with stronger self-regulation, lower writing anxiety, higher perceived value of writing, and better writing outcomes (Pajares, 2003). For example, the recent meta-analysis by Sun et al. (2021) reported a positive relationship between writing self-efficacy and English writing achievement for both L1 and L2 writers, finding also that self-efficacy plays a more facilitative role for L2 writers. Another relevant study is the one by Ruegg (2018), who found that teacher feedback increased writing self-efficacy of Japanese EFL learners to a higher degree as compared to peer feedback.

Self-regulation

In Csizér and Tankó's (2017) survey study with 222 English majors from a university in Hungary, they found that self-regulation was associated with an increased level of motivation, higher self-efficacy, and with a decreased level of writing anxiety. The recent study by Jackson and Park (2020) reported that learner conscientiousness positively contributed to self-regulation, whereas neuroticism negatively contributed to it. Empirical studies have also shown that different types of writing instruction can influence writing self-efficacy and self-regulation. For example, the study by Han and Hiver (2018) with Korean university learners of EFL found that the genre-based L2 writing instruction could benefit writing self-regulation and consolidate writing self-efficacy.

Anxiety

Due to its complex and multifaceted nature, the relationship between writing anxiety and L2 writing can be reciprocal. In other words, the complexity of L2 writing can cause anxiety; conversely, writing anxiety can discourage learners from devoting time and effort to their texts and can negatively affect the quality of L2 written production (Tahmouresi & Papi, 2021). Some studies have also shown that the role of anxiety on L2 written performance can depend on other learner characteristics. For example, anxiety has been associated with less frequent use of self-regulation strategies (Tsao et al., 2017).

Practical implications and suggestions

We now list a number on implications derived from the empirical research briefly reviewed above:
1. Empirical findings suggest that the effects of language aptitude and working memory in L2 writing are positive and that these effects may also depend on learner internal factors (especially proficiency) and external factors (the complexity of the task to be performed and whether tasks are performed in speaking or writing). These insights have important implications for pedagogical-decision making regarding, inter alia, (i) which tasks to assigns to which proficiency groups, and (ii) who would benefit the most from performing tasks in speaking or in writing
2. Self-images of successful past and future experiences have been found to make a positive contribution to writing performance and to the choice of writing strategies. These findings provide a foundation for instructors to consider the use of L2 self-images as a means to improve writing proficiency.
3. Instruction has been found to cause positive changes in learners'

beliefs, and productive beliefs can benefit L2 writing. The empirical evidence has also shown that that L2 writing instruction and/or the type of provided WCF can influence writing self-efficacy and self-regulation. Accordingly, the teaching of writing (including pedagogical decision-making regarding what type of feedback is provided and how) cannot ignore these crucial affective dimensions.
4. Writing anxiety has been shown to have negative effects on L2 writing, which adds another layer of complexity to the teaching of writing instructor ought to be aware of.

Suggestions for action research

An interesting question to explore for action research is to ascertain the effects of the use of technology in L2 writing classroom. The development of technology offers new possibilities for teaching L2 writing, especially the integration of traditional writing skills and digital media into multimodal texts (Lim & Polio, 2020). An example of the use of multimodality in L2 writing classroom is the creation of digital stories, which represent short videos with images, sound/music and text. A digital story project represents a collaborative writing project, in which learners have to select a topic, search for the information on this topic (content, images, sounds), write different types of texts (e.g., a narrative and an argumentative essay) in order to develop their topic, and finally write a script and create a short video (i.e., digital story), which is published online. There is some evidence of the positive effects of digital stories on the development of L2 writing skills (Oskoz & Elola, 2016). However, the complexity of carrying out a multimodal project can also challenge learners in new ways. For this reason, action research should explore how the use of digital stories can influence L2 writers' writing motivation, self-efficacy, self-regulation, and writing anxiety.

The participants of this study should ideally have an upper-intermediate or advanced level of L2 proficiency and can come from one intact class. The data on IDs would be collected by means of questionnaires and interviews. As a first step, and before staring the work on digital stories, teacher-researchers should perform a pre-test consisting of the administration of the following questionnaires (see appendices):

- **L2 writing motivation questionnaire.** As an example, Appendix A shows a scale that includes 7 items which have to be assessed on a 6-point Likert scale ranging from 1 (*Never*) to 6 (*Always*) (see Appendix A). A higher score indicates a higher level of L2 writing motivation.
- **L2 self-efficacy scale**. The scale in Appendix B consists of 7 items measuring learners' beliefs and confidence in their capabilities as L2 writers. It is a 6-point Likert scale ranging from 1 (*Strongly Disagree*) to 6 (*Strongly Agree*). A higher score indicates a higher level of L2 self-efficacy.

- **L2 self-regulation scale.** The scale in Appendix C consists of 9 items measuring the strategic effort of L2 learners to organize and manage their L2 writing goals and processes. It is a 6-point Likert scale ranging from 1 (*Strongly Disagree*) to 6 (*Strongly Agree*). A higher score indicates a higher level of L2 writing self-regulation.
- **L2 writing anxiety scale.** The scale in Appendix D consists of 9 items which have to be assessed on a 6-point Likert scale ranging from 1 (*Strongly Disagree*) to 6 (*Strongly Agree*). A higher score indicates a higher level of L2 writing anxiety.

These questionnaires can be administered during a regular class to the entire group; the teacher-researcher should also collect the students' background information, including their age, years learning L2, and their level of L2 proficiency. After the administration of the questionnaires, the teacher-research can start the implementation of the digital stories project. Because of its complexity, it would be advisable to divide the project into several phases. An optimal procedure would be to connect the project with the official syllabus and implement it over the course of one semester. Table 1 (Appendix E) presents a possible time schedule and the description of the activities in each phase.

After the completion of the multimodal project, a post-test would be performed, which would consist of the administration of the same questionnaires completed in the pre-test. The post-test questionnaire can be complemented with some open-ended questions asking about the learners' experience with the multimodal project. The comparison of the scores from the pre- and post-tests would allow to see the potential effects of a multimedia writing project on learners' L2 writing motivation, self-efficacy, self-regulation, and writing anxiety. To gain deeper insights, the teacher-researcher could also interview some students (see Appendix F for examples of questions). The interviews can be individual or conducted in groups; the teacher-researcher should record the interviews for further analysis.

Conclusion

In conclusion, a key dimension in the teaching of L2 writing is the recognition of the way in which students' cognitive and affective variables may influence their engagement and involvement with writing tasks and with the feedback provided on their writing, as well as the outcome of their task performance. L2 writing instructors are therefore encouraged not only to be updated on the insights obtained in pedagogically-oriented IDs research, but also to engage in well-informed action research in their own classrooms in an effort to cater for their students' IDs in the best possible way in the context of the ecology of their own classrooms.

Further reading

Ahmaddian, M., & Vasylets, O. (2021). The role of cognitive individual differences in writing performance and written corrective feedback processing and use. In R.M. Manchón & C. Polio (Eds.), *Handbook of second language acquisition and writing*. Routledge.

This chapter focuses on the role of working memory and language aptitude in L2 writing. It discusses the way in which these individual traits can influence how L2 learners perform a writing task and use written corrective feedback provided by language teachers. The chapter starts with the discussion of the importance of working memory and language aptitude in instructed second language acquisition. The chapter reviews findings from the relevant empirical studies and concludes with the implications for practice and recommendations for future research.

Kormos, J. (2012). The role of individual differences in L2 writing. *Journal of Second Language Writing*, *21*(4), 390–403. https://doi.org/10.1016/j.jslw.2012.09.003.

This influential paper reviews the most important individual differences which are considered to be relevant in L2 writing. In particular, it explores the effects of cognitive (aptitude, working memory, and self-regulation) and motivational (language learning goals and self-efficacy beliefs) individual traits on L2 writing processes and on the ability of L2 learners to exploit the language learning potential of writing tasks. The author assesses the role of IDs in writing and suggest a comprehensive research agenda for future work in the domain.

Papi, M. (2021). The role of motivational and affective factors in L2 writing performance and written corrective feedback processing and use. In R.M. Manchón & C. Polio (Eds.), *The Routledge handbook of second language acquisition and writing* (pp.152–165). Routledge

This chapter provides a comprehensive review of research exploring the role of affect and motivation in L2 writing processes and outcomes and outlines potential implications of these developments for research and practice. The review covers studies conducted on the role of motivational and affective factors (with a focus on learner beliefs, motivational factors, and emotions) in L2 writing and written corrective feedback.

Papi, M., Vasylets, O., & Ahmaddian, M. (2022). Individual Difference Factors for Second Language Writing. In M. Papi & S. Li (Eds.), *Handbook of Second Language Acquisition and Individual Differences*. Routledge.

This chapter discusses theoretical aspects and empirical findings of research on the role of individual differences in L2 writing, focusing on the effects of cognitive (language aptitude) and conative/affective factors (beliefs, self-efficacy, mindset, achievement goals, future L2 selves, L2 writing experience, and emotions) on L2 writing processes and performance, and written corrective feedback processing. The chapter also discusses data elicitation procedures which are typically employed in the research on individual differences in L2 writing, and provides directions for future research and practical implications for L2 writing teachers and practitioners.

References

Bitchener, J. (2019). The intersection between SLA and feedback research. In K. Hyland & F. Hyland (Eds.), *Feedback in second language writing. Contexts and issues* (pp. 85–105). Cambridge University Press.

Cheng, Y. S. (2017). Development and preliminary validation of four brief measures of L2 language-skill-specific anxiety. *System, 68*, 15–25. https://doi.org/10.1016/j.system.2017.06.009

Cho, M. (2015). The effects of working possible selves on second language performance. *Reading and Writing, 28*(8), 1099–1118. https://doi.org/10.1007/s11145-015-9564-1

Csizér, K., & Tankó, G. (2017). English majors' self-regulatory control strategy use in academic writing and its relation to L2 motivation. *Applied Linguistics, 38*(3), 1–20. https://doi.org/10.1093/applin/amv033

DeKeyser, R. (2019). DeKeyser, R. (2019). The future of language aptitude research. In Z. Wen, P. Skehan, A. Biedron, S. Li, & R.L. Sparks, R. L. (Eds.), *Language aptitude: Advancing theory, testing, research and practice*. Routledge.

Dörnyei, Z. (2006). Individual differences in second language acquisition. *AILA Review, 19*(1), 42–68. https://doi.org/10.1075/aila.19.05dor

Dörnyei, Z. (2009). The L2 motivational self system. In Z. Dörnyei & E. Ushioda (Eds.), *Motivation, language identity and the L2 self* (pp. 9–42). Bristol: Multilingual Matters.

Han, Y. (2017). Mediating and being mediated: Learner beliefs and learner engagement with written corrective feedback. *System, 65*, 133–143. https://doi.org/10.1016/j.system.2017.07.003

Han, J., & Hiver, P. (2018). Genre-based L2 writing instruction and writing-specific psychological factors: The dynamics of change. *Journal of Second Language Writing, 40*, 44–59. https://doi.org/10.1016/j.jslw.2018.03.001

Harklau, L. (2002). The role of writing in classroom second language acquisition. *Journal of second language writing, 11*(4), 329–350. https://doi.org/10.1016/S1060-3743(02)00091-7

Jackson, D. O., & Park, S. (2020). Self-regulation and personality among

L2 writers: Integrating trait, state, and learner perspectives. *Journal of Second Language Writing, 49*, 100731. https://doi.org/10.1016/j.jslw.2020.100731

Jang, Y., & Lee, J. (2019). The effects of ideal and ought-to L2 selves on Korean EFL learners' writing strategy use and writing quality. *Reading and Writing, 32*(5), 1129–1148. https://doi.org/10.1007/s11145-018-9903-0.

Kormos, J., & Sáfár, A. (2008). Phonological short-term memory, working memory and foreign language performance in intensive language learning, *Bilingualism: Language and Cognition, 11*, 261–271. https://doi.org/10.1017/S1366728908003416

Kormos, J. & Trebits, A. (2012). The role of task complexity, modality, and aptitude in narrative task performance. *Language Learning, 62*(2), 439–472. https://doi.org/10.1111/j.1467-9922.2012.00695.x

Li, S. (2019). Six decades of aptitude research: A comprehensive and critical review. In Z. Wen, P. Skehan, A. Biedron, S. Li, & R.L. Sparks (Eds.), *Language aptitude: Advancing theory, testing, research and practice* (pp. 78–96). Routledge.

Lim, J., & Polio, C. (2020). Multimodal assignments in higher education: Implications for multimodal writing tasks for L2 writers. *Journal of Second Language Writing, 47*, 100713. https://doi.org/10.1016/j.jslw.2020.100713

Manchón, R. M. (2009). Individual differences in foreign language learning: The dynamics of beliefs about L2 writing. *RESLA, 22*, 245–268.

Manchón, R. M., & Vasylets, O. (2019). Language learning through writing: Theoretical perspectives and empirical evidence. In A. Benati & J.W. Schwieter (Eds.), *The Cambridge Handbook of Language Learning* (pp.341–363). Cambridge University Press. https://doi.org/10.1017/97811083333603

Michel, M., Kormos, J., Brunfaut, T., & Ratajczak, M. (2019). The role of working memory in young second language learners' written performances. *Journal of Second Language Writing, 45*, 31–45. https://doi.org/10.1016/j.jslw.2019.03.002.

Mills, N., Pajares, F., & Herron, C. (2006). A reevaluation of the role of anxiety: Self-efficacy, anxiety, and their relation to reading and listening proficiency. *Foreign Language Annals, 39*(2), 276–295.

Oskoz, A., & Elola, I. (2016). Digital stories: Bringing multimodal texts to the Spanish writing classroom. *ReCALL, 28*(3), 326–342. https://doi.org/ 10.1017/S0958344016000094

Pajares, F. (2003). Self-efficacy beliefs, motivation, and achievement in writing: A review of the literature. *Reading & Writing Quarterly, 19*(2), 139–158. https://doi.org/10.1080/10573560308222

Papi, M., & Li, S. (Eds.), *Handbook of second language acquisition and individual differences*. Routledge.

Robinson, P. (2012). Individual differences, aptitude complexes, SLA processes, and aptitude test development. In P. Mirosław (Ed.), *New perspectives on individual differences in language learning and teaching* (pp. 57–75). Springer.

Ruegg, R. (2018). The effect of peer and teacher feedback on changes in EFL students' writing self-efficacy. *The Language Learning Journal, 46*(2), 87–102. https://doi.org/10.1080/09571736.2014.958190.

Sun, T., Wang, C., Lambert, R. G., & Liu, L. (2021). Relationship between second language English writing self-efficacy and achievement: A meta-regression analysis. *Journal of Second Language Writing, 53*, 100817. https://doi.org/10.1016/j.jslw.2021.100817

Tahmouresi, S., & Papi, M. (2021). Future selves, enjoyment and anxiety as predictors of L2 writing achievement. *Journal of Second Language Writing, 53*, 100837. https://doi.org/10.1016/j.jslw.2021.100837

Tsao, J. J., Tseng, W. T., & Wang, C. (2017). The effects of writing anxiety and motivation on EFL college students' self-evaluative judgments of corrective feedback. *Psychological Reports, 120*(2), 219–241. https://doi.org/10.1177/0033294116687123

Tseng, W. T., Dörnyei, Z., & Schmitt, N. (2006). A new approach to assessing strategic learning: The case of self-regulation in vocabulary acquisition. *Applied linguistics, 27*(1), 78–102. https://doi.org/10.1093/applin/ami046

Vasylets, O., & Marín, J. (2021). The effects of working memory and L2 proficiency on L2 writing. *Journal of Second Language Writing, 52*. https://doi.org/10.1016/j.jslw.2020.100786

Vasylets, O., Mellado, M., & Plonsky, L. (2022). The role of working memory and language aptitude in digital versus pen-and-paper L2 writing, *Studies in Second Language Learning and Teaching, 12*(4). https://doi.org/10.14746/ssllt.2022.12.4.9

Waller, L., & Papi, M. (2017). Motivation and feedback: How implicit theories of intelligence predict L2 writers' motivation and feedback orientation. *Journal of Second Language Writing, 35*, 54–65. https://doi.org/10.1016/j.jslw.2017.01.004.

Yang, Y., Sun, Y., Chang, P., & Li, Y. (2019). Exploring the relationship between language aptitude, vocabulary size, and EFL graduate students' L2 writing performance. *TESOL Quarterly, 53*(3), 845–856. https://doi.org/10.1002/tesq.510

Appendix A

Second Language Writing Motivation Scale

- I enjoy writing in L2.
- Writing in L2 is very important to me.
- I always look forward to my L2 writing classes.
- I would like to spend lots of time learning to write in L2
- I would like to concentrate on learning to write in L2 more than any

other topic.
- I actively think about what I have learned in my L2 writing class.
- I really try to learn how to write in L2.

The Second Language Writing Motivation Scale has been adapted from Waller and Papi (2017).

Appendix B

Second Language Writing Self-Efficacy Scale

- I feel confident about writing in L2.
- I know how to write well in L2.
- I write L2 with an underlying logical organization.
- If I put in the needed effort, I am sure I can become a good writer in L2.
- I can write essays that are relevant and appropriate to the assignment.
- I present my point of view or arguments accurately and effectively when writing in L2.
- I am sure I can do well on writing courses even if they are difficult.

The Second Language Writing Self-Efficacy Scale has been adapted from Mills et al. (2006).

Appendix C

Second Language Writing Self-Regulation

- I know how to reduce my stress from learning writing in L2.
- I have special techniques to achieve my learning goals when learning writing in L2.
- I feel satisfied with my own special methods for reducing the stress of writing in L2.
- I have special techniques to keep my concentration focused when learning writing in L2.
- I persist until I reach the goals that I make for myself when learning writing in L2.
- I believe I can achieve my goals more quickly than expected when learning writing in L2.
- I can cope with the stress from learning writing in L2 immediately.
- When it comes to learning writing in L2, I think my methods of controlling procrastination are effective.
- I know how to arrange the environment to make learning more efficient when learning writing in L2.

The Second Language Self-Regulation scale has been adapted from Tseng et al. (2006).

Appendix D

Second Language Writing Anxiety

- When writing in L2, I often worry that I will make language mistakes.
- When writing in L2, I often worry that my writing performance is worse than others'.
- As soon as I start writing L2, I begin to worry about not being able to express myself.
- When writing in L2, I often feel my heart pounding.
- When writing in L2, I often get so nervous that I tremble.
- When writing in L2, I often sweat and perspire.
- When practice writing L2 compositions, I often give it up easily.
- I often skimp over L2 composition exercises.
- I usually do my best to avoid writing L2 compositions.

The Second Language Writing Anxiety scale has been adapted from Cheng (2017).

Appendix E

Table 7.1 *Phases and tasks of the digital stories project.*

Phase	Schedule	Tasks
Phase 1	Week 1	• Teacher introduces the project in class, explains its structure and aims, and shows some examples of digital stories • Learners are divided into groups of 3-4 to carry out the project
Phase 2	Week 2-3	• In class, teacher presents different online sources of content, images and sounds, and explains the affordances of collaborative platforms (e.g., Google Docs) and video production tools • Learners start searching for the information for their digital stories and upload it to their group file in Google Docs
Phase 3	Week 4-7	• Teacher introduced the structure and features of a narrative essay • Learners work collaboratively on the narrative essay in Google Docs • Teacher provides feedback on the essay • Learners incorporate the provided feedback into their essays • Teacher grades the essays

Continued...

Phase 4	Week 8-11	• Teacher introduced the structure and features of an argumentative essay • Learners work collaboratively on the argumentative essay in GoogleDocs • Teacher provides feedback on the essay • Learners incorporate the provided feedback into their essays • Teacher grades the essays
Phase 5	Week 12-15	• Learners start working on the scripts for their digital stories. Learners use their narrative and argumentative essays as the basis of the scripts • Learners upload their scripts to Google Docs and the teacher provides feedback • Learner start creating the videos of their digital stories integrating the script, images and sounds
Phase 6	Week 16	• Learners upload their digital stories to the learning platform (e.g., Moodle) and present their stories in class

Appendix F

Questions for the semi-structured interviews

1. Did you enjoy working on digital stories? Why? Why not?
2. What were your favorite tasks in this project?
3. What effects do you think this multimodal project had on your L2 writing?
4. What feelings did you experience when working of this project?
5. Do you feel this project helped you to become a more efficient writer?
6. Do you feel this project helped you to become a better writer?
7. Would you like to participate in more projects like this one?

8
Learner autonomy in writing

Rachael Ruegg

Introduction

The overall aim of developing learner autonomy is for students to be able to take control of their own learning. Taking control of their own learning has benefits for their motivation, engagement, and achievement within the education system. In addition, benefits have been reported not only for students but also for teachers, who have reported increased enjoyment of teaching after introducing autonomy-supportive teaching practices (Reeve, 2016). Moreover, the capacity for autonomy is incredibly useful after students leave the education system in preparing them to identify learning goals, identify materials and methods of learning that are appropriate and evaluate their learning. In this way, teaching that supports the development of learner autonomy will help students this week, but also for the rest of their lives.

Although there is a lot of research evidence of the benefits of autonomy-supportive teaching, there are also obstacles that prevent it from being easy to implement. Institutions have increasing levels of reporting and standardization that make it more difficult to be flexible to students' needs. In addition, when autonomy-supportive teaching methods are first introduced, some students struggle to make decisions about aspects of learning that they have had no choice about in the past. Despite these difficulties, there are pedagogical changes that would increase learner autonomy which are manageable for students and appropriate to different educational contexts.

The purpose of this chapter is to provide an overview of teaching that encourages the development of learner autonomy in L2 writing. This chapter will explain the theoretical background of learner autonomy, discuss what previous literature has found in relation to autonomy-supportive teaching and make general and L2 writing-specific pedagogical recommendations based on the literature. Readers are encouraged to consider this chapter as a general overview to the topic and to consult the sources listed in the reference list to learn about more specific details relating to the development of learner autonomy. It is hoped that the chapter is clear and that it will inspire teachers to try something new in their classrooms and homework assignments.

Theoretical framework

The main theory underpinning autonomy-supportive teaching is self-determination theory. Self-determination theory holds that all social environments should support three different psychological needs: the need for autonomy, the need to be competent and the need for involvement with others (Ryan & Deci, 2017). In order to support learners' autonomy, they should have choice and be encouraged to self-regulate their learning. To support learners' competence, they should have structure and receive relevant feedback. These two kinds of support should be offered through the involvement of at least one other person who cares about them.

The relevant educational theory is social constructivism, which holds that learning occurs socially, through interactions between teachers and students and between students and their peers (Vygotsky, 1978). Social constructivism is most closely related to the third psychological need: for involvement with others. However, the three psychological needs are heavily interrelated. The need for autonomy does not imply a need for complete independence from others. On the contrary, Little (1995) states that the development of learner autonomy depends on the dialogue that takes place between a teacher and student. Social constructivism also holds that competence is best achieved through collaboration between a learner and others, through a process of scaffolding.

In the teaching of language more specifically, the development of learner autonomy would be most likely to occur within the paradigm of communicative language teaching (CLT). In communicative language teaching, language learning takes place through communicative acts which take place in the classroom. Through students communicating with their teacher and their peers in the target language, both confidence and competence in the target language are developed. In the teaching of L2 writing more specifically, CLT is usually implemented through a flipped classroom approach. In order to maximise opportunities for interaction in the classroom, students writing and teachers reading that writing occur outside of the classroom and the time inside the classroom is spent talking about the writing. For example, teachers encourage students to reflect on their past, present and future writing processes and written products. Littlewood (1996) identifies three levels of learner autonomy that are specific to language learning: students first develop autonomy as a communicator, then develop autonomy as a learner (within the education system) and finally develop autonomy as a person (which they take with them after leaving the education system).

Literature review

Before discussing what teachers can do to foster the development of learner autonomy in their students, this section will provide a brief review of concepts and results found in literature on the topic. The overall aim of teaching that fosters the development of learner autonomy is to have students experience educational activities "as emanating from, and an expression of" themselves (Ryan & Deci, 2017, p. 14). From this foundational idea of self-determinism, we can see that the writing classroom is an ideal context in which to apply this theory. From the perspective of the four language skills, classrooms focussing on the receptive skills (listening and reading) will focus on input, whereas classrooms focussing on the productive skills (speaking and writing) will focus on output. Focussing on output allows students a great deal more freedom to express themselves than focussing on input. Indeed, in education more broadly the vast majority of classrooms have certain content which makes up the curriculum. Across educational levels and subject areas, teaching writing is a unique space in which students can meet learning goals without having to focus on specific ideas.

Ryan and Deci (2017) introduce a continuum with teaching that fosters the development of learner autonomy at one end and "controlling teaching" at the other end. Controlling teaching is teaching in which the teacher takes control over every aspect of the learning process. For example, the teacher sets very specific tasks and makes stipulations about every aspect of every task, such as when, where, and how it is to be completed and what materials will be used to complete it. The end goal of autonomy-supportive teaching is to enable learners to take control of their own learning, for example, deciding when and how they will complete a task and what materials they will use to complete it. In this way, autonomy-supportive teaching increases students' agency and their ownership of the learning process.

It seems worthwhile to consider why teachers would control every aspect of learning that takes place in their classroom. There are a wide range of reasons for this tendency. Controlling teaching may be familiar to many teachers as they were also taught in a controlling way. Doing something very different from what is familiar can feel like a big risk. Many are likely to feel that nothing should be left to chance when teaching and may not see this style of teaching as controlling, rather feeling that they are being proactive as teachers, anticipating students' needs in the learning process and questions that they may ask and being prepared to meet those needs. In this sense, controlling teachers may be very hard-working and diligent teachers who are able to quickly and completely offer information that students ask for to help them complete their tasks. In fact, education systems are often set up in a way that encourages controlling teaching. Teachers are required to provide information in advance about what will occur in their courses and institutions often put guidelines in place to ensure a certain level of consistency between teachers, both of which make it difficult to be flexible. In addition, there are increasing levels of accountability for teachers. It is often considered to be their responsibility to ensure that all students pass, for example. Feeling confident that all students will pass while also handing over control to students to choose when, what and how they study entails putting a great deal of trust in students. Finally, the very first time when one offers freedom to students, the students may not know how to use that freedom. Especially in a context in which students are used to controlling teaching, they are likely to be dependent on teacher control. The difficult process in the beginning of training students to take control can often be the biggest obstacle to autonomy-supportive teaching. These are legitimate concerns that many teachers may have about the concept of autonomy-supportive teaching.

In addition to these concerns, some teacher may mischaracterise autonomy-supportive teaching as teaching which lacks any kind of structure or support. Effective autonomy-supportive teaching provides the appropriate level of structure and support for students to successfully meet their learning goals, while encouraging students to take as much control over the process as possible. Finding the ideal balance is probably the most difficult obstacle to effective autonomy-supportive teaching.

However, there is clear research evidence about both the benefits of autonomy-supportive teaching and the problems caused by controlling teaching (Reeve, 2009). Reeve and Cheon (2016) found autonomy-supportive teaching to be effective and easy for teachers to do. A meta-analysis of the overall effectiveness of interventions to support learner autonomy, which combined the results of 19 research studies, found a significant overall effect size of 0.63 (Su & Reeve, 2011). Moreover, research has found that controlling teaching leads to superficial learning, which is less likely to be transferred (Ryan & Deci, 2017). In teaching writing, the likelihood of students transferring what they have learnt to contexts outside of the writing classroom (such as to other classes or high stakes exams) is an important consideration. In addition, students demonstrate lower levels of motivation and engagement and a higher likelihood of dropping out when teaching is controlling (Ryan & Deci, 2017). Thus, although teachers may find handing over control of the learning process to their students to be a difficult concept to accept, there is strong evidence that this is a more effective approach to education. The following section will explain the individual benefits of the approach in more detail.

The most fundamental component of an autonomy-supportive classroom is offering students choice. The most straightforward area in which writing teachers can offer choice is allowing students to choose the topics they will write about in their writing tasks. Previous research has been conducted in the context of English L2 writing instruction which has focussed on the effects of offering topic choice. LeBlanc and Fujieda (2012) investigated differences in lexical variation of the same students' writing when they chose their own topics and when they were writing about teacher-assigned topics. They found significantly more lexical variation in the writing about self-selected topics. Bonyadi (2014) and Neisi et al. (2019) conducted research in which one group of students wrote about a teacher-assigned topic, while another group wrote about topics they had chosen themselves. Both studies found that students who wrote about topics they had chosen themselves significantly outperformed those who wrote about teacher-assigned topics. These three studies show clear evidence of students' increased competence when choice is allowed.

Another study outside of the L2 writing context offered students a choice of homework tasks and found that when students had a choice they had higher levels of motivation for that homework, felt more competent regarding the homework and performed better on a subsequent test than when homework was assigned by a teacher (Patall et al., 2010). Thus, when students are offered more choice they not only perform better, but also *feel* more competent and are more motivated. Similarly, Wang et al. (2016) found that teaching that allowed choice, encouraged feelings of competence and occurred through interaction with others led to significantly higher levels of intrinsic motivation.

The most fundamental benefit of autonomy-supportive teaching is that when students have some choice in their learning, they choose to study about topics that they find most interesting, and in ways that they find engaging. When students are focussing on material that is fundamentally interesting to them in ways that they find engaging, they will be able to tap into their intrinsic motivation for learning and maintain their motivation (Deci, 1995). This takes the responsibility for motivating learners away from teachers.

Increased intrinsic motivation in turn has benefits for learning. When intrinsic motivation was higher and students self-regulated their own learning processes, in combination these two factors had a significant positive effect on competence (Wang et al., 2016). Similarly, Vansteenkiste et al. (2004) found that when students had more intrinsic motivation for a task, they used less superficial processing, more deep processing, increased test scores and increased effort. The positive effects on students use of less superficial learning and more deep learning and on test scores were consistent throughout the study and the students reported being "more fully dedicated and more genuinely engaged in learning activities" (Vansteenkiste et al., 2004, p. 259).The process of becoming more effective in developing students' autonomy thus involves a movement along a continuum from teachers feeling that they should be proactive and dedicated, so that they are prepared to give students any help they need to succeed to students becoming proactive and dedicated in their own learning process, so that they can learn in a way that meets their needs.

Practical implications and suggestions for early-career teachers
General pedagogical recommendations

There are three main studies that have identified specific pedagogical practices which together constitute autonomy-supportive teaching practice. The earliest study (Reeve, 2009) specified five practices: Tapping into students inner motivational resources, providing rationales for activities/tasks and practices, using non-controlling language, allowing student self-pacing of learning and acknowledging and accepting expression of negative feelings during the learning process. The next study (Su & Reeve, 2011) maintained four of those five practices, but removed student self-pacing and replaced it with offering choice. The most recent study (Reeve & Cheon, 2021) included all six practices in the previous two studies, changed student self-pacing to teacher patience and added a final practice: taking students' perspective. Although always taking students' perspective is a sound pedagogical practice, it is significantly vaguer than the other autonomy-supportive teaching practices and thus will not be discussed in this chapter.

The most complete choice students can be given is in the form of a negotiated syllabus (Clarke, 1991). However, the realities discussed above of the need to report detailed information about courses in advance make a negotiated syllabus increasingly less likely to be viable in most contexts. However, students can be offered choice in relation to the topics they write about, and they can be offered a choice of different activities to complete in the classroom or for homework (see Vansteenkiste et al., 2004). Students can be offered a choice about whether they would like to receive feedback from the teacher (see Ruegg, 2018a) as well as choice in the kinds of feedback they would like to receive (see Ruegg, 2020). In addition, even when a syllabus is quite heavily regulated by an institution, small choices can be offered to students such as the order in which the topics are covered or in which the activities are completed. Even smaller choices can be offered to students in the writing classroom. For example, if students are tasked with writing an argument essay or a compare/contrast essay they can be offered a choice between the block method and the point-by-point method rather than only being taught one method of organizing such texts. Small choices such as these are unlikely to have the same effect as more significant choices, but nevertheless students should be offered as many choices as possible, to increase their motivation and engagement.

Unlike offering choice, providing rationales for activities/tasks and practices and acknowledging and accepting expression of negative feelings are closely connected. Providing rationales for activities or tasks is done to manage negative affect. For example, we may know that a task is boring or difficult for students and stress how important the activity or task is to master. Similarly, if we want students to take pedagogical practices seriously, we may explain the reasons for the practice. Providing such rationales may make it easier for students to find the motivation needed to complete a task or allow them to personalize the task to meet their needs. On the other hand, if a teacher has not anticipated how boring or difficult a task will be, then they may have asked students to do it without a clear rationale. In this case, students may express their negative emotions relating to the task and one response from the teacher may be to provide a rationale. We should always provide as many explanations as possible to students about why we are asking them to carry out certain tasks and what we hope they will gain from them. However, in cases where students express negative feelings we should accept and address those negative feelings rather than trying to ignore them.

We should also try to use non-controlling language, instead using invitational language (Vansteenkiste et al., 2004). Instead of telling students what they must do, we can suggest things that they might find effective to do, or even take ownership and explain what we ourselves do as writers. Instead of a directive, we can provide instructions in the form of "I often start my paragraph in this way…". I often share my own personal writing strategies with students in a hope that they will find this less directive and more approachable. This method is likely to have a particularly powerful effect when the teacher shares the same first language background as the students. This kind of language may help to reduce the distance between the teacher and student and increase students' self-efficacy for writing.

L2 Writing-specific pedagogical recommendations

In the field of language learning more specifically, Little et al. (2017) state that autonomous learners should set their own goals, make choices, monitor their learning progress and evaluate their learning outcomes. Furthermore, in relation to the teaching of L2 writing, Ruegg (2018b) discussed specific methods of encouraging learners to take control of different stages of the writing process. For example, assignment introduction, self-review, peer review, teacher feedback, self-assessment and carrying out a personal learning plan. Ruegg (2021) focusses on how to introduce autonomy-supportive teaching practices in contexts where students are not used to having control over their own learning and struggle to know what to do with choice when it is offered to them. Specifically, she focusses on how to support students in choosing an appropriate topic to write about.

Ruegg (2018b) introduced a way in which introducing an assignment to students can become a discovery task, increasing students' engagement and supporting their autonomy. She encouraged the use of guided self-review inside the classroom, allowing opportunities for learner training to support the strengthening of self-review skills. In terms of peer feedback,

Ruegg (2018b) applied the same method used to encourage student-led teacher feedback in Ruegg (2020). In addition, in Ruegg (2018b), students were encouraged to discuss their feedback with each other in groups and then do research to settle differences of opinion between peers. In terms of teacher feedback, Ruegg (2018b) made the focus of feedback progressive, with students receiving comprehensive category-coded feedback on their first assignment, choosing questions from a list to request feedback from the teacher on the second assignment, coming up with their own questions in groups to request feedback on the third assignment and finally, individually writing questions for feedback on the final assignment. This kind of process is an example of an effective way to scaffold students away from teacher-directed feedback and towards student-initiated feedback from their teacher. In order to support the skills needed to utilize assessment criteria for learning, Ruegg (2018b) also incorporated self-assessment of tasks before submission and reflection on that self-assessment after grades were returned, with a specific focus on discrepancies between the self-assessment and teacher assessment of the same assignment. Finally, a Personal Learning Plan (Murray, 2009) was employed, to encourage learners to set their own learning goals, try different methods and materials to work towards those goals, evaluate their own learning and revise their goals. Ruegg (2018b) found that at the end of the semester a majority of the students reported having developed skills in identifying suitable focus areas for study (78%), evaluating and selecting appropriate materials and methods for their study (81%) and evaluating their own progress (72%).

In relation to feedback more specifically, Ruegg (2018a) suggests that there is an overall sum of effort expended in the process of teachers providing feedback on writing and students using that feedback to improve their writing. In general, when teachers use methods of feedback that require a lot of effort (such as direct correction of students' errors), it allows students to be more passive in the process. On the other hand, when teachers provide methods of feedback that require less effort (such as indirect feedback, or indirect coded feedback), the students are required to take a more active role in using the feedback to revise their writing. Clearly, indirect feedback cannot be used for students at all levels of language proficiency, or at all educational levels. However, in general teachers should aim to give less explicit types of feedback in order to encourage students to play an active role in identifying and solving problems in their writing. Relating this idea to self-determination theory, students are likely to be more engaged in a problem-solving activity that will help them improve their writing than in the menial task of copying a teacher's corrections into their text.

Suggestions for action research

In previous literature, Ruegg (2018b) suggested using the student-initiated feedback practice discussed in Ruegg (2020) for the provision of both teacher feedback and peer feedback. Although Ruegg (2020) has provided some specific research evidence about this feedback practice, there is a great deal still unknown. For example, when students use this feedback system repeatedly throughout a course, do they find the feedback they receive to be more useful than when they receive teacher-directed feedback? This would be an interesting area for further action research.

In addition, Campbell and Schumm-Fauster (2013) investigated students' perspectives of a similar student-initiated feedback practice. However, there is little research evidence about students' preferences related to student-led feedback practices. Another fruitful area of further action research would be to use different methods of teacher and or peer feedback and ask students perspectives on those methods.

Another suggestion related to feedback is for action research focussing on self-feedback. Ruegg (2018b) suggests using guided self-feedback inside the classroom and the teacher providing support to students while they review their own work. Action research comparing students who receive this kind of guidance and support with others who are asked to self-review their writing for homework could utilize a word processing programme that keeps track of changes made to texts during self-review and subsequent revision and compare those changes between the groups of students.

Another under-researched area is the various effects of allowing students to choose their own topics. Several studies have been conducted and published (i.e., Bonyadi, 2014; LeBlanc & Fujieda, 2012; Neisi et al., 2019). However, there is a need for many more studies in a range of different contexts which investigate different aspects of this practice.

Indeed, any of the above-mentioned pedagogical suggestions could be investigated in action research projects. If teacher researchers are interested in measuring the relative autonomy of the learners in their classroom (for example, before and after the introduction of a specific pedagogical practice or set of pedagogical practices), a Relative Autonomy Index can be calculated using self-regulation questionnaires (Self-determination theory organization, 2021).

Learner autonomy has been a relatively popular topic in the field of language learning. However, although learner autonomy is particularly relevant to the teaching of writing, there has been relatively less research published about the development of learner autonomy within the L2 writing classroom. There is large scope for future research into the intricacies of different aspects of autonomy-supportive teaching. Moreover, there is a great need for teaching which supports the development of learner autonomy in a large number of teaching contexts around the world. In doing so, we are likely to enhance the intrinsic motivation, engagement and performance of our students.

Further reading

Little, D., Dam, L., & Legenhausen, L. (2017). *Language learner autonomy: Theory, practice and research.* **Multilingual Matters.**

While this book does not focus specifically on L2 writing, many of the ideas in the book can be adapted for the L2 writing classroom. It starts with an overview of the topic, followed by the first part of the book which includes four chapters focussing on practical applications for the classroom. While the first two chapters in this section may be less useful for teaching L2 writing, the third and fourth chapters are indispensable. The second part of the book focusses on research relating to learner autonomy. Again, the first chapter in this section may be less useful for teaching L2 writing, while I would consider the second chapter indispensable. The final part may be less useful than the first two parts.

Overall, this book is highly recommended for anyone interested in learning more about this topic, in particular chapters three, four and six. It will be useful for those who come to the teaching of L2 writing from the perspective of writing to learn language, and those who teach L2 writing within a language programme. It provides a strong theoretical background in learner autonomy and focusses on some key aspects of education that should be considered by teachers.

Littlewood, W. (1996). "Autonomy": An anatomy and a framework. *System, 24(4),* 427–435.

This is an essential text for anyone interested in learner autonomy within the arena of second language learning. Although it was published some time ago now, this is a key text on the topic. It provides ways of thinking about autonomy that may help novice teachers to understand the concept as well as practical applications. In this article, Littlewood provides a progression through which learners can be encouraged to gradually take control of more and more aspects of their learning through time. He also provides a framework which can be used to map teaching and learning activities onto the concept of learner autonomy. All in all, this is a useful and accessible text for novice teachers who would like scaffolding to help them understand the concept of learner autonomy and how they can put it into practice in their teaching contexts.

Liu, W. C., Keng, J., W., C., & Ryan, R. (Eds.). (2016). *Building autonomous learners: Perspectives from research and practice using self-determination theory.* **Springer.**

This is an edited volume on the development of learner autonomy, with fifteen chapters which are all based on self-determination theory. The first chapter is an introduction, which is followed by 14 chapters written by authors from different geographical regions, different disciplines and different levels of the education system. There is a strong focus on increasing learners' motivation, which is a significant concern for those teaching writing, with four of the 14 chapters focussed specifically on this issue. There are a few theoretical chapters, and a preponderance of practical applications, written as either practical recommendations for teaching or empirical research studies conducted in educational contexts.

Although this entire volume may be of interest, for those who are short of time, three chapters in this book in particular are recommended. Anyone interested in increasing autonomy in their learners would benefit greatly from reading the following chapters: Chapter 7 is a practical overview of teaching practices that support the development of learner autonomy. Chapter 8 provides a learning sequence that may be effective in a range of classroom contexts for increasing autonomy. Chapter 12 as an empirical investigation that looks at the effects of autonomy-supportive teaching on self-regulation and student performance.

Ryan, R. M., & Deci, E. L. (2017). *Self-determination theory: Basic psychological needs in motivation, development, and wellness.* **Guilford Publications.**

This is a textbook providing a broad overview of self-determination theory. The book begins with an introduction, followed by a detail section explaining the historical and philosophical background of the theory. This is followed by a section which outlines in detail six theories that are part of self-determination theory. The next section focusses on motivation and its relationship to human development in the contexts of homes, schools and societies. Section five is about practical applications of self-determination theory, although not all practical applications in this section are relevant for educational contexts, much less second language learning contexts. The final section focusses on psychological needs in social contexts, and again, much of the content in this section is not relevant for educators, much less teachers of second language learners. For anyone interested in learning more about self-determination theory in a broad sense, I would recommend reading the introductory chapter and, if time permits, section three which outlines six theories at play in self-determination theory.

References

Bonyadi, A. (2014). The effect of topic selection on EFL students' writing performance. *Sage Open, 4(3),* 1–9. https://doi.org/10.1177/2158244014547176

Campbell, N., & Schumm-Fauster, J. (2013). Learner-centered feedback on writing: Feedback as dialogue. In M. Reitbauer, N. Campbell, S. Mercer, J. Schumm-Fauster, & R. Vaupetitsch (Eds.), *Feedback matters:*

Current feedback practices in the EFL classroom (pp. 55–68). Peter Lang.

Clarke, D. F. (1991). The negotiated syllabus: what is it and how is it likely to work? *Applied Linguistics, 12(1),* 13–28. https://doi.org/10.1093/applin/12.1.13

Deci, E. L. (1995). *Why we do what we do: Understanding self-motivation.* Penguin Books.

LeBlanc, C., & Fujieda, M. (2012). Investigating effects of topic control on lexical variation in Japanese university students' in-class timed writing. *Kwansei Gakuin University Humanities Review, 17,* 241–253.

Little, D. (1995). Learning as dialogue: The dependence of learner autonomy on teacher autonomy. *System, 23*(2), 175-181. https://doi.org/10.1016/0346-251X(95)00006-6

Little, D., Dam, L., & Legenhausen, L. (2017). *Language learner autonomy.* Multilingual Matters.

Littlewood, W. (1996). "Autonomy": An anatomy and a framework. *System, 24*(4), 427–435. https://doi.org/10.1016/S0346-251X(96)00039-5

Murray, G. (2009). Self-access language learning: Structure, control and responsibility. In F. Kjisik, F., P. Voller, N. Aoki, & Y. Nakata (Eds.), *Mapping the terrain of learner autonomy: Learning environments, learning communities and identities* (pp. 118–142). Tampere University Press.

Neisi, L., Nasri, M., Akbari, S., & Namziandost, E. (2019). The comparative effect of teacher-assigned topics and student-selected topics on Iranian upper-intermediate EFL learners' writing skill. *Journal of English Language Teaching and Applied Linguistics, 1(1),* 1–15.

Reeve, J. (2009). Why teachers adopt a controlling motivating style toward students and how they can become more autonomy supportive. *Educational psychologist, 44(3),* 159–175. https://doi.org/10.1080/00461520903028990

Reeve, J. (2016). Autonomy-supportive teaching: What it is, how to do it. In W. C. Liu, J. C. K. Wang, & M. R. Ryan (Eds.), *Building autonomous learners* (pp. 129–152). Springer. https://doi.org/ 10.1007/978-981-287-630-0_7

Reeve, J., & Cheon, S. H. (2016). Teachers become more autonomy supportive after they believe it is easy to do. *Psychology of Sport and Exercise, 22,* 178–189. https://doi.org/10.1016/j.psychsport.2015.08.001

Ruegg, R. (2018a). Providing effective feedback on L2 academic writing. *RumeliDE Dil ve Edebiyat Araştırmaları Dergisi, 13,* 161–178. https://doi.org/10.29000/rumelide.504928

Ruegg, R. (2018b). Increasing autonomy in learners of EAP writing: An exploratory study. In R. Ruegg & C. Williams (Eds.), *Teaching English for Academic Purposes (EAP) in Japan: Studies from an English medium university* (pp. 99–121). Springer.

Ruegg, R. (2020). Student-led feedback on writing: Requests made and feedback received. *Journal of Response to Writing, 6(2),* 69–101.

Ruegg, R. (2021). *Teaching and learning writing in ESL/EFL.* Foreign Language Teaching and Research Press.

Ryan, R. M., & Deci, E. L. (2017). *Self-determination theory: Basic psychological needs in motivation, development, and wellness*. Guilford Publications.

Self-determination theory organization. (2021). *Self-regulation questionnaires.* Retrieved from https://selfdeterminationtheory.org/self-regulation-questionnaires

Su, Y. L., & Reeve, J. (2011). A meta-analysis of the effectiveness of intervention programs designed to support autonomy. *Educational Psychology Review, 23*, 159–188. https://doi.org/10.1007/s10648-010-9142-7

Vansteenkiste, M., Simons, J., Lens, W., Sheldon, K. M., & Deci, E. L. (2004). Motivating learning, performance, and persistence: the synergistic effects of intrinsic goal contents and autonomy-supportive contexts. *Journal of personality and social psychology, 87*(2), 246–260. https://doi.org/10.1037/0022-3514.87.2.246

Vygotsky, L. S. (1978). *Mind in Society: The development of higher psychological processes*. Harvard University Press.

Wang, J. C. K., Ng, B. L., Liu, W. C., & Ryan, R. M. (2016). Can being autonomy-supportive in teaching improve students' self-regulation and performance? In W. Liu, J. Wang, & R. Ryan (Eds.), *Building autonomous learners* (pp. 227–243). Springer. https://doi.org/10.1007/978-981-287-630-0_12

9
Collaborative writing: Theory, research, and implications

Tomohito Hiromori

Introduction

Learning activities involving collaboration with others, such as pair work and group work, have received increasing attention in second/foreign language (L2) learning contexts. If one of the primary purposes of language learning is to develop communication abilities, then it is natural for collaboration to be essential to this process. There are many definitions of collaboration, but the core meaning of the concept is "to labor together" (co-labor). Collaboration is sometimes used synonymously with other terms, notably cooperation. However, the general understanding in the literature is that these two concepts are different. According to Dillenbourg et al. (1996), cooperation is accomplished by dividing labor among participants, whereas collaboration refers to the mutual engagement of participants in a coordinated effort to solve the problem together. In a nutshell, collaboration is considered a series of processes in which there is mutual engagement and coordinated effort by all members participating in the activity.

Writing instruction in L2 classrooms has incorporated a wide range of activities that involve collaboration. The most typical example is collaborative writing, which is the focus of this chapter. Defined as "an activity that requires the co-authors to be involved in all stages of the writing process, sharing the responsibility for and the ownership of the entire text produced" (Storch, 2019, p. 40), the effect of collaborative writing on second language acquisition (SLA) has been confirmed through various theoretical perspectives, such as the interaction hypothesis (Long, 1983), the output hypothesis (Swain, 1993), and sociocultural theory (Lantolf, 2000). The basis of SLA is input, but the negotiation for meaning (e.g., confirmation checks, clarification requests) which occurs during interaction makes the input more comprehensible. Furthermore, through output activities, learners notice what they cannot say or write using their own linguistic knowledge, and generate and test hypotheses about linguistic forms. Although such functions are found in both speaking and writing, they are more pronounced in the latter as learners can often control the amount of time they spend working and deliberating on the task.

In recent research, much attention has been paid to the sociocultural aspects of collaborative writing. Originally informed by Vygotsky's "Zone of Proximal Development" (1978)—which posits that with the help of a teacher or other more capable peers, learners could perform tasks that belong to the next developmental stage, above the one they are currently at—sociocultural theories focus on the context in which learning occurs as well as the interface between learner(s) and social context. Collaborative writing requires agreement between pairs or within a group on what and how to express ideas. In this process, learners are required to deliberate on language choice and grammatical accuracy. Swain (2000, 2006) calls such deliberation about language "collaborative dialogue," and later on, "languaging." Languaging is the act of problem solving through the use of language, such as explaining, reflecting, and describing, when performing cognitively complex tasks. Storch (2013, p. 16) added that "the importance of languaging is not only that it is the means to solve problems but that in the process new knowledge or new understandings are constructed." Collaborative writing is thus an ideal collaborative task to promote languaging through peer interaction.

From a pedagogical perspective, collaborative writing is a good match for recent communication-oriented teaching methods. Communicative language teaching and task-based language teaching are widely adopted in current L2 instruction, where the use of pair and group work to engage learners in communication is a major feature. In this context, instruction should focus primarily on meaning, but careful task design and implementation can also encourage learners to negotiate for form. An instructional technique that focuses on a particular linguistic form (grammar, vocabulary) while conducting meaning-centered activities is called "focus on form" (Doughty & Williams, 1998). A central concept in task-based language teaching, focus on form, has the following characteristics: (1) arises in interactions involving the L2 learner, (2) is incidental (i.e., it is not pre-planned), (3) induces "noticing" (i.e., conscious attention to target linguistic forms), (4) is brief (i.e., it does not interfere with the primary focus on meaning), and (5) is reactive (i.e., occurs in response to a communication problem) (Long, 1991, 2015). When learners experience noticing through focus on form, they are more likely to pay attention to the linguistic form and, as a result, language acquisition will be enhanced. Based on the aforementioned theoretical frameworks, we can appreciate how collaborative writing helps to develop L2 writing skills in directions that other strategies cannot, thanks to its communicative nature.

Literature review on collaborative writing

Research on collaborative writing began in the 1990s. Since then, many studies have been reported in diverse L2 learning contexts. Through a comprehensive review of the timeline of empirical studies on collabora-

Table 9.1 *Factors that influence the nature of collaborative writing and its outcomes*

Factor	Examples
CW vs. Non-CW tasks	Comparison with individual writing
Task variables	Task type, task complexity, task mode
Learner variables	L2 motivation, proficiency
Pattern of interaction	Four patterns of dyadic interaction

Note. CW = collaborative writing

tive writing, Storch (2019) categorized the studies into two periods. During the first period, most researchers were focused on collaborative writing contexts in which learners interacted face-to-face (FTF) in the classroom. With the advancement of information technology during the second period, researchers turned their focus to computer-mediated (CM) collaborative writing. Zhang and Plonsky (2020) reviewed 94 studies on FTF collaborative writing from 1992 to 2017, and Li (2018) examined 21 studies on CM collaborative writing from 2008 to 2017. These two systematic, methodological, and substantive reviews revealed some of the key factors that influence the nature of collaborative writing and its outcomes (see Table 9.1). In the following sections, I examine each of these factors.

Collaborative vs. non-collaborative writing tasks

Many early studies on collaborative writing have attempted to verify its effectiveness by comparing it to individual writing. The underlying assumption was that, compared to individual writing activities where learners have to rely solely on their own linguistic knowledge, working in pairs or groups allows learners to share the knowledge they possess, deals with more cognitively demanding tasks, and consequently results in higher performance. According to the results of a recent meta-analysis (Elabdali, 2021), this assumption was supported by empirical studies, which suggested that, compared to individually written texts, collaboratively written texts were more accurate, with a mean effect size of medium magnitude ($g = 0.73$). Furthermore, texts written individually after the experience of collaborative writing practice scored higher on rubric criteria (e.g., content, organization, and grammar; $g = 0.94$) than those written by individuals without such practice. The findings thus strongly support the theoretical rationales of collaborative writing as a task that facilitates linguistic accuracy, L2 written output, and the development of L2 writing proficiency.

Task variables

Task variables appear to play a major role in determining the nature of collaborative writing. A number of studies have investigated the influence of task type (e.g., dictogloss, jigsaw, text editing), task complexity (e.g., abstract versus concrete topics), and task mode (e.g., FTF versus CM) on learners' engagement during collaborative writing tasks. For example, De la Colina and García Mayo (2007) assessed a group of less proficient L2 learners and how they paid attention to language generated by three task types (dictogloss, jigsaw, and text reconstruction). The study found that although all three collaborative writing tasks were effective in drawing learners' attention to language, the interactions between learners (i.e., language-related episodes or LREs) differed depending on the type of task. Specifically, in the more structured task (text reconstruction), learners discussed, questioned, and corrected each other about the language they produced more frequently than in the other tasks. Although dictogloss has been used in a wide range of studies (Storch, 2013), it tends not to generate many LREs, particularly when used with less proficient learners (e.g., Leeser, 2004; Zhang, 2022). These results suggest that the structured text reconstruction task may be more suitable for learners with relatively low proficiency, while language-focused tasks such as dictogloss are more suitable for advanced L2 learners.

Due to recent developments in information technology and the unprecedented global crisis brought about by COVID-19, online instruction has been attracting more attention than ever before, and language education is no exception. In the case of collaborative writing, a number of studies have examined the effect of mode of communication (FTF vs. CM) on learners' engagement in the task. The results of this research indicate that both FTF and CM classes have advantages and disadvantages, and how each mode is perceived varies from learner to learner (Li, 2018; Storch, 2019). Since some learners may not be fully accustomed to online instruction, it is still too early to judge which mode is better at this point. However, studies have repeatedly highlighted that it appears difficult for learners in the CM mode to engage deeply in collaborative writing tasks (Baralt et al., 2016; Carver et al., 2021). This may be because CM collaborative writing tends to be accompanied by an incoherent flow of conversation, with difficulties in determining co-authorship, and unequal participation (Jiang et al., 2021). Therefore, in the pedagogical implications that follow, I will discuss how to enhance learners' engagement, especially in CM classes.

Learner variables

The approach to collaborative writing tasks varies among learners. One of the factors behind this difference is their attitude and motivation toward the task. Chen and Yu (2019) investigated how changes in student attitudes affected patterns of interaction and language learning opportunities in collaborative writing over multiple observations. The results showed that students' attitudes changed based on the levels of exposure to the activities, and positive attitudes led to more learning opportunities. In a pair or group task, the motivation of the partner or group members also has an impact on the learner's motivation. Here, my colleagues and I recently conducted a study (Hiromori et al., 2021a) to investigate whether the transmission of motivation between students in a pair (i.e., "motivation contagion") occurs in collaborative writing tasks. The results revealed that students' motivation can be impacted by merely observing the motivational orientation of their partners, and their effects were moderated by students' motivation levels—less motivated learners were greatly influenced by the motivation demonstrated by their partner, while highly motivated learners showed no such influence. Therefore, it is suggested that the motivation of learners in pairs or groups should be carefully considered when conducting collaborative writing tasks, noting that this applies more strongly to learners with low motivation.

Another thing to keep in mind when pairing and grouping is the proficiency level of the learners. In general, learners of various proficiency levels learn together in an ordinary L2 classroom, but how can we best pair/group learners in a collaborative task? Aldosari (2008) investigated the impact of proficiency pairing and task type on learners' interactions. The results demonstrated that collaboration tended to occur mainly among pairs with similar proficiency (i.e., low-low and high-high) rather than those with mixed proficiency. Additionally, the highest number of LREs was generated by the high-high pairs, and the lowest by the low-low pairs. One possible explanation is that the low-low pairs were more preoccupied with task completion—such as sharing ideas for the composition—than with deliberation over the language, resulting in a low number of LREs. Similarly, Fernández Dobao (2012, 2014) investigated whether pairs or groups are better for collaborative writing tasks. In her 2012 study, she compared the LREs and L2 text (complexity, accuracy, fluency) produced by pairs and small groups using a modified jigsaw task. The findings showed that small groups produced more LREs than pairs, and consequently, the texts written by the small groups were more accurate than those written in pairs. Although Fernández Dobao points out that small groups may provide more opportunities for language learning than pairs, she also notes that in group interaction, not all members necessarily work on the task in the same way. As seen in pair work, some learners are not willing to contribute much to the shared task.

Taken together, these results demonstrate that in detailing learners' engagement in collaborative writing tasks, it is necessary to examine how they interact in pairs and groups in the actual process of working on the tasks, and what kind of relationship they form as a result. Therefore, I discuss this point in the next section.

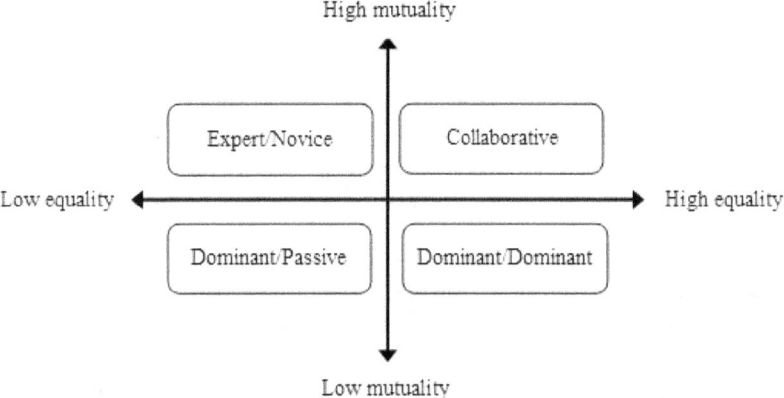

Figure 9.1 *A model of dyadic interaction (Storch, 2002, p. 128)*

Pattern of interaction and relationships formed

Several SLA studies have investigated patterns of interaction in pair and group work, but the model proposed by Storch (2002, 2009) has been the most influential among them. Focusing on the socially constructed nature of interaction, Storch (2002) investigated the relationships that learners formed when working on a range of collaborative writing tasks. She found that there were some fixed patterns in dyadic interaction, and once these patterns were established, they tended to persist. These patterns were classified into four types based on the concepts of "mutuality" (learners' level of engagement with each other's contribution) and "equality" (learners' level of contribution and control over the task): (1) collaborative (+mutuality, +equality), (2) expert/novice (+mutuality, −equality), (3) dominant/dominant (−mutuality, +equality), and (4) dominant/passive (−mutuality, −equality) (see Figure 9.1 for a visual representation). According to her model, the first two patterns (i.e., collaborative and expert/novice) result in a more collaborative attitude, more knowledge transfer, and greater language learning, whereas the other two (i.e., dominant/dominant and dominant/passive) are less favorable for collaborative tasks.

Although Storch's model has been applied and validated in various studies (see Azkarai & Kopinska, 2020 for a recent review), it should be noted that social, cultural, and educational contexts may influence the pairing patterns seen in the model. The four patterns involve both or either student playing a leading role in the pair work—whether collaborative, expert, or dominant. However, in my recent study of Japanese university students, eight out of the 30 pairs studied revealed that no such role was taken up in their pairs (Hiromori, 2021). In contrast, these pairs were labeled passive/passive. In these pairs, the number of words produced, turns exchanged, and LREs generated tended to be low, implying that both students were quiet around each other and did not contribute much willingly. A similar study by King (2013), which was based on 48 hours of lesson observation in Japanese university English classrooms, found that Japanese students rarely initiated communication in English (0.24 per cent of the total hours observed). These results show that simply pairing learners does not necessarily lead to collaboration or engagement in the task.

The above is true, not only for pairs, but also for groups. Simply assigning learners to groups does not mean that they will work "as a group" rather than "in a group" (Fernández Dobao, 2012, 2014). Here, the concept of assigned leadership, whose role is officially assigned by teachers and so forth (Northouse, 2009), may provide useful insights to facilitate successful learning in groups. Hiromori et al. (2021b) investigated how L2 learners' motivation and group work dynamics differ in a collaborative writing task between an experimental group that included a leader-role student and a control group that did not. The results demonstrated that it was possible to design group work that intentionally assigned a leadership role to promote group work dynamics. Interestingly, the study also found that group work could go well even without granting leadership, but under a specific condition: full equality in terms of contribution to the conversation within the group. In other words, group work is more likely to proceed well "if there is an equal relationship where each member of the group participates in the activity and proactively expresses their opinions" (Hiromori et al., 2021b, p. 64). These findings have useful implications for teaching collaborative writing in L2 classrooms.

Practical implications and suggestions

Now, I will discuss three points to consider when implementing collaborative writing in L2 classrooms. First, learners' engagement in collaborative writing is significantly influenced by the nature of the task—its level of difficulty, purposes, duration, and so forth. Thus, you need to carefully select which tasks to use depending on what you are trying to achieve in your writing instruction (e.g., L2 use and its development, motivation enhancement, collaborative learning experiences). Although you may be concerned about students' use of their first language (L1), previous studies have shown that learners do not use their L1 to a large extent, and that L1 use is more related to task type than to L2 proficiency (Storch & Aldosari, 2013). Therefore, it is advisable that you construct a course syllabus based on the development and continuity of what tasks are used and in what order. In addition, Storch (2013, p. 159) pointed out that teachers should consider writing tasks that "do not easily lend themselves to a division of labor so that learners collaborate rather than cooperate" (see difference between collaboration and cooperation in Section 1).

A good example of this is an information gap task, which uses information gaps to elicit active language use by participants. In such a task, pair or group interaction is essential to complete the task because each learner possesses different information. The key to the success of collaborative writing tasks is to create awareness of the differences in information and perceptions among learners and to create the inevitability of communication and collaboration.

We have seen how simply pairing/grouping learners does not guarantee successful pair or group work. Therefore, the next point to consider is how you can design a task that encourages learners' active participation and engagement. The first thing that you can do is to prepare a psychologically safe environment for mutual learning. Chang (2010) found that learning with a group of students who showed little interest in each other and were unresponsive could lead to a decrease in motivation. This finding indicates that good relationships within a group are closely related to the proactive engagement of learners in group work. Further, you may want to assign a student to play the role of leader in pair and group work. Although some learners are not good at speaking up or leading activities on their own, many of them will perform their roles if they are formally appointed and are clearly informed of the ultimate goal (Hiromori et al., 2021b; Selcuk et al., 2021). In particular, it often takes a long time for learners to cognitively/emotionally engage in a task in a CM condition, but pre-appointing a leader can be an effective teaching strategy to motivate learners to engage in the task and to activate group work dynamics from the beginning of the activity.

Finally, as is true for any activity, learners' perceptions of the task have a significant impact on their engagement with it. Although learners generally have positive attitudes toward collaborative writing (e.g., Fernández Dobao & Blum, 2013; Shehadeh, 2011), they do not always perceive it favorably and sometimes have difficulty changing their long-established beliefs (e.g., writing is essentially an individual activity, pair work with less proficient learners is not worthwhile). Therefore, teachers need to explicitly explain the benefits of collaborative learning among students. For example, you can exchange ideas with students about the advantages of collaborative writing, and have students experience actual writing tasks that incorporate the benefits. You may want to show role-play movies that display desired behaviors in collaboration and then prompt students to reflect on good or bad collaboration. Kim and McDonough (2011) found that students who viewed videotaped models of collaborative interaction adopted more collaborative patterns of interaction and produced more LREs than those who did not view such models, which clearly shows the importance of pre-task training in collaborative writing. However, it is also important to understand that students will not be able to do (or change their minds) immediately after being taught. They will need persistent and continuous guidance, and sometimes, personalized assistance. When students buy into the potential of pair or group work, they will be more inclined to appreciate such learning benefits.

Suggestions for action research or case study
Pairing based on a partner's level of L2 motivation

Previous research on collaborative writing has examined pairing based on learners' proficiency, but little has been done to investigate the effects of pairing based on their level of motivation. Dörnyei (2002) examined how a fellow participant's level of motivation influenced actual task engagement in an oral argumentative task. The results showed that a partner's motivational orientation exerted a "pulling force" on the task attitude of an individual, concluding that "students' task motivation was *co-constructed* by the task participants" (p. 156; italics in original). As such, unmotivated learners should be able to improve their performance by being paired with motivated learners. Alternatively, in a partial follow-up study of Dörnyei's 2002 work, Konno and Koga (2017) showed that highly motivated learners performed better when paired with similarly motivated learners than with less motivated ones. Specifically, the authors agreed with Dörnyei (2002) that task motivation is co-constructed with task participants, but this is true only for pairs with high motivation. Examining which of these arguments is correct in the actual classroom setting will lead to useful insights for more effective collaborative writing practices.

Effects of long-term intervention

Most studies that have examined the effects of collaborative writing have been cross-sectional in nature (i.e., one-shot design studies). More longitudinal studies are required to clarify the circumstances under which learners collaborate more with each other and the factors that promote group work dynamics. Such a study will also allow us to see if the benefits of writing collaboratively can endure beyond a single writing experience. Further, it is also possible to investigate whether pairing/grouping randomly each time is more pedagogically effective than doing the activity continuously with fixed pair/group members. For example, when focus is more on enhancing pair/group work experience, fixing members may be a better option because it can help enhance pair/group cohesion and reduce anxiety by working with the same peer(s). On the other hand, working with the same partner all the time can lead to boredom and sometimes overreliance on hardworking peers. Therefore, if we can clarify how fixing or changing group members transforms learners' approaches to collaborative writing tasks, then we can design more targeted pedagogical interventions.

Further reading

Storch, N. (2013). *Collaborative writing in L2 classrooms*. Multilingual Matters.

This is the first book-length treatment of collaborative writing in the field of L2 education. One of the central aims of this book is "to encourage language teachers to consider implementing collaborative writing activities in their classes" (p. 1). For readers who are interested in the contents of this chapter, I highly recommend reading this book first.

Storch, N. (2019). Collaborative writing. *Language Teaching***, 52(1), 40–59. https://doi.org/10.1017/S0261444818000320**

This article systematically reviews research on collaborative L2 writing. Based on a total of seven themes (e.g., learner interaction during collaborative writing, the outcomes of collaborative writing), this paper presents a concise list of studies in chronological order. It is very useful for readers to know how the focus of research on collaborative writing has changed and what kind of research has been conducted since the 1990s.

Li, M. (2022). *Researching and teaching second language writing in the digital age***. Palgrave Macmillan.**

Mimi Li, who has been leading the way in the field of L2 writing and technology, summarizes the latest research, covering not only CM collaborative writing but also relatively new topics, such as online teacher/peer feedback and automated writing evaluation. This is a good book for integrating digital tools into L2 writing instruction.

References

Aldosari, A. (2008). *The influence of proficiency levels, task type and social relationships on pair interaction: An EFL context* (Unpublished doctoral dissertation). University of Melbourne, Australia.

Azkarai, A., & Kopinska, M. (2020). Young EFL learners and collaborative writing: A study on patterns of interaction, engagement in LREs, and task motivation. *System, 94*, 1–15. https://doi.org/10.1016/j.system.2020.102338

Baralt, M., Gurzynski-Weiss, L., & Kim, Y. (2016). Engagement with language: How examining learners' affective and social engagement explains successful learner-generated attention to form. In M. Sato & S. Ballinger (Eds.), *Peer interaction and second language learning: Pedagogical potential and research agenda* (pp. 209–240). John Benjamins.

Carver, C., Jung, D., & Gurzynski-Weiss, L. (2021). Examining learner engagement in relationship to learning and communication mode. In P. Hiver, A. H. Al-Hoorie, & S. Mercer (Eds.), *Student engagement in the language classroom* (pp. 120–142). Multilingual Matters.

Chang, L. Y. H. (2010). Group processes and EFL learners' motivation: A study of group dynamics in EFL classrooms. *TESOL Quarterly, 44*

(1), 129–154. https://doi.org/10.5054/tq.2010.213780

Chen, W., & Yu, S. (2019). A longitudinal case study of changes in students' attitudes, participation, and learning in collaborative writing. *System*, *82*, 83–96. https://doi.org/10.1016/j.system.2019.03.005

De la Colina, A. A., & García Mayo, M. P. (2007). Attention to form across collaborative tasks by low-proficiency learners in an EFL setting. In M. P. García Mayo (Ed.), *Investigating tasks in formal language learning* (pp. 91–116). Multilingual Matters.

Dillenbourg, P., Baker, M., Blaye, A., & O'malley, C. (1996). The evolution of research on collaborative learning. In P. Reimann & H. Spada (Eds.), *Learning in humans and machine: Towards an interdisciplinary learning science* (pp. 189–211). Elsevier.

Dörnyei, Z. (2002). The motivational basis of language learning tasks. In P. Robinson (Ed.), *Individual differences and instructed language learning* (pp. 137–158). John Benjamins.

Doughty, C., & Williams, J. (Eds.) (1998). *Focus-on-form in classroom second language acquisition*. Cambridge University Press.

Elabdali, R. (2021). Are two heads really better than one? A meta-analysis of the L2 learning benefits of collaborative writing. *Journal of Second Language Writing*, *52*. Early View. https://doi.org/10.1016/j.jslw.2020.100788

Fernández Dobao, A. (2012). Collaborative writing tasks in the L2 classroom: Comparing group, pair, and individual work. *Journal of Second Language Writing*, *21*(1), 40–58. https://doi.org/10.1016/j.jslw.2011.12.002

Fernández Dobao, A. (2014). Vocabulary learning in collaborative tasks: A comparison of pair and small group work. *Language Teaching Research*, *18*(4), 497–520. https://doi.org/10.1177/1362168813519730

Fernández Dobao, A., & Blum, A. (2013). Collaborative writing in pairs and small groups: Learners' attitudes and perceptions. *System*, *41*(2), 365–378. https://doi.org/10.1016/j.system.2013.02.002

Hiromori, T. (2021). Anatomizing students' task engagement in pair work in the language classroom. *Journal for the Psychology of Language Learning*, *3*(1), 88–106. https://doi.org//10.52598/jpll/3/1/5

Hiromori, T., Yoshimura, M., Mitsugi, M., & Kirimura, R. (2021a). Watch your partner's behaviors: Motivation contagion in L2 pair work. *Journal of Pan-Pacific Association of Applied Linguistics*, *25*(1), 25–47. https://doi.org/10.25256/PAAL.25.1.2

Hiromori, T., Yoshimura, M., Mitsugi, M., & Kirimura, R. (2021b). Roles of leadership and L2 learner motivation in group work activities. *JACET Journal*, *65*, 47–67. https://doi.org/10.32234/jacetjournal.65.0_47

Jiang, D., Kalyuga, S., & Sweller, J. (2021). Comparing face-to-face and computer-mediated collaboration when teaching EFL writing skills. *Educational Psychology*, *41*(1), 5–24. https://doi.org/10.1080/01443410.

2020.1785399

Kim, Y., & McDonough, K. (2011). Using pretask modelling to encourage collaborative learning opportunities. *Language Teaching Research*, *15*(2), 183–199. https://doi.org/10.1177/1362168810388711

King, J. (2013). Silence in the second language classrooms of Japanese universities. *Applied Linguistics*, *34*(3), 352–343. https://doi.org/10.1093/applin/ams043

Konno, K., & Koga, T. (2017). Exploring the relationships between motivation and on-task behavior during interactive tasks. *Language Education & Technology*, *54*, 223–247.

Lantolf, J. P. (2000). *Sociocultural theory and second language learning*. Oxford University Press.

Leeser, M. J. (2004). Learner proficiency and focus on form during collaborative dialogue. *Language Teaching Research*, *8*(1), 55–81. https://doi.org/10.1191/1362168804lr134oa

Li, M. (2018). Computer-mediated collaborative writing in L2 contexts: An analysis of empirical research. *Computer Assisted Language Learning*, *31*(8), 882–904. https://doi.org/10.1080/09588221.2018.1465981

Long, M. H. (1983). Linguistic and conversational adjustments to non-native speakers. *Studies in Second Language Acquisition*, *5*(2), 177–193. https://doi.org/10.1017/S0272263100004848

Long, M. H. (1991). Focus on form: A design feature in language teaching methodology. In K. de Bot, R. B. Ginsberg & C. Kramsch (Eds.), *Foreign language research in cross-cultural perspective* (pp. 39–52). John Benjamins.

Long, M. H. (2015). *Second language acquisition and task-based language teaching*. Wiley Blackwell.

Northouse, P. G. (2009). *Leadership: Theory and practice*. Sage.

Selcuk, H., Jones, J., & Vonkova, H. (2021). The emergence and influence of group leaders in web-based collaborative writing: Self-reported accounts of EFL learners. *Computer Assisted Language Learning*, *34*(8), 1040–1060. https://doi.org/10.1080/09588221.2019.1650781

Shehadeh, A. (2011). Effects and student perceptions of collaborative writing in L2. *Journal of Second Language Writing*, *20*(4), 286–305. https://doi.org/10.1016/j.jslw.2011.05.010

Storch, N. (2002). Patterns of interaction in ESL pair work. *Language Learning*, *52*(1), 119–158. https://doi.org/10.1111/1467-9922.00179

Storch, N. (2009). *The nature of pair interaction. Learners' interaction in an ESL class: Its nature and impact on grammatical development*. VDM Verlag.

Storch, N. (2013). *Collaborative writing in L2 classrooms*. Multilingual Matters.

Storch, N. (2019). Collaborative writing. *Language Teaching*, *52*(1), 40–59. https://doi.org/10.1017/S0261444818000320

Storch, N., & Aldosari, A. (2013). Pairing learners in pair work activity. *Language Teaching Research*, *17*(1), 31–48. https://doi.org/10.1177/

1362168812457530

Swain, M. (1993). The output hypothesis: Just speaking and writing aren't enough. *The Canadian Modern Language Review*, *50*(1), 158–164. https://doi.org/10.3138/cmlr.50.1.158

Swain, M. (2000). The output hypothesis and beyond: Mediating acquisition through collaborative dialogue. In J. P. Lantolf (Ed.), *Sociocultural theory and second language learning* (pp. 97–114). Oxford University Press.

Swain, M. (2006). Languaging, agency and collaboration in advanced second language learning. In H. Byrnes (Ed.), *Advanced language learning: The contributions of Halliday and Vygotsky* (pp. 95–108). Continuum.

Vygotsky, L. S. (1978). *Mind in society: The development of higher psychological processes*. Harvard University Press.

Zhang, M. (2022). A re-examination of pair dynamics and L2 learning opportunities in collaborative writing. *Language Teaching Research*, *26*(1), 10–33. https://doi.org/10.1177/1362168819890949

Zhang, M., & Plonsky, L. (2020). Collaborative writing in face-to-face settings: A substantive and methodological review. *Journal of Second Language Writing*, *49*, 100753. https://doi.org/10.1016/j.jslw.2020.100753

10
Written corrective feedback

Minh Thi Thuy Nguyen
Willy Ardian Renandya

Introduction

Feedback is an important part of learning. Rarely, if ever, can students learn everything that the teacher has just taught. Some may remember some of the concepts discussed in a lesson. Some may understand these concepts but only at a rather superficial level, while others may completely miss the key points of the lesson. Feedback therefore provides an opportunity for teachers to re-teach concepts that students missed and for students to revisit important learning points that they have not completely learned the first time round. While it is universally acknowledged that feedback plays a critical role in learning, how to give effective feedback is a contentious issue, not only in general education but also in second language education. In second language writing, for example, teachers are often unsure about what kinds of feedback and how much feedback they should give to students' first drafts. Many have expressed dissatisfaction with their own feedback practices and wanted to learn more about how to give more effective feedback, the kind of feedback that can lead to significant improvement in students' final drafts (Lee, 2020a).

In L2 writing classrooms, feedback may target both content and language of the learner's written work. That said, second language acquisition (SLA) research to date has concentrated primarily on language-focused feedback, or feedback on linguistic errors (Li & Vuono, 2019). For the purposes of this chapter, the term "written corrective feedback" (WCF) is used to discuss this type of feedback, which is also referred to as "error feedback," "negative feedback," "error correction" or "error treatment" elsewhere. It is worth noting that WCF can be provided in either written (e.g., corrections or comments provided in the learner's essay) or oral form (e.g., verbal feedback given during individual conferencing) and can be conducted by the teacher (teacher feedback), peer (peer feedback) or the computer (e.g., automated feedback). However, this chapter focuses only on WCF provided in the written form by the teacher.

Theoretical perspectives

Despite the widespread acknowledgement that teacher feedback is an indispensable component of classroom learning and is often expected by the learner, there has been a controversy in SLA research surrounding the value of WCF in improving L2 writing. This controversy is related to the long-standing debate in the field over the type of language input (language that learners hear or read) that is required for L2 acquisition (Nassaji & Kartchava, 2021). From a cognitive perspective on L2 development, there are two types of language input that is available to the learner in acquiring a L2. The first type is positive evidence, or information about what is linguistically possible or acceptable in the target language (TL). Learners receive positive evidence when they encounter spoken and written TL texts in communicative contexts. The second type of input that the learner may receive is negative evidence. That is information about what is not possible or unacceptable linguistically in the TL and is typically provided through grammar teaching or corrective feedback (CF) (Long & Robinson, 1998). (But note that while some CF types contain only negative evidence, others can contain both types of linguistic evidence – see the next section).

While it seems to be generally agreed among SLA scholars that positive evidence is beneficial for L2 acquisition, there has been less consensus about the role of negative evidence (Nassaji & Kartchava, 2021). For example, in one of the earliest theories in SLA, the Monitor Model, Krashen (1985) claims that simple exposure to language input that one can understand is sufficient for learners to develop the ability to use the TL for real world communication. On the other hand, he argues that CF only caters to conscious knowledge of grammar rules that is only useful for 'monitoring and 'editing' language production but does not help learners to develop implicit knowledge that can be drawn upon for automatic language production in the real world. In other words, from the lens of the Monitor Model, consciousness of grammar does not aid language acquisition which relies exclusively on positive evidence. Drawing on the Monitor Model, opponents of WCF such as Truscott (1996) assert that WCF "has no place in writing courses and should be abandoned" (p. 328) because not only that it is ineffective, but it may also adversely affect learners' confidence. We will see later that this view is not supported by cumulative evidence from current SLA research on the effectiveness of WCF.

On the other hand, some theorists argue that positive evidence alone is not sufficient for developing advanced L2 knowledge and that learners also need to attend to language forms (DeKeyser, 2014; Schmidt, 1990; Swain, 1985, 1995). In this regard, CF is believed to play an important role. Proponents of the skill acquisition theory, for example, maintain that L2 development involves a gradual transformation of conscious knowledge of grammar rules into unconscious knowledge that is available for automatic language use, and the feedback that learners receive on their linguistic errors plays a vital role in facilitating this transition (DeKeyser, 2014; Lyster & Sato, 2013). Support for WCF can also be found in interaction theories such as the Noticing Hypothesis (Schmidt, 1990) and Output Hypothesis (Swain, 1985, 1995). According to the Noticing Hypothesis, the feedback that learners receive on their language production can help them notice the gap in their L2 knowledge, which is crucial for intake (Schmidt, 1990). The Output Hypothesis adds further that when learners are "pushed" to modify their language production upon receiving feedback (e.g., when learners are required to revise their writing based on the received feedback), they can attend to problematic forms that might otherwise go unnoticed and try out alternative ways of expressing their meaning. This helps learners to process language forms at a deeper level and hence enables them to develop an awareness of how and why particular forms are used, which is beneficial to L2 learning (Swain, 1985, 1995). Proponents of WCF such as Shintani et al. (2014), drawing on these theories, recommend that it is important for learners to not only notice feedback but also have the opportunity to revise their written production using feedback so that they can benefit from it.

Finally, from the perspective of sociocultural theory (Vygotsky, 1978), CF is also regarded as a powerful tool for mediating learning. Sociocultural theory considers L2 learning as occurring through scaffolding or support from a more knowledgeable person such as the teacher or a higher proficiency peer to the learner as they interact or work collaboratively to solve a learning problem. It is argued that this process enables the learner to progress from their current level of linguistic ability and gradually reach a higher level of competence where they can use the L2 independently and autonomously. From this perspective, feedback is seen as a scaffolding strategy to help the learner accomplish a learning task that they may not be able to complete without assistance (Nassaji, 2021). Proponents of sociocultural theory contend that WCF is effective when it is given within the learner's 'zone of proximal development', that is when it is appropriate for the learner's level (Storch, 2018).

Literature review

Types of WCF

WCF can be categorised in many different ways. Based on the manner in which WCF is given, SLA scholars distinguish between direct, indirect, and metalinguistic feedback (e.g., Bitchener, 2021; Bitchener & Storch, 2016; Ellis, 2009; Lee, 2020a, 2022). Direct feedback, or error correction, indicates that an error has been made (e.g., by crossing out the error) and provides the learner with the correction. In contrast, indirect feedback only indicates the presence of the error but does not correct it. The third type, metalinguistic feedback, also does not show the learner how to correct an error but only provides information on the nature of the error, by means of error codes (e.g., T means verb tense) or metalinguistic explanation (e.g., "Use the simple past tense because you are describing an event that finished at a specific point of time"). For this reason, some researchers consider metalinguistic feedback as another form of indirect feedback (e.g., Lee, 2020b). Metalinguistic feedback may be combined with direct feedback to provide the learners with both metalinguistic information on the nature of the error and the correct form (e.g., Hassan & Abbas, 2022; Sheen, 2007).

Additionally, feedback can be categorised as either focused or unfocused (comprehensive). As its name suggests, focused feedback involves the teacher selecting only one or a few error types that they consider important to address, while unfocused (comprehensive) feedback may address all or most errors in the learner's text (Lee, 2020b). Another important consideration when providing feedback is **whether learners are required to** respond to the feedback by revising their texts, or whether they are only expected to attend to the correction (Ellis, 2009).

The distinction between different WCF types is important from both a theoretical and pedagogical perspective. Theoretically, direct feedback is considered to provide both positive and negative evidence while indirect feedback and metalinguistic feedback only contain negative evidence. Research into the relative effectiveness of each type, therefore, can contribute to shedding light on the key issues regarding the type of input that is required for L2 acquisition. The theoretical significance of metalinguistic feedback is also related to the distinction made by Schmidt (1990) between noticing and understanding. Whereas noticing only involves attention to a specific form in the input, understanding requires the generation of the rules underlying the use of the form, which is a higher level of awareness. Feedback containing metalinguistic information has been found to promote both noticing and understanding and lead to a deeper level of input processing (Hassan & Abbas, 2022; Sheen, 2007).

In a similar vein, WCF with or without the opportunity to revise draws on different theoretical approaches that emphasise the role of input versus output in L2 acquisition (Shintani et al., 2014). While revision is a form of 'pushed output' which, based on the Output Hypothesis, can contribute to noticing and learning (Swain, 1985, 1995), it might also be possible for the learner who receives only WCF to notice the corrections (Ekanayaka & Ellis, 2020; Ellis, 2009). Therefore, research into these feedback options may provide an answer to the question concerning whether input alone is sufficient for learning or whether output is also required.

Theoretically, there is also a solid reason for distinguishing focused and unfocused (comprehensive) WCF. Unfocused (comprehensive) WCF addresses a larger number of errors compared to focused WCF. This can result in cognitive overload for the learner, which may hinder their ability to attend to the teacher's feedback to develop an understanding of the nature of the errors and how to correct them (Mao & Lee, 2020). From a practical standpoint, understanding the relative efficacy of the different WCF options can assist the teacher to make informed decisions in a way to suit not only the learners' needs and goals but also the teachers' own timetables.

Effectiveness of WCF

The effectiveness of WCF in improving L2 writing was strongly refuted by Truscott (1996, 2007), who argued that WCF had a limited role to play in L2 grammatical development. Truscott's position was based on his observation that early studies only showed that WCF could lead to an elimination of errors in a second draft. However, they did not demonstrate whether learners could apply these corrections in a new writing task, which was generally considered as stronger evidence of learning. Truscott also found it problematic that prior research on WCF did not use a control group to provide baseline data, hence making it difficult to ascertain the effect of WCF on L2 writing development.

Truscott's refutation of the effectiveness of WCF subsequently led to a surge of interest in WCF research. A number of recent studies have resolved the issues that he raised and provided evidence that WCF can indeed contribute to L2 development (see Bitchener, 2021; Li & Vuono, 2019; Karim & Nassaji, 2020a for a detailed review). Two meta-analysis studies by Kang and Han (2015) and Lim and Renandya (2020) have demonstrated that not only that WCF produces a positive effect on writing accuracy, but this effect is also retained in the long term.

Another question that many recent studies have attempted to address is concerning the relative effectiveness of different WCF options. The results to date, however, have been relatively mixed (Lee, 2022; Li & Vuono, 2019). For example, while many studies have found an advantage for direct feedback over indirect feedback because of its higher degree of explicitness (e.g., Bagheri & Rassaei, 2022; Karim & Nassaji, 2020a), some have found that both types are equally effective (e.g., Sinha & Nassaji, 2021; Suzuki et al., 2019; Zabihi & Erfanitabar, 2021).

Controversies have also been observed surrounding feedback with and without metalinguistic information. Sheen (2007), for example, found that while both direct feedback with and without metalinguistic information was effective in the short term, the former produced a stronger effect in the long term. Shintani and Ellis (2013) also found a superior effect for metalinguistic explanation over direct feedback alone in developing learners' awareness of grammatical rules. Zabihi and Erfanitabar (2021) found that metalinguistic information could enhance the effectiveness of both direct and indirect feedback. Similarly, Hassan and Abbas (2022) reported a stronger effect for a combination of direct and indirect feedback with metalinguistic information than direct and indirect feedback alone. Other studies, however, have found a superior effect for feedback without metalinguistic information (e.g., Benson & DeKeyser, 2019; Guo & Barrot, 2019; Lopez et al., 2018) or that one is not more efficacious than another (e.g., Karim & Nassaji, 2020b). The two meta-analysis studies by Kang and Han (2015) and Lim and Renandya (2020) have also shown that there is no clear advantage of one WCF option over another.

Several factors have been identified to mediate the effect of WCF and contribute to the variations in the findings of the existing studies. These factors include not only contextual factors such as foreign language versus second language learning contexts, but also learner-related factors such as proficiency levels and language analytic ability, as well as feedback-related factors such as types of linguistic targets and scope of feedback (focused versus unfocused) (Kang & Han, 2015; Karim & Nassaji, 2020a; Lee, 2022; Lim & Renandya, 2020; Li & Vuono, 2019). In terms of learner-related factors, for example, Kang and Han (2015)'s meta-analysis has shown that advanced learners may benefit more from WCF than their lower proficiency peers. Other studies have also shown that different proficiency groups may benefit from different WCF types. For instance, while direct feedback is considered more useful to low proficiency learners because it provides them with correct target forms, indirect feedback is believed to work better with higher proficiency learners who possess more knowledge to self-correct (Bitchener, 2021). In Sheen's (2007) study, metalinguistic feedback was found to be more beneficial for learners with higher language analytical ability. Shalizar and Rezaei (2022) have demonstrated that feedback may prove most helpful when it is provided within the learner's 'zone of proximal development'.

Furthermore, the effectiveness of WCF may also depend on the linguistic target. Generally, WCF seems to work better for salient (e.g., hypothetical conditionals) than non-salient features (e.g., indefinite articles) (Shintani et al., 2014). Metalinguistic feedback may not work for non-rule-based items such as irregular past tense (Zhang, 2021). Guo and Barrot (2019) found that such idiosyncratic features seem more amenable to direct feedback while rule-based features (e.g., the regular past tense) seem to benefit more from metalinguistic feedback. For complex features (e.g., articles), giving partial feedback (feedback on some but not all the functions) may even produce unintended negative effects on accuracy development (Gennaro & Ekiert, 2021).

In terms of the feedback scope, findings of the limited number of existing studies are inconclusive regarding whether focused or unfocused (comprehensive) feedback is more efficacious (Kang & Han, 2015; Karim & Nassaji, 2020a; Mao & Lee, 2020), although the meta-analysis by Lim and Renandya (2020) seems to indicate an advantage for focused feedback. Finally, feedback in conjunction with revision also seems more beneficial than feedback without the opportunity to rewrite (Ekanayaka & Ellis, 2020; Shintani et al., 2014).

Practical implications for teachers

Despite theoretical controversies about the usefulness of WCF, there is cumulative evidence from current SLA research that WCF is effective in improving L2 writing accuracy (Lee, 2022). From a pedagogical perspective, WCF as a form of formative assessment is also valued by both teachers and learners (see Li & Vuono, 2019). As such, there is a clear case for language-focused feedback in L2 writing classrooms.

The next question to ask then is how teachers can ensure that their feedback practices are effective and what effective practices generally look like. In terms of 'dose', for example, how much correction is too much? Although research on teacher and learner beliefs shows that comprehensive feedback is preferred by both groups, this kind of feedback is in fact onerous for teachers, while not more efficacious than selective and focused corrections (Lee, 2019). From both a cognitive and affective perspective, comprehensive feedback may also overwhelm and demotivate learners. In contrast, a selective approach to feedback may help teachers and learners focus on error types that require most urgent attention in each lesson, allowing learners to address gaps in knowledge in a gradual and less cognitively demanding manner (Mao & Lee, 2020).

In terms of strategies for delivering WCF, the inconclusiveness of research has led scholars to conclude that WCF options "should be considered more as a matter of suitability than superiority" (Karim & Nassaji, 2020a, p. 35). It is therefore recommended that teachers carefully consider their choices to suit learner needs in specific situations. For instance, direct feedback can be a useful option when treating errors that learners fail to self-correct (e.g., new linguistic forms or idiosyncratic structures). However, learners should be encouraged to self-edit if they already possess knowledge of the target features, and indirect feedback can be useful for this purpose. Depending on learners' proficiency levels, they may also be encouraged to locate errors or have the errors located for them. The former option can lead to deeper processing but is more challenging for low level learners (Ellis, 2009). Further, while metalinguistic feedback may help learners understand the causes of their errors, it is also a laborious method. One way to save time for teachers using this method is to collectively provide metalinguistic explanations in the form of handouts which learners can then use for self-correction (see Shintani et al., 2014). Regardless of WCF options, learners should also be encouraged to use teacher feedback for rewriting as there is evidence that opportunity to rewrite can facilitate learning (Ekanayaka & Ellis, 2020).

Suggestions for action research

Given that there is no 'one-size-fits-all' solution when dealing with written errors, teachers should be encouraged to reflect on their feedback practices and gather evidence about the effectiveness of their practices (Lee, 2019). To assist their reflections, teachers can consider planning and carrying out a series of small-scale action research studies with their own students. By reflecting on their own practices via action research, teachers can better understand the link between theory and practice, and more importantly, find out the kind of feedback that works or does not work for their unique contexts. Lee (2020a, p. 80-81) suggests a number of research questions that can be used to guide classroom-based action research, some of which are reproduced below:

1. What are the effects of focused WCF on students' motivation and written accuracy development?
2. How do teachers and students perceive the effectiveness of focused WCF?
3. How do students engage with teacher feedback delivered on feedback forms? How do they perceive the usefulness of feedback forms?
4. How do teachers deliver commentary that contains praise and criticism? How do students perceive such differential comments?
5. How do teachers provide training in peer feedback? What are the effects of peer feedback training on students' peer feedback and revision behaviours?
6. In what ways does students' self-evaluation help them take charge of and improve their writing?
7. How do students perceive the usefulness of technology-enhanced feedback?

Conclusion

Feedback is essential to move learners forward in their learning and to help them improve their performance. Good writing teachers know this and strive to provide learners with the right amount of feedback, the right kind of feedback and at the right time. They also understand that while research shows that WCF can have positive effects on students' writing, they will need to find out for themselves which feedback types and scopes are most effective for their students. By continuously reflecting on their own feedback practices, teachers can gradually become more confident in providing the kind of feedback that makes a real difference in their students' writing.

Further reading

Lee, I. (2020). *Feedback in L2 writing classrooms.* **TEFLIN.**
  This book discusses key aspects of writing feedback and provides practical advice for improving the quality of teacher feedback. For example, what purposes feedback serves in classroom writing assessment, what

effective teacher feedback practices are like, how different types of teacher feedback, and peer and self-feedback may be used to facilitate learners' writing development, how technology may be leveraged to enhance feedback effectiveness and what changes teachers may consider in order to improve their feedback practices. The book, which is written in a highly accessible manner, is useful for teachers who want to enhance their feedback literacy and practices.

Nassaji, H., & Kartchava, E. (Eds.) (2021). *The Cambridge handbook of corrective feedback in second language teaching and learning*. Cambridge University Press.

This edited volume provides comprehensive research on written corrective feedback in second language acquisition. Its 36 chapters cover theoretical foundations of corrective feedback, address methodological issues, as well as provide up-to-date research findings regarding the effectiveness of corrective feedback for various linguistic domains. Among the key issues discussed are modes of corrective feedback, feedback providers, scope, timing, explicitness, individual differences and learner and teacher training in using corrective feedback to enhance second language learning. The volume is a highly useful reference for novice researchers and teachers who want to learn more about the topic.

References

Bagheri, M., & Rassaei, E. (2022). The effects of two forms of written corrective feedback and ambiguity tolerance on EFL learners' writing accuracy. *English Teaching & Learning, 46*, 19–38. https://doi.org/10.1007/s42321-021-00082-6

Benson, S., & DeKeyser, R. (2019). Effects of written corrective feedback and language aptitude on verb tense accuracy. *Language Teaching Research, 23*(6), 702–726. https://doi.org/10.1177/1362168818770921

Bitchener, J. (2021). Written corrective feedback. In H. Nassaji & E. Kartchava (Eds.), *The Cambridge handbook of corrective feedback in second language teaching and learning* (pp. 207–225). Cambridge University Press. https://doi.org/10.1017/9781108589789

Bitchener, J., & Storch, N. (2016). *Written corrective feedback for L2 development*. Multilingual Matters. https://doi.org/10.21832/9781783095056

DeKeyser, R. M. (2014). Skill acquisition theory. In B. VanPatten & J. Williams (Eds.), *Theories in second language acquisition: An introduction* (2nd ed., pp. 94–112). Routledge. https://doi.org/10.4324/9780203628942

Ekanayaka, W.I., & Ellis, R. (2020). Does asking learners to revise add to the effect of written corrective feedback on L2 acquisition? *System, 94*, 1–12. https://doi.org/10.1016/j.system.2020.102341

Ellis, R. (2009). A typology of written corrective feedback. *ELT Journal, 63*(2), 97–107. https://doi.org/10.1093/elt/ccn023

Gennaro, K., Ekiert, M. (2021). The impact of corrective feedback on English articles. *ETL Journal, 75*(3), 290–299. https://doi.org/10.1093/elt/ccaa074

Guo, Q., & Barrot, J.S. (2019). Effects of metalinguistic explanation and direct correction on EFL learners' linguistic accuracy. *Reading and Writing Quarterly, 35*(3), 261–276. https://doi.org/10.1080/10573569.2018.1540320

Hassan, A., & Abbas, A. (2022). The impact of written corrective feedback on second language composition in English. In N. A. Raza & C. Coombe (Eds.), *English language teaching in Pakistan* (pp.181–201). Springer. https://doi.org/10.1007/978-981-16-7826-4

Kang, E., & Han, Z. (2015). The efficacy of written corrective feedback in improving L2 written accuracy: A meta-analysis. *The Modern Language Journal, 99*(1), 1–18. https://doi.org/10.1111/modl.12189

Karim, K., & Nassaji, H. (2020a). The effect of written corrective feedback: A critical synthesis of past and present research. *Instructed Second Language Acquisition, 3*(1), 28–52. https://doi.org/10.1558/isla.37949

Karim, K., & Nassaji, H. (2020b). The revision and transfer effects of direct and indirect comprehensive corrective feedback on English-as-a-second-language (ESL) students' writing. *Language Teaching Research, 4*(4), 519–539. https://doi.org/10.1177/1362168818802469

Krashen, S. D. (1985). *The input hypothesis: Issues and implications.* Longman.

Lee, I. (2019). Teacher written corrective feedback: Less is more. *Language Teaching, 52*, 524–536. https://doi:10.1017/S0261444819000247

Lee, I. (2020a). *Feedback in L2 writing classrooms.* TEFLIN Publication.

Lee, I. (2020b). Utility of focused/comprehensive written corrective feedback research for authentic L2 writing classrooms. *Journal of Second Language Writing, 49*, 1–7. https://doi.org/10.1016/j.jslw.2020.100734

Lee, I. (2022). Written corrective feedback. In H. Mohebbi & C. Coombe (Eds.), *Research questions in language education and applied linguistics* (pp. 425–429). Springer. https://doi.org/10.1007/978-3-030-79143-8

Li, S., & Vuono, A. (2019). Twenty-five years of research on oral and written corrective feedback in *System*. *System, 84*(1), 93–109. https://doi.org/10.1016/j.system.2019.05.006

Lim, S.C., & Renandya, W. (2020). Efficacy of written corrective feedback in writing instruction: A meta-analysis. *TESL-EJ, 24*(3), 1–26.

Long, M., & Robinson, P. (1998). Focus on form: Theory, research and practice. In C. Doughty & J. Williams (Eds.), *Focus on form in classroom second language acquisition* (pp. 15–41). Cambridge University Press.

Lopez, M. B., Steendam, E. V., Speelman, D., & Buyse, K. (2018). The differential effects of comprehensive feedback forms in the second language writing class. *Language Learning, 68*, 813–850. https://doi.org/10.1111/lang.12295

Lyster, R., & Sato, M. (2013). Skill acquisition theory and the role of practice in L2 development. In M. P. García Mayo, J. Gutierrez–

Mangado, & M. Martínez Adrián (Eds.), *Contemporary approaches to second language acquisition* (pp. 71–92). John Benjamins. https://doi.org/10.1075/aals.9

Mao, Z., & Lee, I. (2020). Feedback scope in written corrective feedback: Analysis of empirical research in L2 contexts. *Assessing Writing, 45*, 1–14. https://doi.org/10.1016/j.asw.2020.100469

Nassaji, H. (2021). Corrective feedback from a sociocultural perspective. In Nassaji, H., & Kartchava, E. (Eds.), *The Cambridge handbook of corrective feedback in second language teaching and learning* (pp. 85–107). Cambridge University Press. https://doi.org/10.1017/9781108589789

Nassaji, H., & Kartchava, E. (Eds.), *The Cambridge handbook of corrective feedback in second language teaching and learning.* Cambridge University Press. https://doi.org/10.1017/9781108589789

Schmidt, R. (1990). The role of consciousness in second language learning. *Applied Linguistics, 11*(2), 129–158. https://doi.org/10.1093/applin/11.2.129

Shalizar, R., & Rezaei, A. (2022). Examining the differential effects of focused vs. unfocused ZPD and explicit feedback on second language writing. *The Language Learning Journal*, 1–17. https://doi.org/10.1080/09571736.2022.2042366

Sheen, Y. (2007). The effect of focused written corrective feedback and language aptitude on ESL learners' acquisition of articles. *TESOL Quarterly, 41*, 255–283. https://doi.org/10.1002/j.1545-7249.2007.tb00059.x

Shintani, N., & Ellis, R. (2013). The comparative effect of direct written corrective feedback and metalinguistic explanation on learners' explicit and implicit knowledge of the English indefinite articles. *Journal of Second Language Writing, 22*, 286–306. https://doi.org/10.1016/j.jslw.2013.03.011

Shintani, N., Ellis, R., & Suzuki, W. (2014). Effects of written feedback and revision on learners' accuracy in using two English grammatical structures. *Language Learning 64*(1), 103–131. https://doi.org/10.1111/lang.12029

Sinha, T.S., & Nassaji, H. (2021). ESL learners' perception and its relationship with the efficacy of written corrective feedback. *International Journal of Applied Linguistics, 32*, 41–56. https://doi.org/10.1111/ijal.12378

Storch, N. (2018). Written corrective feedback from sociocultural theoretical perspectives: A research agenda. *Language Teaching, 51*(2), 262–277. https://doi.org/10.1017/S0261444818000034

Suzuki, W., Nassaji, H., & Sato,K. (2019). The effects of feedback explicitness and type of target structure on accuracy in revision and new pieces of writing. *System, 81*, 135–145. https://doi.org/10.1016/j.system.2018.12.017

Swain, M. (1985). Communicative competence: Some roles of comprehensible input and comprehensible output in its development. In S. M. Gass, & C. G. Madden (Eds.), *Input in second language acquisition* (pp. 235–253). Newbury House.

Swain, M. (1995). Three functions of output in second language learning. In G. Cook, & B. Seidlhofer (Eds.), *Principles and practice in the study of language: Studies in honour of H. G Widdowson* (pp. 125–144). Oxford University Press.

Truscott, J. (1996). The case against grammar correction in L2 writing classes. *Language Learning, 46*(2), 327–369. https://doi.org/10.1111/j.1467-1770.1996.tb01238.x

Truscott, J. (2007). The effect of error correction on learners' ability to write accurately. *Journal of Second Language Writing, 16*, 255–272. https://doi.org/10.1016/j.jslw.2007.06.003

Vygotsky, L. S., (1978). *Mind in society: The development of higher psychological processes*. Harvard University Press

Zabihi, R., & Erfanitabar, D. (2021). The revision effects of varying degrees of written corrective feedback explicitness on L2 learners' writings. *RELC Journal*, 1–15. https://doi.org/10.1177/00336882211054649

Zhang, T. (2021). The effect of highly focused versus mid-focused written corrective feedback on EFL learners' explicit and implicit knowledge development. *System, 99*, 1–16. https://doi.org/10.1016/j.system.2021.102493

11
Insights into dynamic written corrective feedback

Kendon Kurzer

Introduction

Many second language (L2) writing instructors are interested in written corrective feedback (WCF), believing that WCF—which primarily addresses grammatical accuracy in L2 writing contexts (Ferris, 2006)—supports multilingual writers as they work to reduce linguistic/grammatical errors. Indeed, a robust body of literature on WCF indicates that WCF can promote accuracy and thus a primary question among L2 writing instructors is how to best deliver WCF (Ferris & Kurzer, 2019). One promising WCF method is Dynamic Written Corrective Feedback (DWCF) (outlined originally in Evans et al., 2010).

Via DWCF, instructors promote writing accuracy by utilizing feedback practices that are "manageable, meaningful, timely, and constant" (Hartshorn & Evans, 2012, p. 30) for students and teachers. While these aims may seem lofty, DWCF prioritizes keeping feedback practices manageable for teachers and accessible for students. As originally conceived, students write short paragraphs during each class period. The teacher codes all errors in the student texts using a coding system that is taught explicitly to the students (Appendix A contains a sample coding system). Students individually edit their initial paragraphs and resubmit edited drafts to their teacher. The teacher then codes any remaining or newly introduced student errors, and the process repeats until the student produces an error free draft. Students simultaneously tally the different error types from their texts in an error log (Appendix B) to identify their individual error patterns; being able to see error patterns may help students develop increased autonomy (Ferris, 2006; Lalande, 1982).

DWCF and cognitive/second language acquisition theoretical frameworks

Coding systems such as DWCF adhere to prominent cognitive/SLA theories in several manners. For example, to acquire a target language, multilingual students must first foster declarative knowledge—what they intellectually know—before they can obtain procedural knowledge: the ability to apply declarative knowledge to authentic contexts (DeKeyser, 2001). Instructors should include deliberate practice-based pedagogies to help multilingual students obtain procedural knowledge and then automatize grammatical features of the target language (DeKeyser, 2001). The drafting done via DWCF may help multilingual students transfer procedural knowledge to new environments and thus automatize grammatical features in future writing contexts.

DWCF can also be a tool to help instructors interact successfully with individual multilingual students' Zone of Proximal Development and help these students internalize (Vygotsky, 1978) grammatical concepts and transfer these principles to their own writing. Coded WCF approaches like DWCF can be used to scaffold grammar feedback, helping lift students beyond their current capabilities.

Prioritizing comprehensible input—providing instruction that is only slightly beyond students' current mastery of the concepts at question, or $i+1$—is important to ensure that learning is kept meaningful (Krashen, 1985). Instructors can use DWCF to provide feedback that adheres to the ideals of comprehensible input, while still encouraging students to efficiently acquire the target grammatical concepts. Long (1996) explicitly encouraged corrective feedback as a logical extension of Krashen's Input Hypothesis, believing that corrective feedback may facilitate effectual language acquisition, "at least for vocabulary, morphology, and language-specific syntax" (Long, 1996, p. 414). DWCF may be such an approach.

DWCF and established best practices of written corrective feedback

As mentioned earlier, the central tenant of DWCF is to provide pedagogical interventions that are "manageable, meaningful, timely, and constant" (Hartshorn & Evans, 2012, p. 30). As such, DWCF adheres to best pedagogical practices as emphasized in current WCF literature.

Focused vs. unfocused WCF

Focused WCF—that addresses only specific error types—may promote increased accuracy compared to more comprehensive *unfocused* WCF that addresses all grammatical error types (Bitchener, 2008; Lee, 2020). For example, some studies investigated only articles/determiners and found meaningful gains (e.g., Bitchener & Knoch, 2010; Ellis et al., 2008). At first glance, DWCF may seem inappropriate, as it is a comprehensive coding system. However, WCF researchers increasingly recognize that studies that investigate overly narrowly focused WCF practices may not reflect authentic classrooms in which instructors likely do not limit their feedback to only a single grammatical feature or two (Ferris & Kurzer, 2019) or feel that arguments against comprehensive WCF are based on limited evidence (Falhasiri, 2021).

Using a comprehensive coding approach like DWCF may help instructors identify all students' error types in their writing while the explicit codes may adequately scaffold student learning (Hartshorn & Evans, 2012; Kurzer, 2018a; Kurzer, 2022) similar to focused WCF; studies on DWCF reflect meaningful gains in accuracy despite being comprehensive.

Indirect vs. direct WCF

Indirect WCF—highlighting or otherwise marking but not correcting errors—may more effectively encourage long-term mastery/production of linguistic features in writing than *direct* WCF—providing a correction (Ferris, 2006; Lalande, 1982) Students addressing their errors without relying on teacher corrections likely promotes internalization of the target grammatical features (Lalande, 1982). Per the DWCF process, the teacher marks errors in student writing using a coding system but requires students to edit their marked errors individually. Students receive scaffolded support from the code to guide their corrections and record their errors on each draft, which likely helps them recognize their patterns of error along with any improvements in accuracy over time. Thus, indirect feedback as done via DWCF may help students automate their accurate L2 production (DeKeyser, 2001), and promote stronger self-monitoring capabilities in the students (Lalande, 1982).

Explicit vs. unlabeled WCF

WCF that is *explicit*—employing, for example, a coding system like DWCF—may prompt previously received formal grammar instruction compared to *unlabeled* WCF, since multilingual students with previous instruction may access the knowledge of syntactic terms needed to understand such codes (Bitchener, 2008; Bitchener & Knoch, 2010; Ferris, 2006). DWCF could remind such students of their previously received training and help connect it to their actual produced language. Additionally, multilingual students have indicated that they appreciate explicit WCF (Lee, 2005).

Untreatable grammatical features and DWCF

Some grammatical features with idiosyncratic systems are thought to be *untreatable*, whereas grammatical features with methodical rules—or *treatable* features—may be easier to explicitly teach (Bitchener, 2008; Ferris, 2006). Errors in some untreatable features such as "word order, sentence boundaries, phrase construction, word choice, or collocations" may "obscure meaning," although errors in others such as prepositions and articles may not (Ferris, 2010, p. 193). Past research on DWCF has found that students in classes that employed DWCF demonstrated increased accuracy of untreatable features, even when the classes lacked formal grammatical instruction (Hartshorn & Evans, 2012).

Table 11.1 Summary of previous research on DWCF

Study	Control	Large N (>30)	Context	Longitudinal
Evans et al., 2010	No	No	IEP	No
Hartshorn et al., 2010	Yes	No	IEP	No
Evans et al., 2011	Yes	No	Undergrad	No
Hartshorn & Evans, 2012	Yes	No	IEP	No
Marzban & Arabahmadi, 2013	Yes	No	?*	No
Hartshorn & Evans, 2015	Yes	No	IEP	Yes
Kurzer, 2018a	Yes	Yes	Undergrad	No
Kurzer, 2018b	Yes	Yes	Undergrad	No
Kurzer, 2019	No	No	CC	No
Eckstein et al., 2020	No	No	Grad	No
Messenger et al., 2020	No	No	IEP Instructor	No
Eckstein & Bell, 2021	Yes	No	Undergrad	No
Kurzer, 2022	Yes	Yes	Undergrad	No

Note: The context of this study was unclear to me, with the authors indicating only that the study was of "two intact intermediate classes at the private institute in Iran" (p. 1001).

Research on dynamic written corrective feedback

The research literature on DWCF has grown in recent years, with 13 articles published through 2022 in various contexts. As noted in Table 11.1, nine of the 13 empirical articles on DWCF so far have been quasi-experimental studies with control and treatment groups although most also had small sample sizes. The initial studies on DWCF were conducted in an Intensive English Program (IEP) in the United States, although one investigated DWCF in credit-bearing, elective language support courses for matriculated multilingual students, with strong outcomes in favor of DWCF (Evans et al., 2011). Another recent study investigated DWCF in first-year composition (FYC) contexts, finding that students in classes with DWCF did not produce more accurate writing than did the control group (Eckstein & Bell, 2021). The authors hypothesize that this lack of improvement might be due to the aims of FYC moving beyond linguistic accuracy to expose students to varied genres and audience expectations; accuracy may temporarily wane due to these unfamiliar contexts (Eckstein & Bell, 2021).

With the exception of Eckstein and Bell (2021), these small studies found statistically significant improvements in the DWCF treatment groups regarding linguistic accuracy generally (Evans et al., 2010; Evans et al., 2011; Hartshorn & Evans, 2015; Hartshorn et al., 2010), and on the following individual linguistic/grammatical features: lexical accuracy, verb accuracy, semantic accuracy, sentence structures, determiners, numeric agreement, and mechanical accuracy (Hartshorn & Evans, 2012), with medium to large effect sizes. An additional IEP-based study of DWCF that lacked a control group identified statistically significant improvements in accuracy of students in a grammar class (Evans et al., 2010). However, we lack evidence of long-term gains; only one study on DWCF has followed students over more than one semester (Hartshorn & Evans, 2015).

My research explored DWCF in a developmental writing program that supported matriculated multilingual students' language and writing skills via three credit-bearing courses taken prior to mainstream first-year composition using much larger sample sizes than represented in other studies (treatment n=214 and control n=111) (Kurzer, 2018a). While the previous studies on DWCF investigated narrow error types, I initially elected to categorize grammatical errors as global, local (per Bates et al., 1993), and mechanical, and compared the groups' abilities to produce accurate writing regarding those general categories (Kurzer, 2018a). Treatment students produced more accurate writing on all error categories across all three levels of developmental writing, and they demonstrated better self-editing skills, supporting the idea that DWCF may support more autonomous writing/self-editing (Ferris, 2006; Lalande, 1982). Then, in a more fine-grained analysis of the data from the intermediate and advanced classes (treatment n=130 and control n=79), I found statistically significant differences in favor of the treatment students in term-final student writing regarding all specific error types except for prepositions at the intermediate level, again with moderate to large effect sizes attributable to the DWCF treatment (Kurzer, 2022).

Taken collectively, the research investigating DWCF reveals a largely positive impact on students' abilities to produce more accurate writing, at least with certain students and in certain writing contexts. However, accuracy gain is only one facet of what makes a WCF-based pedagogical activity impactful or meaningful to enhance students' language learning. We should also consider student and instructor opinions regarding a particular pedagogy. Drawing on the same student population of the study outlined earlier, I contrasted treatment and control student responses on a number of survey items, finding that students in classes with DWCF more highly rated the quality of general class instruction, quality of grammar feedback, and value of peer feedback, although they did not rate their own grammar abilities more strongly, perhaps due to having a more accurate understanding of their error patterns (Kurzer, 2018b).

In an action research study in an L2 writing class at a community college (CC), I employed and evaluated students' perceptions of DWCF as a complement to my traditional grammar instruction (Kurzer, 2019). Via a term-end survey, I found that the students responded positively to DWCF as a method of applying grammatical concepts and practicing grammar in their own writing. Despite the small sample size ($n=25$) of students who completed the survey, this first study of DWCF in a CC provides more evidence that DWCF is well received when coupled with traditional grammar instruction. Students specifically mentioned that DWCF matched them at their personal level better than did the grammar textbook for the class, supporting the conclusion that teachers using DWCF can meet students where they are grammatically. However, many multilingual students may perceive that they need traditional grammar instruction and feedback (Lee, 2005) although approaches like DWCF may be more effective; combining the two may best help students feel that their needs are being adequately met while still encouraging more meaningful practice.

One study explored the timing of delivering DWCF (either biweekly or postponed until the end of the term) with a small number of graduate students, finding that graduate students of classes that employed timely DWCF resulted in improvements in fluency and complexity in student writing, but neither treatment resulted in statistically significant improvements in grammatical accuracy (Eckstein et al, 2020). This may indicate a possible ceiling level at which DWCF is no longer effective at promoting grammatical accuracy (although the writing practice and feedback from the process may still positively affect other measures).

Finally, a single published study has addressed teacher perspectives of DWCF (Messenger et al., 2020). Interviews with five experienced ESL teachers revealed trends supporting DWCF as a pedagogical intervention to promote meaningful uptake of grammatical concepts, although these teachers also offered some suggestions to keep it manageable as well (discussed later in this chapter).

Practical implications and suggestions

DWCF is a practical pedagogy that can be adapted to a wide variety of student needs and contexts. To review the process in more depth, DWCF is a particular system of delivering written corrective feedback targeting students' individual grammatical errors on their own writing that is "manageable, meaningful, timely, and constant" (Hartshorn & Evans, 2012, p. 30), that, as originally developed, followed this system:

1. Students write first drafts of timed paragraphs (for 10 minutes) on an assigned topic in class and turn them in to the teacher.
2. The teacher codes all errors present in the drafts.
3. The teacher returns the coded drafts to the students and the students record their errors in an error log.

4. The students self-edit their paragraphs, altering only the grammar, and turn the new drafts in to the teacher.
5. The teacher codes all remaining or newly introduced errors in the second drafts.
6. The teacher returns the coded second drafts to the students and the students record their remaining errors.
7. If students have yet to reach an established threshold of accuracy (as originally implemented, all errors had to be edited out), they repeat the editing process on new drafts until they reach that threshold.
8. The entire process repeats at regular intervals across the course of the term (e.g., daily or weekly).

The DWCF process can be tailored to meet student needs for a variety of contexts and approaches.

Adapt number of DWCF rounds/edited drafts for different programs/contexts

Research on DWCF has thus far primarily been conducted in the United States in an IEP, developmental writing (pre-first year composition) at a research university and a community college, first-year composition, general grammar classes for matriculated multilingual students, and support classes for multilingual graduate students, with typically promising results. While less effective at fostering accuracy among FYC (Eckstein & Bell, 2021) and graduate students (Eckstein et al., 2020), at least according to these two smaller studies, DWCF likely may be effective in other contexts such as TOEFL/IELTS preparation programs, EFL contexts, or discipline-specific writing classes for undergraduate multilingual students.

As originally implemented in an IEP, DWCF replaced traditional grammar classes entirely. In the writing program in which I work, an institution with 10-week quarters, we elected to augment our (primarily writing-focused, but with language/grammar support) instruction with rounds of DWCF. This necessitated requiring many fewer rounds of DWCF in each term in this context than originally suggested, and we elected to adjust based on level: 14 rounds at the beginning level, 10 at the intermediate level, and only five at the advanced level (Kurzer, 2018a, 2018b, 2022). While I initially hypothesized that I would not see meaningful improvements at the advanced level with only five rounds, that ended up not being the case. I similarly adjusted DWCF in my community college writing class, which had a much higher focus on grammar and relied primarily on a grammar textbook, requiring one round of DWCF per week, so 14 over the course of the semester. Thus, it seems reasonable to adjust the rounds of DWCF required based on student language level and institutional constraints/values.

As mentioned earlier, via the original DWCF system, instructors required students to edit out all errors to finish a particular round and no longer create new drafts. Stakeholders in our developmental writing program felt that such an approach could be demotivating (if three, four, or even five drafts were required to reach that threshold) so we elected to require just two drafts of each round. Students were still required to record their errors from each draft, but they no longer needed to edit out all remaining errors. The required number of edited drafts within each round can accordingly be adapted based on programmatic/student needs in several ways. In addition to the two approaches that have thus far been researched (requiring all errors removed on final drafts and requiring no more than two drafts), another feasible approach could be requiring students to remove all global grammatical errors but not local grammatical errors (Bates et al., 1993).

Tailor DWCF codes/writing prompts based on student needs

In addition to adjusting the number of DWCF rounds/drafts, instructors can tailor the coding system to prioritize certain grammatical features most necessary to foster communication skills, not native-like accuracy. I adjusted the original 20 codes down to 16 for my studies/classes by combining some to better match our program foci. I also grouped the errors per global, local, and mechanical categories, with the aim of prioritizing the grammatical features most central for effective communication.

Instructors—especially those of lower levels—may also elect to focus only on patterns of error commonly present in a particular student's writing, rather than coding all errors present. A conscious decision to avoid marking only occasional errors may help students focus more thoroughly on their own patterns of error. Such a focus could better keep feedback comprehensible for students, or $i+1$ (Krashen, 1985).

Finally, depending on the level of the students, I would consider further revising the DWCF codes in a few manners. I regularly teach discipline-specific writing classes for upper-division undergraduates (e.g., writing for nursing students, education students, or food science students). In classes with a high proportion of multilingual students, I have considered developing a DWCF coding system that, on top of the typical codes, includes codes for collocates issues, discipline-specific jargon misuse, and ineffective/missing transitions. Such adaptations based on student needs in particular curricular ecologies seems wise.

As originally devised, the prompts used to elicit student texts via DWCF were basic, everyday topics, so students would not need to spend time and mental effort on content but could focus on grammar (e.g., "tell me about the weather today"). For our program, we selected topics that were slightly more advanced due to the higher language level of most of our matriculated students (see Appendix C for the list of topics used in our beginning and intermediate classes; I did not dictate topics for the advanced classes but left them up to the instructors). Several students in my research recommended that the DWCF topics could be more effectively integrated with the other assignments in the class (Kurzer, 2018b). I have since started doing exactly that in my classes. I have found that using DWCF drafts as pre-writing activities, reading responses, or to check for understanding about major assignments provides opportunities for valuable scaffolding or formative assessment.

Approaches to grading DWCF

Throughout its iterations, DWCF has typically been graded on a completion system, meaning students earn full points if they do all the work. However, some instructors in our program felt that awarding points based on number of remaining errors in second drafts would be one method of motivating students to take the editing seriously. We lack research on how to best grade DWCF. I recommend grading on a completion basis to create an environment in which students can take chances with their language that they might not be able to in more formal, higher stakes contexts. Regardless, DWCF should likely not be worth a high proportion of a final course grade, especially in contexts in which it is a supplementary pedagogy to other instruction. That said, if DWCF is the primary mode of instruction, assigning more weight to DWCF drafts would be logical.

In my experience, some teachers (myself included) have struggled to keep students consistently recording their errors on the error log. I recommend that a grading scheme build in points for filling out and reflecting on the error log and patterns of error. I would also regularly check students' logs to help ensure that they are recording errors to encourage students to reflect on and learn from their patterns of error.

Suggestions for action research or case study

As a pedagogical approach suitable for various contexts, DWCF may prove to be an intriguing focus of action research/case studies. Such research exploring each of the adaptations I outlined above would contribute to our knowledge of DWCF. A particularly salient focus for future research would be to explore students' reactions and opinions toward various approaches of implementing or grading DWCF. By better understanding which facets of DWCF students find most valuable, we can further hone our approaches to be more effective.

In-depth case studies looking at exactly how students interact with DWCF codes, perhaps via retrospective interviews that ask students what their processes were after receiving coded errors on a particular draft, would show how students respond to coded feedback. To extend that approach, a case study in which the teacher/researcher observes students as they work through coded feedback would also be very meaningful to the larger body of research on WCF as well as with DWCF specifically.

Further reading

Evans, N. W., Hartshorn, K. J., McCollum, R., Wolfersberger, M. (2010). Contextualizing corrective feedback in L2 writing pedagogy. *Language Teaching Research,* 14, 445–463.

In this first research article featuring DWCF, the researchers shared their approach to replacing an intermediate grammar class of an intensive English program with a course devoted exclusively to DWCF. This quasi-experimental study also reported the largely positive outcomes attributable to the DWCF treatment regarding many error types, despite the small sample sizes represented.

Evans, N. W., Hartshorn, K. J., Strong-Krause, D. (2011) The efficacy of dynamic written corrective feedback for university-matriculated ESL learners. *System,* 39, 229–239.

This study was the first to look at DWCF among matriculated undergraduate students. The quasi-experimental study contrasted outcomes among credit-bearing but optional language support/writing classes for multilingual students offered by a linguistics department. In this study, the control group's course focused on writing process (with rhetorical aspects of several student papers being the primary focus of feedback) while the treatment group replaced the instruction and feedback with DWCF. The researchers identified several improvements in accuracy attributable to DWCF, despite the small sample sizes.

Kurzer, K. (2018). Dynamic written corrective feedback in developmental ESL writing classes. *TESOL Quarterly,* 52(1), 5–33.

In this paper, I reported the results of a much larger study in terms of sample sizes investigating DWCF in beginning, intermediate, and advanced developmental writing classes (pre-first-year composition). Rather than looking at specific error types, I grouped the errors by category (global, local, and mechanical) and found statistically significant improvements and medium to large effect sizes attributable to the DWCF treatment across all error categories at all levels.

Kurzer, K. (2019). Dynamic written corrective feedback in a community college ESL writing class setting. In S. M. Anwaruddin (Ed.) *Knowledge mobilization in TESOL: Connecting research and practice* (pp. 59–75). Brill.

In this book chapter, I presented the results of a small action research study I conducted in an intermediate ESL writing class with a heavy grammar emphasis I taught at a community college. In addition to process writing, the course included grammar exercises from a common grammar textbook, and I implemented DWCF on top of that. This study consisted of student survey responses in which they shared their opinions and preferences for coursework, ranking DWCF highly due in large part to the opportunity to apply grammatical themes in their own writing and how DWCF matched their current level of linguistic mastery better than the grammar textbook.

References

Bates, L., Lane, J., & Lange, E. (1993). *Writing clearly: Responding to ESL compositions*. Heinle & Heinle.

Bitchener, J. (2008). Evidence in support of written corrective feedback. *Journal of Second Language Writing, 17*, 102–118. https://doi.org/10.1016/j.jslw.2007.11.004

Bitchener, J., & Knoch, U. (2010). The contribution of written corrective feedback to language development: A ten month investigation. *Applied Linguistics, 31*, 193–214. https://doi.org/10.1093/applin/amp016

DeKeyser, R. (2001). Automaticity and automatization. In P. Robinson (Ed.), *Cognition and second language instruction* (pp. 97–113). Lawrence Erlbaum. https://doi.org/10.1017/CBO9781139524780.007

Eckstein, G., Sims, M., & Rohm, L. (2020). Dynamic Written Corrective Feedback among graduate students: The effects of feedback timing. *TESL Canada Journal, 37*(2), 78–102.

Eckstein, G., & Bell, L. (2021). Dynamic Written Corrective Feedback in first-year composition: Accuracy and lexical and syntactic complexity. *RELC Journal*. https://doi.org/10.1177/00336882211061624

Ellis, R., Sheen, Y., Murakami, M., & Takashima, H. (2008). The effects of focused and unfocused written corrective feedback in an English as a foreign language context. *System, 36*, 353–371. https://doi.org/10.1016/j.system.2008.02.001

Evans, N. W., Hartshorn, K. J., & Strong-Krause, D. (2011) The efficacy of dynamic written corrective feedback for university-matriculated ESL learners. *System, 39*, 229–239. https://doi.org/10.1016/j.system.2011.04.012

Evans, N. W., Hartshorn, K. J., McCollum, R., & Wolfersberger, M. (2010). Contextualizing corrective feedback in L2 writing pedagogy. *Language Teaching Research, 14*(4), 445–463. https://doi.org/10.1177/1362168810375

Falhasiri, M. (2021). Is less really more? The case for comprehensive written corrective feedback. *Canadian Journal of Applied Linguistics/Revue canadienne de linguistique appliquée, 24*(3), 145–165. https://doi.org/10.37213/cjal.2021.31242

Ferris, D. R. (2006). Does error feedback help student writers? New evidence on the short- and long-term effects of written error correction. In K. Hyland & F. Hyland (Eds.), *Feedback in second language writing: Contexts and issues* (pp. 81–104). Cambridge University Press.

Ferris, D. R. (2010). Second language writing research and written corrective feedback in SLA. *Studies in Second Language Acquisition, 32*, 181–201. https://doi.org/10.1017/S0272263109990490

Ferris, D. R. & Kurzer, K. (2019). Does error feedback help L2 writers? Latest evidence on the efficacy of written corrective feedback. In K. Hyland & F. Hyland (Eds.) *Feedback in second language writing: Contexts and issues* (2nd ed). (pp. 106–124). Cambridge University Press.

Hartshorn, K. J., Evans, N. W. (2012) The differential effects of comprehensive corrective feedback on L2 writing accuracy. *Journal of Linguistics and Language Teaching, 3*, 16–46.

Hartshorn, K. J., & Evans, N. W. (2015). The effects of dynamic written corrective feedback: A 30 week study. *Journal of Response to Writing, 1*, 6–34.

Hartshorn, K. J., Evans, N. W., Merrill, P. F., Sudweeks, R. R., Strong-Krause, D., Anderson, N. J. (2010). The effects of dynamic corrective feedback on ESL writing accuracy. *TESOL Quarterly, 44*, 84–108. https://doi.org/10.5054/tq.2010.213781

Krashen, S. D. (1985). *The input hypothesis: Issues and implications.* Pergamon.

Kurzer, K. (2018a). Dynamic written corrective feedback in developmental ESL writing classes. *TESOL Quarterly, 52*(1), 5–33.

Kurzer, K. (2018b). Student perceptions of dynamic written corrective feedback in developmental multilingual writing classes. *Journal of Response to Writing, 4*(2), 34–68.

Kurzer, K. (2019). Dynamic written corrective feedback in a community college ESL writing class setting. In S. M. Anwaruddin (Ed.), *Knowledge mobilization in TESOL: Connecting research and practice* (pp. 59–75). Brill.

Kurzer, K. (2022). Accuracy gains from unfocused feedback: Dynamic Written Corrective Feedback as meaningful pedagogy. *Journal of Language and Education. 8*(4), 107121. https://doi.org/10.17323/jle.2022.13380

Lalande, J. F. II (1982). Reducing composition errors: An experiment. *Modern Language Journal 66*, 140–149. https://doi.org/10.1111/j.1540-4781.1982.tb06973.x

Lee, I. (2005). Error correction in the L2 writing classroom: What do students think? *TESL Canada Journal, 22*(2), 1–16. https://doi.org/10.18806/tesl.v22i2.84

Lee, I. (2020). Utility of focused/comprehensive written corrective feedback research for authentic L2 writing classrooms. *Journal of Second Language Writing, 49*, 1–7. https://doi.org/10.1016/j.jslw.2020.100734

Long, M. H. (1996). The role of linguistic environment in second language acquisition. In W. Ritchie & T. Bhatia (Eds.), *Handbook of second language acquisition* (pp. 413–468). San Diego, CA: Academic Press. https://doi.org/10.1016/B978-012589042-7/50015-3

Messenger, R., Evans, N., & Hartshorn, K. (2020). Managing dynamic written corrective feedback: Perspectives of experienced teachers. *Journal of Response to Writing, 6*(1), 108–138.

Vygotsky, L. (1978). Interaction between learning and development. *Readings on the Development of Children*, 23, 34–41.

Appendix A: DWCF writing correction marks

		Error Type	Example
Global Errors	VF	Verb Form	It was happened yesterday. Psychology expose you to behavior.
	VT	Verb Time	It happen yesterday.
	SS	Sentence Structure (incl. Run-on and incomplete)	They brought the man who them him found. Because they thought it was good. Because friendship takes effort, so it is time-consuming.
	W\O	Word Order	Especially, I miss home.
	WC	Word Choice	She says that raising a pet needs responsibility.
Local Errors	PP	Prepositions	I was responsible of everything.
	D	Determiner (articles)	The trip to United States was enjoyable.
	NF	Noun Form	All family member are supposed to get along. She limited the amount of candies I could eat.
	WF	Word Form	Money brings themselves more opportunities.
Other Errors (Mechanical)	SPG	Spelling	I never worried about my teech getting bad.
	P	Punctuation	When I was visiting; one morning scared me.
	C	Capital letter	Students love to party. they also love to eat pizza.
	^	Insert something	A good major helps you earn a lot money.
	℮	Omit something (Use with SS)	I chose this major is because it is interesting.
	?	Meaning is not clear	He borrowed some smoke.
	AWK	Awkward wording	Candy makes children feel a sweet taste.

Appendix B: Error log

		1	2	3	4	5	6	7	8	9	10	Total
Paragraph Score:												
Global Errors	VF											
	VT											
	SS											
	WO											
	WC											
Local Errors	PP											
	D											
	NF											
	WF											
Other Errors (Mechanical)	SPG											
	P											
	C											
	^											
	ℯ											
	?											
	AWK											

Appendix C: DWCF paragraph prompts

Beginning:

Diagnostic: Discuss two goals you hope to accomplish this quarter and why they are important to you. (Remember that these paragraphs **shouldn't** be returned to the students for editing until the end of the quarter, for our study.)

1. Describe an activity you enjoy and explain why you enjoy it. (Verb tense)
2. Write about a historical event that was significant to your culture. (Verb time)
3. What suggestions do you have for someone who is going to visit your home country? Where should they go and why? (Modals)
4. What is one of the most important discoveries or inventions? How has society benefited from it? (Passive voice)
5. Write about something you have always wanted to do, but haven't yet done it. Why do you want to do it? What has prevented you from doing it? (Sentence structure)
6. What qualities are important in friends? (Word order)
7. Describe a custom from your home culture or the United States that you like or dislike. Why do you like or dislike it? (Connecting words/phrases)
8. Think of someone you respect or admire. What are his/her qualities that you admire? (Subject/verb agreement)
9. Describe your childhood home in as much detail as you can. (Determiners and nouns)
10. How can one become a successful student? (Prepositions)
11. Describe a couple of strategies that can help you improve your English. How will these strategies help? (Word choice)
12. Describe a book or a movie you enjoy. Why do you like it? (Word choice)

Intermediate:

Diagnostic: Discuss what you want to accomplish this quarter. What do you need to do in order to accomplish these goals? (Remember that these paragraphs **shouldn't** be returned to the students for editing until the end of the quarter, for our study.)

1. Describe your week so far. What have you accomplished? What do you still want to do? (Verb tense)
2. Write about your most recent vacation. What did you do? Where did you go? (Verb time)
3. What is a regret you have? What should you have done and why? (Modals)
4. What is the best gift you have ever received and why? (Passive voice)
5. Think of a prominent historical figure. What are his/her qualities?

(Subject/verb agreement)
6. What is your definition of success? What makes a successful person? (Word order)
7. If you were given the chance to change your life at this moment, what would you do and why? (Conditional sentences)
8. Describe an embarrassing moment you've experienced. (Clauses)

12
Feedback on student writing for early career teachers: Effective strategies for teacher, peer, and self-feedback

Grant Eckstein

Introduction

Feedback on student writing consists of information provided to a writer in response to some aspect of the writing. The end objective of providing feedback is to improve a piece of writing, but this objective is usually accompanied by helping the writer improve future pieces too. While improving students' writing and their writing skills are obvious objectives of feedback, there are numerous factors that can support or limit the effectiveness of feedback. The present chapter will explore some of these complicating factors and then present current pedagogical practices and innovations regarding teacher, peer, and self-feedback that can help early career teachers support student writing development.

Theoretical framework

L2 feedback practices need to be contextualized within the broader field of composition studies, a field that has largely been focused on L1 writers for the last half-decade or more (Matsuda, 1999). This focus is relevant because the field of second-language writing is situated "at the intersection of second language studies and composition studies" (Silva et al., 1997, p. 399) and has borrowed extensively from composition theories (Kroll, 1998). In fact, a great deal of L2 writing theory involves critically determining how L1 approaches can and should be different for L2 learners.

An important innovation, and one that helped unify the composition field, is the shift in the 1960s and 1970s from the so-called product approach (or current-traditional rhetoric) to a process approach for writing. Matsuda (2003) describes the earlier product approach rather reductively as a system in which students learned a particular discourse mode (narrative, compare/contrast, etc.), were assigned a topic by the teacher, wrote and submitted a single draft of a theme, and received a grade without opportunity for revision. The process approach is a radical rethinking of writing instruction that has crystalized as a way to help students see and engage with writing as a process. That process involves planning, drafting, revising, and publishing (Seow, 2002), but the process is rarely linear, so students are asked to reflect on and get to know their own unique process for composing. The process approach also encourages writers to find their unique voice; to select their own topics for writing; and, importantly, to get feedback from their teacher, peers, and tutors. Thus, the process approach led composition teachers to begin providing feedback in a concerted and substantial way.

Literature review

Seeing the value of L1 composition recommendations for feedback, L2 scholars have sought to determine whether such recommendations can also address L2 writers' feedback needs. Zamel (1985) was an ardent early supporter of such transfer. In her work, she recommended that L2 writing teachers adopt a process orientation, establish priorities by responding to "meaning-level" issues on early drafts while delaying feedback on language issues until final drafts (giving students authority over their own writing), and conduct face-to-face writing conferences. In short, she favored adopting all the suggestions from L1 composition pedagogy. On the other hand, Silva (1993, 1997, 1988) argued that L2 writers are so distinct that they need their own feedback pedagogy, and that at the very least, L1 composition approaches should be carefully examined before use with L2 writers.

Silva's position proved very influential, and researchers have laid out a number of ways that L1 composition advice overlaps with, falls short of, or directly contradicts the needs of L2 learners (see Ferris, 2003). One such case is the issue of prioritizing meaning-level feedback before language feedback. Ferris (1995) acknowledged that L2 writers are aware of their language needs and may be eager to address both language and content simultaneously. In fact, delaying language feedback can be especially frustrating for these students and their teachers, particularly if there are so many language errors that they interfere with meaning. But L2 students also show preferences for feedback similar to those of L1 students. Like L1 students, L2 writers dislike confusing, unclear, and vague feedback (Ferris, 1995). Of course, some comments are more effective than others. The most effective are text-specific requests for information and directive statements, and the least effective are items of praise, questions (which students seem to misunderstand), and informative statements that do not include a directive for change (Ferris, 1997).

The three sources of feedback mentioned previously have also been explored by L2 scholars. Goldstein and Conrad (1999) agreed with L1 scholars about the value of face-to-face conferences between L2 writers and teachers since this mode can address revision and language issues that are hard to describe in written feedback. However, Conrad and Goldstein (1990) also acknowledge that L2 writers can struggle to effectively interact and negotiate with a teacher they view as the ultimate authority on their writing. Peer feedback has remained somewhat controversial in L2 writing research because the cultural and linguistic backgrounds of students can complicate its effectiveness. For example, though L2 students seem to welcome peer review as a complement to (not a replacement for) teacher feedback and do benefit from it, researchers worry that language learners don't have the language skills and credibility to always offer effective feedback on peer writing (Wang, 2014), especially if they don't receive training on how to do it well. Moreover, researchers observe that L2 students far prefer authoritative teacher feedback over peer feedback when given the option (Hu & Lam, 2010). In terms of self-feedback, researchers find the practice to be transferable to L2 writers and encourage its practice (Shvidko, 2015).

Practical implications and suggestions

The field of second-language writing has generated a number of resources through which teachers can obtain up-to-date information on these issues. Perhaps the best-recognized venues for L2 writing information are the flagship *Journal of Second Language Writing* and the yearly *Symposium on Second Language Writing*. The newer *Journal of Response to Writing* in particular offers focused insights into feedback options for new and experienced teachers of L2 writers. The remainder of this chapter provides research-based, practical suggestions meant to help newer writing instructors provide effective feedback on L2 student writing.

Establish feedback criteria

To establish expectations of what "good writing" looks like (Casanave, 2017, p. 143), teachers should develop thoughtful rubrics for each writing assignment and ensure that students have access to these rubrics and can understand them (see Brookhart, 2013). Rubrics should include criteria for evaluating student writing using well-written performance descriptions. Comments on student writing can then be connected to the rubric's expectations for "good writing." For L2 writers in particular, rubrics should be comprehensible and use language that does not exceed students' language proficiency.

Design clear feedback

Feedback on student papers should be clear and easy to understand, which may mean avoiding abbreviations, shorthand, technical terms, and jargon (Ferris, 2003). Of course, these can be used effectively so long as students and teachers understand one another. Thus, it is best to explain important metalinguistic phrases, such as "topic sentence" or "thesis statement" before using them in feedback (Reid, 1994). Alternatively, teachers can use more generic language to describe concepts that have not been covered in class. Teachers should also use vocabulary and syntax in their feedback that will be comprehensible for their L2 students.

Choose when to comment on what

Teachers should provide feedback for L2 writers on intermediate drafts when multi-draft writing is assigned. When feedback is provided only on finished products, it might serve little purpose in improving students' subsequent writing (Laflen, 2019). When deciding the content of feedback, L2 writers often appreciate and can handle both language-based and rhetorical feedback even in early drafts, though there appears to be a cline by which low-proficiency writers prefer more language feedback while higher-proficiency writers prefer more rhetorical feedback (Eckstein, 2013). Teachers should therefore be sensitive to students' needs and abilities when deciding what feedback to provide and prioritize between drafts.

Give the right amount of feedback

Feedback that is especially short (e.g., "Great!" and "Needs work") can be unhelpful for L2 writers because of its lack of specificity or direction. Instead, L2 writers need feedback that identifies specific areas for improvement with suggestions for how to improve. Moreover, L2 writers generally appreciate extensive feedback; this is partially because L2 students often have far fewer options for getting feedback on their writing. They may not have friends, classmates, or family members who can quickly offer a word or two of advice. As a result, teacher feedback may be the only feedback they get, and thus they appreciate receiving a lot of it. On the other hand, busy teachers might limit themselves to thoughtful feedback on just two or three priority issues in a paper.

Select the right location for feedback

Written feedback can be provided in essentially two locations: in-text and at the end of the text. In-text feedback might take the form of marginal comments, notes between lines, or codes that link particular information to a section of the text. End-of-text comments are usually larger comments, left at the end of the paper (or sometimes the beginning), with feedback about the text as a whole or patterns of concern. While both locations are viable, when feedback is left only in-text, writers can struggle to distinguish between important and trivial comments. When left only at the end, writers may be unsure where to make specific changes. Ferris (2003) explains that her approach is to read the whole paper through and craft an endnote that summarizes several priority issues for the writer to address. Only after completing the endnote does she provide in-text comments that demonstrate specific locations where the endnote suggestions can be applied.

Provide feedback in effective forms

The three primary syntactic forms for feedback are questions, indirect statements, and direct statements. Questions are usually intended to offer polite revision requests, but L2 writers can often be confused by questions or take questions too literally, thereby missing the implied request for revision (Thonus, 1999). Questions asking for explicit information (e.g., "What is the author of this source?") are more useful than questions meant to probe the writer's thinking (e.g., "Are you sure this is the best way to express your emotions?") (Ferris, 1995). Indirect statements include phrases like, "You might consider moving this sentence to the top of the paragraph." Indirect statements also carry an amount of politeness that can be confusing for L2 writers to process as a directive (Hyland & Hyland, 2001). Directive statements, such as, "Use this idea to introduce your paragraph," are the least polite but also the easiest to understand. L2 writers typically prefer this level of directiveness when seeking feedback (Eckstein, 2019). Teachers may be reluctant to offer such feedback because of institutional policies against directiveness, social pressure to be polite, or anxiety about directly instructing writers where and how to reconstruct their text for fear of exerting too much control over their text (i.e., appropriation). A helpful overarching suggestion is to couple questions and indirect statements with suggestions for revision; this way, writers are more likely to understand not only that the request is for revision, but also how to go about revising.

Consider oral/audio feedback

Oral feedback, as typically offered in teacher-student conferences, one-to-one tutorials in the writing center, or peer feedback sessions, gives the feedback provider an opportunity to ask clarifying questions about the writer's meaning and negotiate revision requests, particularly if the interaction is synchronous. Teachers might also provide asynchronous oral feedback by using an audio file or producing a video that includes a screenshare image of the writer's work as the feedback provider marks the paper in real time or summarizes feedback. This approach is useful for writers in that they can understand both the point in the text designated for revision and the teacher's emotional attitude toward the writer and the writing. L2 writers in particular can benefit linguistically by hearing the stress and intonation patterns of the feedback and noticing syntactic structures provided by their teacher.

Use peer feedback

Writers improve by discussing their writing with others, and peers can provide that "other" voice, which can offer a wide variety of benefits to both writer and peer reviewer. For instance, reviewers can benefit from

Table 12.1 *Sample language for feedback giver and receiver*

Feedback-Giver Language	Feedback-Receiver Language
<ul><li>"I really liked this spot where…"</li><li>"I was expecting XXX, and that's what you explained here. Nice job!"</li><li>"Here's what I understood from your text: XXX. Is that right?"</li><li>"I didn't understand this part here. Could you provide more detail?"</li><li>"I was expecting XXX, but it never came. Maybe you could add it."</li><li>"The organization confused me. Perhaps change things like this…"</li></ul>	<ul><li>"I'm glad you liked it! Can you tell me what exactly you liked? Is there anything else I can do to improve the good stuff?"</li><li>"Oops, that's not what I meant. Here's what I was thinking; can you help me phrase it better?"</li><li>"What was the most confusing for you? Could you state what you think you understood?"</li><li>"Where would be the best place to add it? Can you suggest some wording?"</li><li>"Thanks for looking at organization. Any suggestions for how to revise?"</li></ul>

seeing others' writing and comparing it to their own (Eckstein et al., 2011), and writers can benefit from getting more feedback while practicing their language skills (Lundstrom & Baker, 2009). Peer feedback sessions in general encourage students to be more engaged with assignment criteria and in class (Hyland, 2000) and to develop critical thinking and learner autonomy (Yang et al., 2006). Despite these advantages, researchers and practitioners have worried about the value of L2 peer review because L2 writers tend to focus on grammar and surface errors. These writers may not be qualified to address such errors, and focusing on these errors may not lead to effective revisions (Storch, 2005). Also, L2 writers tend to prefer the authoritative comments of teachers and dislike or disregard peer feedback (Tsui & Ng, 2000), which is usually biased based on things like friendship and social closeness (Saito & Fujita, 2004). Additionally, cultural issues including those associated with collectivism, power, face-threatening acts, and interpersonal harmony might make some students less willing to provide critical comments or take on authoritative stances as readers (Nelson & Carson, 2006).

To overcome some of these drawbacks of peer review, scholars urge teachers to offer students peer feedback training. Such training sessions should discuss at least three things: 1) benefits of peer feedback as a learning/writing activity, 2) best approaches to working well in a pair or group, and 3) appropriate language to use as a feedback giver and receiver (Rollinson, 2005). On this third point, helpful phrases can include those listed in Table 12.1. These phrases may need to be adapted to the language level of particular writers. In addition, teachers can offer rubrics, checklists, or other guidelines to help reviewers know what to focus on and what to overlook when providing feedback.

After peer-review training, students can provide peer feedback in pairs or small groups. Typically, these feedback sessions are done by having writers exchange papers either in person (e.g., in class) or electronically using a learning management system or an automated peer feedback system, such as Peerceptiv (https://peerceptiv.com/). Once writers are finished with the peer feedback task, teachers can further legitimize peer feedback by asking students to submit a short memo explaining what they learned from their peers' feedback and how they plan to change or revise their writing.

Design self-feedback opportunities

Self-feedback involves L2 writers examining their own writing either generally or in relation to specific feedback features. These feedback features can include features the students identify themselves or features they are instructed to examine by a teacher. Charles (1990) proposed an early version of self-monitoring in which students annotate their texts with doubts or concerns about their writing, which teachers could then address in feedback. This method is similar to the "letter to the reviewer" assignment discussed by Shvidko (2015) in which students write a letter expressing concerns about their writing. In either instance, writers initiate the review process that teachers or peers complete. There is very limited research on self-monitoring or self-feedback, though Xiang (2004) found it to be effective for improving organization among higher proficiency writers, and Yu et al. (2020) showed that peer and self-feedback increased L2 students' motivation for and engagement in writing. Others view self-feedback as a form of self-assessment (Panadero et al., 2019) in which writers can learn to provide their own feedback on any part of their writing in preparation to improve it. When designing self-feedback activities, teachers should provide students with assessment criteria and standards for the task the students are set to perform. The teachers can then provide students with or help students locate exemplars of good products. Teachers can also support students by helping them practice self-feedback in class, perhaps as a rubric training or use activity and then provide feedback on students' self-feedback.

Conclusion

L2 feedback approaches have been and continue to be heavily influenced by L1 approaches, though scholars and practitioners are right to consider ways in which L1 approaches can or should be modified to support L2 writers. Some obvious changes relate to language differences: feedback needs to be communicated in ways that are comprehensible and pragmatically interpretable by L2 writers. Additionally, teachers need not shy away from language-based feedback since many L2 writers struggle with this issue. Beyond these concerns, teachers should express their feedback approach to their students and then provide feedback in manners and formats that help students take advantage of the help they are provided. In terms of manners and formats of support, and as a brief summary to this chapter, consider this list. Teachers who work with L2 writing should establish feedback criteria, respond to intermediate drafts, offer substantive feedback on a few select points, include both end-of-text and in-text comments, use direct statements and clear questions, offer suggestions for revision, include oral and audio feedback, build student motivation, and employ thoughtful peer and self-feedback options.

Suggestions for future research

Though the information in this chapter provides a review of best practices for new teachers, it also presents areas where more research is needed. More research based on more students in more contexts can help demonstrate more ways in which L2 writing feedback can be effective. For example, we need more research that examines how L2 writers interact with both praise and criticism in feedback. Although some research has demonstrated general trends, it is unclear if writers interpret comments and questions differently based on their language backgrounds and language proficiency. We also need additional research on how writers engage with feedback both in cross-sectional and longitudinal studies to help confirm and expand what we know about what writers do with feedback. Moreover, there is exceptionally little research that examines long-term writing development in response to feedback. Action research and case studies that follow one or more students over several semesters and collect both written products and student reflections would be extremely valuable in documenting specific writing development trajectories. We must also pay attention to the emotional effect of feedback and design studies that investigate writers' emotions when engaging with feedback. Additional investigations that explore feedback-provision are also needed; scholars have begun investigating whether teachers change their feedback type and quantity in oral versus written feedback, but this research line should be extended to peer and self-feedback and should include additional modes, such as synchronous and asynchronous feedback.

Although L2 feedback research is expanding, there is still far too little of it in general. Hopefully new teachers will be inspired to complete—and ideally publish—action research as well as carefully controlled experimental or quasi-experimental research to help the L2 writing community learn what works best for L2 writing feedback.

Further reading

Ferris, D. R. (2003). *Response to student writing: Implications for second language students.* Lawrence Erlbaum Associates.

This book is a definitive volume on feedback to second language writing. Ferris provides an essential historical overview of English composition feedback theories and practices and demonstrates how these have strongly influenced complementary developments in L2 response theories and practices. The book then dives deeply into L2 feedback scholarship by reviewing basic L2 feedback theory and error correction and peer review research. It also examines how students think and feel about the feedback they receive to their writing. Additionally, the book provides important practical suggestions for helping teachers respond to student writing and implement peer review. The book is meticulously researched and provides an outstanding mixture of helpful practical suggestions with exhaustive reference to authoritative literature so that both teachers and researchers can benefit from reading it.

Ferris, D. R., & Hedgcock, J. S. (2023). *Teaching L2 composition: Purpose, process, and practice* **(4th Ed.). Routledge.**

This textbook offers theory and pedagogical applications for teachers of L2 composition students. Since composition is generally taught in higher education, the text is most applicable to college and university teachers, but it also works well for those teaching in intensive English programs and adult education environments. While the text deeply examines many aspects of writing instruction, including writer backgrounds, writing task design, curriculum creation, and writing assessment, the authors provide an in-depth discussion of feedback and response practices in chapter 7 that can aid beginning and experienced teachers. Feedback topics covered include principles and guidelines for written feedback, holding teacher-student writing conferences, implementing peer review, and facilitating student self-feedback. The information on feedback and response is supported by both author experience and a wealth of academic scholarship.

Hyland, K. (2019). *Second language writing* **(2nd Ed.). Cambridge University Press.**

Hyland's textbook provides an easy entry point to L2 writing instruction. Like the Ferris and Hedgcock book, Hyland's volume provides a broad overview of second language writing instruction, much of which is relevant to designing a good environment that supports effective feedback practices. In his focused chapter on responding to student writing (chapter 7), Hyland explores the question of what feedback is, whether it leads to writing improvement, and other considerations such as student preferences for feedback, its pragmatic purposes, and the interpersonal aspect of teacher feedback. Hyland also discusses processes for implementing teacher-student conferences and peer review and offers insights into the pros and cons of automatic writing evaluation.

Matsuda, P. K., Cox, M., Jordan, J., & Ortmeier-Hooper, C. (2011).

Second-language writing in the composition classroom: A critical sourcebook. **Bedford St. Martin's.**

This edited volume is a collection and reprinting of some of the most influential articles written by leaders in the field of L2 writing. Although the book is ostensibly meant for composition teachers, principles can be applied in various L2 writing settings and with a variety of learners. The book covers a wide range of issues across five major sections that ends in five chapters specifically dedicated to responding to (and assessing) L2 writing. These chapters explore ways teachers can work with diverse learners, grade them fairly, and attend to their specific feedback needs in ethical, empowering, and favorable ways.

References

Brookhart, S. (2013). How to create and use rubrics for formative assessment and grading. *ASCD.* www.ascd.org/publications/books/112001.aspx

Casanave, C. P. (2017). *Controversies in second language writing: Dilemmas and decisions in research and instruction* (2nd ed.). University of Michigan Press.

Charles, M (1990). Responding to problems in written English using a student self-monitoring technique. *ELT Journal, 44*(4), 286–293. https://doi.org/10.1093/elt/44.4.286

Conrad, S. M., & Goldstein, L. M. (1999). ESL student revision after teacher-written comments: Text, contexts, and individuals. *Journal of Second Language Writing, 8*(2), 147–179. https://doi.org/10.1016/S1060-3743(99)80126-X

Eckstein, G. (2013). Implementing and evaluating a writing conference program for international L2 writers across language proficiency levels. *Journal of Second Language Writing, 22*(3), 231–239. https://doi.org/10.1016/j.jslw.2013.03.001

Eckstein, G. (2019). Directiveness in the center: L1, L2, and generation 1.5 expectations. *The Writing Center Journal, 37*(2), 61–92. Retrieved from https://www.jstor.org/stable/26922018

Eckstein, G., Chariton, J., & McCollum, R. M. (2011). Multi-draft composing: An iterative model for academic argument writing. *Journal of English for Academic Purposes, 10*(3), 162–172. https://doi.org/10.1016/j.jeap.2011.05.004

Ferris, D. R. (1995). Student reactions to teacher response in multiple-draft composition classrooms. *TESOL Quarterly, 29*(1), 33–53. https://doi.org/10.2307/3587804

Ferris, D. R. (1997). The influence of teacher commentary on student revision. *TESOL Quarterly, 31*(2), 315–339. https://doi.org/10.2307/3588049

Ferris, D. R. (2003). *Response to student writing: Implications for second language students.* Lawrence Erlbaum Associates.

Goldstein, L. M., & Conrad, S. M. (1990). Student input and negotiation of meaning in ESL writing conferences. *TESOL Quarterly, 24*(3), 443–460.

Hu, G. W., & Lam, S. T. E. (2010). Issues of cultural appropriateness and pedagogical efficacy: Exploring peer review in a second language writing class. *Instructional Science, 38*, 371–394. https://doi.org/10.1007/s11251-008-9086-1

Hyland, P. (2000). Learning from feedback on assessment. In A. Booth & P. Hyland (Eds.), *The practice of university history teaching* (pp. 233–247). Manchester University Press.

Hyland, F., & Hyland, K. (2001). Sugaring the pill: Praise and criticism in written feedback. *Journal of Second Language Writing, 10*(3), 185–212. https://doi.org/10.1016/S1060-3743(01)00038-8

Kroll, B. (1998). Assessing writing abilities. *Annual Review of Applied Linguistics, 18*, 219–242.

Laflen, A. (2019). What LMS site statistics tell us about timing instructor feedback on student writing. *Journal of Response to Writing, 5*(2), 46–71.

Lundstorm, K., & Baker, W. (2009). To give is better than to receive: The benefits of peer review to the reviewer's own writing. *Journal of Second Language Writing, 18*(1), 30–43. http://doi.org/10.1016/j.jslw.2008.06.002

Matsuda, P. K. (1999). Composition studies and ESL writing: A disciplinary division of labor. *College Composition and Communication, 50*(4), 699–721.

Matsuda, P. K. (2003). Process and post-process: A discursive history. *Journal of Second Language Writing, 12*(1), 65–83. https://doi.org/10.1016/S1060-3743(02)00127-3

Nelson, G. L. & J. G. Carson (2006). Cultural issues in peer response: Revisiting "culture." In K. Hyland & F. Hyland (Eds.), *Feedback in second language writing: Contexts and issues* (pp. 42–59). Cambridge University Press.

Panadero, E., Lipnevich, A., & Broabent, J. (2019). Turning self-assessment into self-feedback. In M. Henderson, A. Rola, D. Boud, & E. Molloy (Eds.), *The impact of feedback in higher education* (pp. 147–163). Palgrave McMillan.

Reid, J. (1994). Responding to ESL students' texts: The myth of appropriation. *TESOL Quarterly, 28*, 273–292. https://doi.org/10.2307/3587434

Rollinson, P. (2005). Using peer feedback in the ESL writing class. *ELT Journal* 59, 23–30.

Saito, H., & Fujita, T. (2004). Characteristics and user acceptance of peer rating in EFL writing classrooms. In *Language Teaching Research, 8*(1), 31–54, https://doi.org/10.1191/1362168804lr133oa

Seow, A. (2002). The writing process and process writing. In J. Richards & W. A. Renandya (Eds.), *Methodology in language teaching: An anthology of current practice* (pp. 315–320). Cambridge University Press. https://doi.org/10.1017/CBO9780511667190.044

Shvidko, E. (2015). Beyond "giver-receiver" relationships: Facilitating an interactive revision process. *Journal of Response to Writing, 1*(2), 55–74.

Silva, T. (1988). Comments on Vivian Zamel's "Recent Research on Writing Pedagogy". A reader reacts. *TESOL Quarterly, 22*(3), 517–520. https://doi.org/10.2307/3587296

Silva, T. (1993). Toward an understanding of the distinct nature of L2 writing: ESL research and its implications. *TESOL Quarterly, 27*(4), 657–677. https://doi.org/10.2307/3587400

Silva, T. (1997). On the ethical treatment of ESL writers. *TESOL Quarterly, 31*(2), 359–363. https://doi.org/10.2307/3588052

Storch, N. (2005). Collaborative writing: Product, process, and students' reflections. *Journal of Second Language Writing, 14*(3), 153–173. https://doi.org/10.1016/j.jslw.2005.05.002

Thonus, T. (1999). How to communicate politely and be a tutor, too: NS-NNS interaction and writing center practice. *Text - Interdisciplinary Journal for the Study of Discourse, 19*(2), 253–280. https://doi.org/10.1515/text.1.1999.19.2.253

Tsui, A. B., & Ng, M. (2000). Do secondary L2 writers benefit from peer comments? *Journal of Second Language Writing, 9*(2), 147–170. http://doi.org/10.1016/S1060-3743(00)00022-9

Wang, W. (2014). Students' perceptions of rubric-referenced peer feedback on EFL writing: A longitudinal inquiry. *Assessing Writing, 12*, 80–96. https://doi.org/10.1016/j.asw.2013.11.008

Xiang, W. (2004). Encouraging self-monitoring in writing by Chinese students. *ELT Journal, 58*(3), 238–246. https://doi.org/10.1093/elt/58.3.238

Yang, M., Badger, R., & Yu, Z. (2006). A comparative study of peer and teacher feedback in Chinese EFL writing class. *Journal of Second Language Learning, 15*(3), 179–200. http://doi.org/10.1016/j.jslw.2006.09.004

Yu, S., Jiang, L., & Zhou, N. (2020). Investigating what feedback practices contribute to students' writing motivation and engagement in Chinese EFL context: A large scale study. *Assessing Writing, 44*, 1-15. https://doi.org/10.1016/j.asw.2020.100451

Zamel, V. (1985). Responding to student writing. *TESOL Quarterly, 19*(1), 79–101. https://doi.org/10.2307/3586773

13
Technology and L2 writing instruction

Yijen Wang
Ali Panahi

Introduction

Technology has changed writing instruction in several ways (Nation & Macalister, 2021), influencing the spread of literacy skills, styles of written communication, and the process of writing (Adams, 2022). Regarding the change in the writing process, digital devices have transformed the writing process by offering much more than just a shift from handwriting to typing. Early literature on the impact of technology on writing instruction predominantly compared digital devices to traditional methods, such as computers versus paper-and-pencil. These comparative studies suggest that students who use technology show significant improvements in their writing outcomes, including increased fluency, accuracy, creativity, engagement, and motivation (Daskalovska, 2015; Li, 2018; Ma, Tang, & Lin, 2015). Recent research has further highlighted the benefits of digital devices for writing. For instance, online writing platforms, writing apps, and computer-assisted writing programs can provide students with access to a wide range of learning resources, facilitate collaboration and feedback, and offer real-time support and guidance as students write. These findings indicate that technology can play a valuable role in supporting the L2 (L2) writing process.

Shifts in writing purpose and literacy have also been brought about by the evolution of technology. For instance, Web 2.0 tools enable L2 learners to not only write for academic purposes, but also to produce texts, short messages on social networking services (SNS), and emails. As a result, the language used in these different contexts may vary. The use of multimedia also provides learners with the opportunity to express their thoughts in ways that extend beyond texts. This has led to changes in writing formats, which may now include visual and audio elements, emphasizing the importance of teaching multimodal composition for 21st-century digital competence (Nation & Macalister, 2021; Rahimi & Tafazoli, 2022).

In line with this, technology has had a considerable influence on literacy by transforming how we access, consume, and deliver information. L2 learners can take advantage of the internet to access a wide range of information, to use various digital tools to express themselves, and to share their ideas with a wider audience. As writing can be undertaken in a variety of online and offline formats, the objectives of writing instruction have changed. Technology has created new forms of literacy that go beyond traditional reading and writing skills (Elola & Oskoz, 2017). For example, Adams (2022) states that "digital literacy encompass the linguistics knowledge and writing skills associated with pen and paper writing as well as knowledge of technology tools and design knowledge developed from experiences both consuming and producing digital text (p. 187)".

As the process and format of writing have changed, technology-enriched environments have come to be considered more effective for writing education. For example, writing classes may happen in a computer lab, in a bring-your-own-devise (BYOD) environment, or even outside of the classroom (Alirezabeigi, Masschelein, & Decuypere, 2020; Thomas, 2020). With the use of mobile devices, ubiquitous learning takes place for both formal and informal instruction. Students have more opportunities to publish their work online on social media and e-publishing platforms. Technology has also changed the ways of evaluating writing outcomes. For example, automated assessment tools using machine learning technology can be used to analyze text and provide feedback on the grammar, vocabulary, tone, coherence, and other aspects of L2 writing. This can help both teachers and students to save time on the assessing process and enhance accuracy of their writing. Writing assessment can be conducted remotely too, with which teachers are able to provide a more personalized and effective assessment experience for each student.

The impact of technology-based writing instruction on writing outcomes was investigated in literature (e.g., Little, Clark, Tani, & Connor, 2018; Xu, Banerjee, Ramirez, Zhu, & Wijekumar, 2019) with use of meta-analytic methods. Results confirmed the effect of education technology on writing outcomes. More specifically, with the breakout of Coronavirus, the effective dominance of technology is strongly visible in the development of L2 writing instruction and writing proficiency which has explicit and implicit implications for the early-career teachers. This given, for the early-career teachers, as Bloch (2018) indicates, the implications of technological use in the teaching of writing can consequently be observed in three directions: as a tool for literacy development, as a rhetorical space for the development of digital literacy, and as an innovative approach to being literate.

Theoretical framework: Integration of technology into writing instruction

Researchers have viewed writing development in various perspectives, and the two most widely applied theories are *cognitive theory* and *sociocultural theory*. Understanding the theories can help teachers explicitly use technology for writing education. Here, we outlined a variety of digital tools/devices for writing development coping with the theories mentioned above.

Cognitive theory of writing and technology

In Flower and Hayes's model (1981), *cognitive theory* views writing as a thinking process, emphasizing a writer's internal mental activities, namely "planning," "translating/drafting," and "revising," and these processes should be under control of a monitor. Technology can play an important role in these stages, and here are some examples:

In the planning stage, to generate ideas from long-term memory, students can recall their memories from photos, notes, files saved in their digital devices, or blogs and social networking services (SNSs). Technology also benefits students in searching for writing sources, with which they can access to an enormous amount of information via a simple click on the internet. There are also many useful digital tools to help students brainstorm, for example, using mind mapping applications to link the relationships among ideas. Freewriting and listing students' rough thoughts on note applications/software also help with the planning, for example, Microsoft OneNote, Notion, Evernote, and built-in note-taking applications. With the use of mobile devices, students can easily engage in the planning process, making writing activities more ubiquitous. When any thoughts come across students' mind, they can use their smartphone to record through texts, audios, and photos.

In the second writing stage, translating acts as a function that puts the writer's ideas into meaningful sentences (Flower & Hayes, 1981), which is also known as drafting. Microsoft Word and Google Docs may be the most common tools for students to write their draft. However, writing a first draft is usually the most painful stage for students. It is not rare to see L2 learners use their first language to undertake the planning stage and use the target language for drafting. These days, when transforming their thoughts into sentences, it is likely that some students use machine translation tools. The other artificial intelligence (AI) tools, such as ChatGPT, are also starting to be used by students to complete writing assignments. The concerns about the use of these tools will be discussed later.

Finally, to improve the writing, revising and editing are required. In this stage, accuracy of grammar and word choices are reviewed, and the clarifications are examined. These can be easily checked with the use of technology. The most frequently used one may be Microsoft Word, which was equipped with spelling and grammar check, and even provides word-choice suggestions for the users.

Sociocultural theory of writing and technology

In contrast to *cognitive theory*, which focuses on the individual writer's cognitive process of writing, *sociocultural theory* looks at motivation, affect, as well as social influences on writing (Hodges, 2017). According to Vygotsky (1978), learning is a social process where students can learn better with peers and are scaffolded by teachers. In other words, in a writing class, students need socializing to develop their writing.

In line with the theory, Brindley and Schneider (2002) state the effective writing instruction should include "modelling, shared writing, guided writing, and interactive writing" (p.330). These writing instructional strategies can be undertaken with technology. For example, teachers can use Google Docs to share and write with students (Alharbi, 2019). Some applications mentioned above also provide collaborating functions for multiple writers to compose a text together in real-time. In this way, teacher and students are able to work on a document and share their writing with each other for review and feedback from different places synchronously and asynchronously. Interactions between teacher and students, as well as students and students can be further facilitated.

Literature review: Effects of technology on writing instruction

With regard to the effectiveness of technology-supported learning and writing instruction, the results of previous studies have shown optimistic results (Al-Wasy, 2020; Choy & Cheung, 2022; Little et. al., 2018; Lv, Ren, & Xie, 2021). As Bloch (2018) indicates, writing teachers nowadays explore how writers investigate and utilize technology for literacy development inside and outside the classroom. This renders the role of technology in writing instruction much more significant. Given that technology can be generally categorized into two main domains: tutor and tool (Hubbard & Siskin, 2004; Stošić, 2015), the related literature is thematically reviewed concerning the role technology plays in teaching and learning writing in different contexts.

Technology as a tutor for writing instruction

Technology can be viewed as a tutor for learners to retrieve information, practice drills, and receive feedback (Cennamo, Ross, & Ertmer, 2014). These days, online writing tutorial programs are accessible through massive open online courses (MOOCs), YouTube, Udemy, Coursera, and even a variety of websites. With the use of these tutorial technologies, students have more chances to practice their self-directed learning. In writing classrooms, providing online instructions before in-class learning allows students to gain background knowledge of wiring, with which class time can be used more effectively for collaborative activities. Teachers can assign videos and online materials for students to view prior to the class time and focus on group discussions or feedback in the classroom learning. This kind of approach is called flipped classroom. In literature, a vast number of studies have been conducted on the importance of digital tools in inspiring and instructing learners to write and boost the quality and quantity of their writing (Alghasab, 2020). Furthermore, one of the recent studies on L2 writing has been conducted by Choy and Cheung (2022) on primary school students' perceptions towards self-directed learning and collaborative learning with and without technology in English writing lessons in Singapore. The results displayed that the use of technology is effective in teaching writing.

The other growing trend is the use for receiving feedback on writing from technology. For instance, computer-automated measurement of syntactic complexity in L2 writing (Lu, 2017), metalinguistic corrective feedback (Gao & Ma, 2019), automated written corrective feedback (Ranalli, 2018). In Gao and Ma's (2019) study, the investigation into computer-automated metalinguistic corrective feedback and L2 writing indicated that metalinguistic corrective feedback on L2 writing influences learners' performance. In this sense, teachers can use technology as a tutor to support their writing instructions.

Technology as a tool for writing instruction

Unlike the tutor role, technology does not evaluate but is used as a tool to assist in teaching writing and engage students in writing process. The tool we select can make an impact on our writing process and the way we think about writing (Adams, 2022). Writing tools such as search engines, corpus, and word processing software have been widely used in L2 education. As a tool, technology can be utilized to enhance writing process and facilitate interactions. To be more specific, we categorized digital tools into three key features:

Online dictionaries and corpora

For L2 writers, online dictionaries are frequently used for looking up words meaning in their writing process, and online thesauri are also useful for selecting synonyms and antonyms of word. Given that choosing appropriate words without contexts from a dictionary is difficult for language learners, corpora may be an alternative. Corpora are computerized databases of collections of verbal and written texts, produced in authentic contexts. With corpus-based tools, students are able to make better choices of words through checking concordances, collocations and words frequency (Adam, 2022). Research has shown that with appropriate scaffolding provided by teachers, students are more likely to utilize corpus-based tools, and further improve fluency and accuracy in terms of syntactic and lexical aspects (Daskalovska, 2015; Ma, Tang, & Lin, 2015).

Collaborative writing

Collaborative writing is defined as "an activity that can be simply defined as the involvement of two or more writers in the production of a single text" (Storch, 2019, p. 40). Wikis were the most common tool used for collaborative writing (Chao & Lo, 2011) in early literature. The past several years have seen online collaborative writing tools such as Google Docs and Microsoft Word Online enable multiple students to co-work on a writing synchronously, which means that students can share their writing and provide/receive feedback on the writing from each other and their teacher through the online word processing tools and the built-in real-time chat box. Abrams (2019), using Google Docs, researched the relationship between computer-mediated writing and task-based collaborative L2 writing, and the study demonstrated that the collaboration-based activities make a significant contribution to writing improvement, as it engages the learners and motivates meaning-making, leading in the end to L2 writing development. Many learning management systems (LMS), such as Moodle and Google Classroom are also equipped with chat rooms and discussion forums, which can be used to make improvements and revisions in real-time (see also Hafour & Al-Rashidy, 2020).

Online feedback

Regarding technology-supported feedback for L2 writing instruction, Lv, Ren, and Xie's (2021) meta-analysis investigated the results of 17 primary studies on students' English SL/FL writing quality (i.e., a sample size of 1568 students) after online feedback and the results indicated the effectiveness of written feedback in general. More specifically, they found out that educational levels and task genre mitigate the influence of online feedback on writing quality. After all, the results make a contribution to a better realization of the influence of online feedback on ESL/EFL writing and help gain some insights into technology supported ESL/EFL writing instruction.

Research into online feedback through Computer-Mediated Communication (CMC) tools such as e-mail and chat rooms in early literature have shown optimistic results (Li, 2018; Wu, Petit, & Chen, 2015). Resent research trends look at the use of social networking services (SNS) such as Facebook, YouTube, and Twitter on providing feedback and sharing information to enhance interactions between teachers and students (Dizon, 2016). With the use of SNS, students have more opportunities to access the real-world, where they can seek advice on their writing outside of the classrooms. For example, online communities such as HiNative are platforms for language learners to ask questions to "native speakers". Online feedback can be undertaken not only through textual feedback, but also visual and oral feedback, as immersive simulations achieve greater learning outcomes. In line with this, online teleconference tools enable teachers to provide screencast feedback (Anson, 2018; Cunningham, 2019; Tseng & Yeh 2019), with which the process of corrections and feedback can be shown on a screen. In Cheng and Li's study (2020), they investigated students' perceptions of using screencast video-based feedback and text-based feedback on EFL writing. The findings indicated that teacher social presence was promoted through screencast video feedback.

Technology as an agent for writing instruction

With the rapid progress of technology, the third role technology plays in education has emerged, which can be seen as a writing agent on behalf of both teachers and students, with which they act as a role of selecting/evaluating the outcomes created by technology. Powered by machine learning, AI technology can provide suggestions on grammar, word choices, tones, styles, paraphrasing (e.g., Grammarly, Wordtune, Quillbot), and offer autosuggest/autocomplete (e.g., Gmail), generate citations, and generate abstract or summary (e.g., InstaText, Abstract Generator) during the writing process. Chatbots such as ChatGPT even can produce (mostly) meaningful texts based on the instructions given to it by users. Machine translation tools such as Google Translate can be used for drafting (Tsai, 2019) and post-editing (Chang, Chen, & Lai, 2022; Koponen, 2016). Automatic writing evaluation (AWE) technologies are also frequently used by students (Adam, 2022). For example, Dizon and Gayed's (2021) study showed that students' use of an AWE system enhanced their L2 writing quality through reducing grammatical and lexical errors and increasing their lexical variation. On the other hand, teachers can also use these AI technologies to assist their grading and provide feedback on students' writing. In this sense, technology may make writing instruction more efficient by reducing teachers' workload on marking papers.

Practical implications and suggestions

As innovative technology continuously emerges, teachers face new challenges. It is time for educators to reconsider writing instruction regarding how to teach, what to teach, and how to assess writing. Although technology empowers writing education, some issues around the use of technology in writing education have been raised. Since learners can use digital tools to copy and paste texts easily, plagiarism has become a serious issue (Nation & Macalister, 2021). Thus, teachers should emphasize ethical concerns and teach learners how to avoid plagiarism. Another concern is related to the rise of using AI tools for writing. As students may become more reliant on AI tools, there is the risk that they will not be able to improve their writing skills due to their over-relyiance on these tools, which may hamper their critical thinking skills and L2 writing competence. Fairness of accessibility to AI tools is also under debate. It is likely that the students who have access to AI tools will have better writing products compared with those who do not. How to assess writing outcomes/products has also become a challenge. Assessment beyond accuracy and fluency, that is, evaluating the writing process rather than only the product may be an idea. For instance, process-tracing technology (Ranalli, Feng, & Chukharev-Hudilainen, 2019), digital portfolio (Barrot, 2020), and progress recording within LMS allow teachers to easily track students' progress, making it easier to provide individualized feedback and support.

A particular technology takes on different roles in different writing processes, depending on how it is used. Consistent with sociocultural perspectives, since the cognitive processes in writing remain largely the same, the role teachers play in scaffolding are highly unlikely to be replaced in the foreseeable future. In order to keep up with the changing demands of writing instruction, regardless of whether teachers are pre-service or in-service, every teacher should equip themselves with technological skills. To be prepared for 21st-centrury digital competence, teachers should keep learning how to adopt and evaluate technology and how to train themselves as well as their learners to use technology for writing purposes. Choy and Cheung (2022) point out that with the sweeping of the Covid-19 pandemic across the world, more classes have shifted to online or blended formats. Technology-driven learning writing lessons are well suited to these formats, facilitating the development of writing-related collaborative and self-directed learning skills. As technology becomes more accessible and familiar, teachers can incorporate digital tools into their writing instruction process on a daily basis. This can potentially move early-career teachers towards autonomy, giving them professional independence to make decisions about what technology to use and how to use it, ultimately helping them to boost and scaffold their students' writing in terms of both products and processes. Early-career teachers need to be aware of the changes in technologies and the tentative expectations regarding effectiveness of these technologies for L2 writing instruction and seek out professional feedback from technologically proficient teachers with experience in using technology in real language and teaching environments. Achieving this requires ongoing evaluation of the technology and open communication among teachers, students, policymakers, and developers.

Suggestions for action research or case study

L2 writing instruction should be well-planned and grounded in practical teaching and research. To further explore the potential of technology in L2 writing instruction, early-career teachers may consider conducting action research or a case study. Teachers can choose to teach with a specific online system and then invite more experienced teachers and get feedback about how they are proceeding forward in terms of the process of technology use and relating it to writing instruction. Likewise, they can do case studies using candidate technologies over the course of sever sessions. Then, based on the performance of their learners as a consequence of the technological tool in use, the results of the action research by the colleagues can be formally reported and the related concern or challenge can be well-managed or at least the degree of challenge can be mitigated, and the teaching practice may be further improved.

To improve current teaching practices, teachers must understand how their students learn, yet longitudinal research into how students engage in the writing process using technology in naturalistic contexts remains scarce. While research into teachers' and students' perceptions and actual usage of a specific technology have been widely studied, the role of technology as an agent may be a research topic which is timely yet less explored. Ethnographic research may also be helpful to explore the interplay between technology, teachers, and students in writing instruction.

Further reading

Kessler, M. (2020). Technology mediated writing: exploring incoming graduate students' L2 writing strategies with activity theory. *Computer and Composition, 55.* https://doi.org/10.1016/j.compcom.2020.102542

The study explores two Chinese L2 English writers as they compose assignments in order to better realize the existing learner practices surrounding digital composition. The results reveal that students' writing processes are positively affected by varying numbers of factors. Also, implications related to writers' artifact-mediated strategies are elaborated in detail.

Li, J., Link, S., & Hegelheimer, V. (2015). Rethinking the role of automated writing evaluation feedback in ESL writing instruction. *Journal of L2 Writing, 27,* 1–18. https://doi.org/10.1016/j.jslw.2014.10.004

The study presents that technological tool contributes to automated writing evaluation and provides feedback on both content and language in addition to an automated score. The results of the study revealed that technology helps develop corrective feedback, so there are potential benefits for technology use in L2 writing assessment and instruction.

Rowland, A., Smith, S. J., & Lowrey, K. A. (2020). Pairing technology with 6 traits of writing instruction. *Journal of Special Education Technology, 37* (1), 135-142. https://doi.org/10.1177/

0162643420945600

The study explores the issue that individuals with disabilities keep on struggling with writing skills. The results of the study show that technology provides supportive tools for writing instruction, but plenty of teachers are not confident enough to use technological tools in teaching writing. On the ground of the 6 Traits of Writing model as a framework, this study presents and justifies how students with disabilities are challenged in each trait and supplies technological assistance that can be supportive to the achievement of the skills within that specified trait domain.

Yangın-Ekşi, G., Akayoglu, S., & Anyango. L. (2023). *New directions in technology for writing instruction: Practices for English language teaching classrooms.* Springer.

This book may be the most up to date one which focuses on technology in EFL/ESL writing instruction from conceptual, theoretical, and practical perspectives. Providing specific examples of writing approach with technology usage and research in a variety of contexts, the book may be useful for early-career teachers who desire to gain in-depth knowledge of integration technology into writing instruction.

References

Abrams, Z. I. (2019). Collaborative writing and text quality in Google Docs. *Language Learning & Technology, 23*(2), 22–42. https://doi.org/10125/44681

Adams, R. (2022). L2 Technology and Writing. In N. Ziegler. & M. González-Lloret. (Eds.), *The Routledge handbook of L2 acquisition and technology.* Routledge. https://doi.org/10.4324/9781351117586-17

Alharbi, M. A. (2019). Exploring the potential of google doc in facilitating innovative teaching and learning practices in an EFL writing course. *Innovation in Language Learning and Teaching, 14*(3), 227–242. https://doi.org/10.1080/17501229.2019.1572157

Al-Wasy, B. Q. (2020). The effectiveness of integrating technology in EFL/ESL writing: a meta-analysis. *Interactive Technology and Smart Education, 17*(4), 435–454. https://doi.org/10.1108/ITSE-03-2020-0033

Alirezabeigi. S., Masschelein, J., & Decuypere, M. (2020). The agencement of taskification: On new forms of reading and writing in BYOD schools. *Educational Philosophy and Theory. 52*(14), 1514–1525, https://doi.orrg/10.1080/00131857.2020.1716335

Anson, C. M. (2018). She really took the time: Students' opinions of screen-capture response to their writing in online courses. In C. Weaver, & P. Jackson (Eds.), *Writing in online courses: How the Online Environment Shapes Writing Practices.* Hampton Press.

Barrot, J. S. (2020). Effects of Facebook-based e-portfolio on ESL learners' writing performance, *Language. Culture and Curriculum, 34*(1), 95–111. https://doi.org/10.1080/07908318.2020.1745822

Bloch, J. (2018). Technology for Teaching English as a Second Language (ESL) Writing. In J. I. Liontas (Ed.), *The TESOL encyclopedia of English language teaching* (pp.1–8). John Wiley & Sons, Inc. http://doi.org/10.1002/9781118784235.eelt0440

Brindley, R., & Schneider, J. J. (2002). Writing instruction or destruction: Lessons to be learned from fourth grade teachers' perspectives on teaching writing. *Journal of Teacher Education, 53*(4), 328–341. https://doi.org/10.1177/0022487102053004005

Cennamo, K., Ertmer, P. A., & Ross, J. (2013). *Technology integration for meaningful classroom use: A standards-based approach, international edition.* Wadsworth Publishing.

Chang, P., Chen, P-J., & Lai, L-L. (2022). Recursive editing with Google Translate: the impact on writing and error correction. *Computer Assisted Language Learning.* https://doi.org/10.1080/09588221.2022.2147192

Chao, Y-C. J., & Lo, H-C. (2011). Students' perceptions of Wiki-based collaborative writing for learners of English as a foreign language. *Interactive Learning Environments, 19*(4), 395–411, https://doi.org/10.1080/10494820903298662

Cheng, D., & Li, M. (2020). Screencast video feedback in online TESOL classes. *Computers and Composition, 58,* 102612. https://doi.org/10.1016/j.compcom.2020.102612

Choy, D., & Cheung, Y-L. (2022). Comparison of primary four students' perception towards self-directed learning and collaborative learning with technology in their English writing lessons. *Journal of Computers in Education, 9,* 783–806. https://doi.org/10.1007/s40692-022-00220-4

Cunningham, K. J. (2019). Student perceptions and use of technology-mediated text and screencast feedback in ESL writing. *Computers and Composition, 52,* 222–241. https://doi.org/10.1016/j.compcom.2019.02.003

Daskalovska, N. (2015). Corpus-based versus traditional learning of collocations. *Computer Assisted Language Learning, 28*(2), 130–144. https://doi.org/10.1080/09588221.2013.803982

Dizon, G. & Gayed, J. (2021). Examining the impact of Grammarly on the quality of mobile L2 writing. *The JALT CALL Journal, 17*(2), 74–92. https://doi.org/10.29140/jaltcall.v17n2.336

Dizon, G. (2016). A comparative study of Facebook vs. paper-and-pencil writing to improve L2 writing skills. *Computer Assisted Language Learning, 29*(8), 1249–1258. https://doi.org/10.1080/09588221.2016.1266369

Elola, I., & Oskoz, A. (2017). Writing with 21st century social tools in the L2 classroom: new literacies, genres, and writing practices. *Journal of L2 Writing, 36,* 52–60. https://doi.org/10.1016/j.jslw.2017.04.002

Flower, L., & Hayes, J. R. (1981). A cognitive process theory of writing. *College Composition and Communication, 32*(4), 365–387. http://

dx.doi.org/10.2307/356600

Gao, J., & Ma, S. (2019). The effect of two forms of computer-automated metalinguistic corrective feedback. *Language Learning & Technology, 23*(2), 65–83. https://doi.org/10125/44683

Hafour, M., & Al-Rashidy, A. M. (2020). Storyboarding-based collaborative narratives on Google Docs: Fostering EFL learners' writing fluency, syntactic complexity, and overall performance. *The JALT CALL Journal. 16*(3), 123–146. https://doi.org/10.29140/jaltcall.v16n3.393

Hodges, T. S. (2017). Theoretically speaking: An examination of four theories and how they support writing in the classroom. *The Clearing House: A Journal of Educational Strategies, Issues and Ideas. 90*(4), 139–146. http://doi.org/10.1080/00098655.2017.1326228

Hubbard, P., & Siskin, C. (2004). Another look at tutorial CALL. *ReCALL, 16*(2), 448–461. https://doi.org/10.1017/S095834400400 1326

Koponen, M. (2016). Is machine translation post-editing worth the effort? A survey of research into post-editing and effort. *The Journal of Specialised Translation, 25*(2) 131–148.

Li, M. (2018). Computer-mediated collaborative writing in L2 contexts: an analysis of empirical research. *Computer Assisted Language Learning, 31* (8), 882–904. https://doi.org/10.1080/09588221.2018.1465981

Little, C. W., Clark, J. C., Tani, N.E., & Connor, C.M. (2018). Improving writing skills through technology-based instruction: A meta-analysis. *Review of Education, 6*(2), 183–201. https://doi.org /10.1002/rev3.3114

Lu, X. (2017). Automated measurement of syntactic complexity in corpus-based L2 writing research and implications for writing assessment. *Language Testing, 34*, 493–511. https://doi.org /10.1177/026553221 7710675

Lv, X., Ren, W., & Xie, Y. (2021). The effects of online feedback on ESL/EFL writing: A meta-analysis. *Asia-Pacific Education Researcher, 30*, 643–653. https://doi.org/10.1007/s40299-021-00594-6

Ma, Q., Tang, J., & Lin, S. (2022). The development of corpus-based language pedagogy for TESOL teachers: a two-step training approach facilitated by online collaboration. *Computer Assisted Language Learning, 35*(9), 2731–2760. https://doi.org/10.1080/09588221.2021.1895225

Nation, I. S. P., & Macalister, J. (2021). *Teaching ESL/EFL reading and writing.* Routledge.

Rahimi, A. R., & Tafazoli, D. (2022). The role of university teachers' 21st -century digital competence in their attitudes toward ICT integration in higher education: Extending the theory of planned behavior. *The JALT CALL Journal. 18*(2), 238–263. https://doi.org/10.29140/jaltcall. v18n2.632

Ranalli, J. (2018). Automated written corrective feedback: How well can students make use of it. *Computer Assisted Language Learning, 31*(7), 653 –674. https://doi.org/10. 1080/09588221.2018.1428994

Ranalli, J., Feng, H-H., & Chukharev-Hudilainen, E. (2019). The affordances of process-tracing technologies for supporting L2 writing instruction. *Language Learning & Technology, 23*(2), 1–11. https://dr.lib.iastate.edu/handle/20.500.12876/23555

Storch, N. (2019). Collaborative writing. *Language Teaching, 52*(1), 40–59. https://doi.org/10.1017/S0261444818000320

Stošić, L. (2015). The importance of educational technology in teaching. *International Journal of Cognitive Research in Science, Engineering and Education, 3*(1), 111–114. https://orcid.org/0000-0003-0039-7370

Thomas, S. (2020). Student's evaluation of a classroom bring-your-own-device (BYOD) policy. *The JALT CALL Journal. 16*(1), 29–49. https://doi.org/10.29140/jaltcall.v16n1.208

Tseng, S.-S., & Yeh, H.-C. (2019). The impact of video and written feedback on student preferences of English speaking practice. *Language Learning & Technology, 23*(2), 145–158. https://doi.org/10125/44687

Tsai, S-C. (2019). Using Google Translate in EFL drafts: A preliminary investigation. *Computer Assisted Language Learning, 32*(5-6), 510–526. https://doi.org/10.1080/09588221.2018.1527361

Vygotsky, L. S. (1978). Interaction between learning and development. In M. Cole., V. John-Steiner., S. Scribner., & E. Souberman (Eds.), *Mind in society: The development of higher psychological processes* (pp. 79–91). Harvard University Press.

Wu, W-C. V., Petit, E., & Chen, C-H. (2015). EFL writing revision with blind expert and peer review using a CMC open forum. *Computer Assisted Language Learning, 28*(1), 58–80. https://doi.org/10.1080/09588221.2014.937442

Xu, Z., Banerjee, M., Ramirez, G., Zhu, G., Wijekumar, K. (2019). The effectiveness of educational technology applications on adult English language learners' writing quality: a meta-analysis. *Computer Assisted Language Learning, 32*(1-2), 1–31. https://doi.org/10.1080/09588221.2018.1501069

14
Future directions in writing research

Ronald P. Leow
Rosa M. Manchón

Introduction

Recently, there have been some shifts in the foci of the second/foreign language (L2) writing strand of research, namely, 1) the perspective of writing in an additional language as a potential for learning or what is called "learning *through* writing" (Cumming, 2020) or "writing-to-learn" versus "learning-to-write" (Manchón, 2011), 2) the need for a process-oriented approach to the study of writing to elucidate how L2 writers do process the L2 as they compose and review their written production (e.g., Leow, 2020; Manchón & Leow, 2020), and 3) the location of writing research designs within the language curriculum and, as an extension, within an instructed second language acquisition (ISLA) framework (e.g., Leow, 2020; Leow & Manchón, 2021; Manchón & Leow, 2020). This chapter reports succinctly on the current literature of the writing and written corrective feedback (WCF) strands of research along the lines of these recent perspectives and provides a future agenda for writing and WCF investigations, followed by pedagogical suggestions and potential action research.

Theoretical framework
Writing

The language learning potential of L2 writing in instructed SLA (ISLA) settings is based on two main assumptions: 1) Writing activity constitutes the kind of communicative practice in using the L2 that may lead to the consolidation (i.e., gradual proceduralization) of L2 knowledge. Writing may also provide the opportunity to expand L2 knowledge (e.g., via the use of external resources). 2) Writing activity (in contrast to speaking) possesses certain characteristics that may offer more favorable conditions for the learning functions of output predicted in the original formulation of Swain's Output Hypothesis (Swain, 2005), that is, the noticing, hypothesis-testing, and metalinguistic function of output. Thus, the greater availability of time and pace in the writing condition, as well as the permanent nature of the written text, allow for potential greater attention to be devoted to language-related concerns. Additionally, the intense problem-solving nature of many forms has been found to induce more intense linguistic encoding processes (see Manchón, 2023; Manchón & Cerezo, 2018; Manchón & Vasylets, 2019; Manchón & Williams, 2016).

Three debatable issues have arisen from these assumptions that warrant future investigation, namely the kind of language learning that may derive from written output practice,[1] the status of the L2 knowledge (explicit or implicit) drawn on while writing, and the possibility of explicit L2 knowledge eventually becoming implicit. Empirical investigations into each issue are clearly warranted for future development of this research strand.

Written corrective feedback (WCF)

Several theoretical underpinnings have been postulated to account for feedback processing from mainly two perspectives, namely, cognitive (see Leow & Suh, 2021 for a recent review) and sociocultural (see Storch, 2021 for a recent review). Among the cognitive theoretical underpinnings are two recent ones (Bitchener, 2021, and Leow, 2020) that address directly the role of WCF.

Bitchener (2021) adopts the various stages of the L2 learning process postulated by Gass's (1997) Model of Second Language Acquisition and elaborates on each processing stage in relation to additional moderating variables: At the attention stage (feedback type preference), at the noticing stage (explicitness of WCF types), at the understanding stage (informativeness of WCF and long-term memory), at the analyzing stage (working memory processing capacities, long-term memory store, language learning aptitude, and type of WCF), and at the hypothesis formation/testing stage (affective factors and prior experiences). Based on these processes and moderating variables, the hypothesis may be accepted or not, which in turn leads to consolidation or a repetition of the episode.

Leow's (2020) Feedback Processing Framework, based on his 2015 Model of the L2 Learning Process in ISLA, provides a framework that offers a cognitive explanation for the role of feedback (written or oral) in subsequent L2 development with a strong focus on how such feedback is processed by L2 writers (or speakers). The crucial aspects of the framework lie in the several early stages of feedback processing linked to the potential activation of prior knowledge, the potential for restructuring, the type of learning (item vs. system), the products potentially existing in the L2 learners' internal system, and an explanation for type of subsequent L2 output produced. In addition, he includes several cognitive processes and variables such as depth of processing, levels of awareness, activation of appropriate prior knowledge, hypothesis testing, rule formulation, and/or metacognition that may play a role in whether or how the feedback was indeed processed.

Literature review

Writing

Two relevant lines of research that have directly or indirectly provided empirical evidence on the purported language learning effects of writing are those corresponding to task-modality studies, on the one hand, and empirical research on macro- and micro-writing processes, on the other.

Task-modality studies have provided empirical evidence for the purported advantage of speaking over writing. The bulk of this research has investigated whether performing the same task in speaking and in writing results in linguistic differences (often in terms of CAF measures, i.e. complexity, accuracy and fluency of production). Relevant for instruction is the finding that the written mode brings about the use of more accurate and at times more complex language (although the picture is rather complex because of conflicting findings; see Manchón, 2023; Vasylets & Gilabert, 2021, for recent reviews), as well as longer-lasting effects on the learning of new grammatical forms.

Some studies have also looked into the potential interaction of task complexity and task modality (i.e., performing more and less complex tasks in speaking and writing, e.g. Vasylets, Gilabert, & Manchón, 2017, 2019; Zalbidea, 2017, 2020) and have found that task modality appears to play "a more robust role than task complexity in promoting improved linguistic performance" (Zalbidea 2017, p. 348). Yet, these research findings should be viewed cautiously due to limited research and some important methodological issues. Importantly, the effect of task complexity on the processing dimension of writing is almost uncharted territory.

Linguistic processing while writing and potential learning outcomes

Recent studies of L2 writing processes fall into two main categories in terms of whether they inspect writing primarily at the point of inscription, or beyond and above the point of inscription (Manchón, 2023 for a recent review). The former (see contributions to Révész & Michel, 2019) have provided abundant empirical evidence on on-line writing behaviors, especially fluency and pausing. In contrast, the few existing ISLA-oriented studies on writing processes beyond the point of inscription (e.g. López-Serrano, Roca de Larios & Manchón, 2019; Tabari, 2022) are concerned with higher-order writing processes such as L2 writers' problem-solving behavior while writing. Collectively, studies of writing processes have gradually expanded the methodological procedures and now include concurrent and retrospective introspection data, and data collection procedures such as keystroke logging, eye tracking, and screen capture technologies.

Studies of writing processes above and beyond the point of inscription have inspected macro-writing processes (planning, formulation, revision, and monitoring), primarily in terms of their distinctive nature (at times comparing processes in L1 and L2 writing) and their temporal distribution (see Michel et al., 2021, for a review). López Serrano, Roca de Larios and Manchón (2019) have provided a detailed account of the language reflection individual writers engage in in their problem-solving activity, which includes both a theoretically-motivated and empirically-based coding scheme (useful for future inquiry into the connection between writing and language learning) and, importantly, a problem-solving theoretical proposal for the type of problem-solving behavior that could lead to advances language competences. Testing these predictions would be a worthy avenue to explore in future research. Another relevant line of work that ought to be further pursued in future research is the potential mediation of individual differences (see Ahmadian & Vasylets, 2021; Papi, 2021: Papi, Vasylets, & Ahmadian, 2022 for reviews) and the effect of task-related factors on linguistic processing while writing.

WCF strand of research

The role of WCF in L2 writers' subsequent L2 development has been a major source for theoretical, empirical, and pedagogical debate for decades (see Leow, 2020; Manchón & Vasylets, 2019, for recent reviews). Most WCF studies have addressed type (direct vs. indirect vs. metalinguistic, see, for example, Caras, 2019) and amount (focused vs. unfocused, see, Shepherd, O'Meara, & Snyder, 2016) of WCF over the last four decades. Some studies have also investigated WCF and collaborative writing conditions (e.g., Manchón, Nicólas-Conesa, Cerezo, & Criado, 2020), although this strand of research is typically subsumed under a sociocultural perspective (e.g., Kim & Emelivanova, 2021; Wigglesworth & Storch, 2012). There is also interest in the role of digital or computer-mediated WCF in L2 development under the auspices of Automated Writing Evaluation (AWE) (e.g., Ranalli, 2021), as well as studies on the timing of feedback (e.g., Fu & Li, 2022).

Type of WCF: What the research reveals

The overall results reveal that studies comparing types of WCF varying in directness have produced inconsistent results. According to Leow (2020), several plausible explanations can be made to account for such inconsistencies, for example, the length of the study, the level of language proficiency, individual differences, task type, the incomparability and/or robustness of the research designs, type of linguistic item and so on. In addition, several assumptions have been made regarding how the written feedback was processed by the L2 writers. For example, advocates for direct WCF assume that the provision of such feedback is an opportunity for L2 writers to immediately confirm or disconfirm their original hypotheses on the L2 and view the absence of direct WCF as detrimental to the learning process. Advocates for indirect WCF have assumed that indirect WCF benefits L2 writers more given that they need to be cognitively engaged while processing the feedback, which can lead to information retention (see Leow, 2020 for further elaboration).

Amount of WCF: What the research reveals

Similar to type of WCF, overall inconsistent findings have been reported by studies addressing the effect of unfocused feedback studies conducted within a comparison of type of feedback (Leow, 2020). On the other hand, focused feedback studies have offered overall a more positive result with the caveat that several of these studies investigated only English articles.

Like the direct versus indirect comparison, researchers have made different assumptions with respect to the differential effectiveness of focused and unfocused WCF. Advocates for focused WCF assume that focused WCF when compared to unfocused WCF has greater potential not only to attract L2 writers' noticing of the WCF but also lead to understanding the corrective information due to the smaller amount of feedback provided. It is also assumed that asking L2 writers to correct a large range of linguistic errors found in unfocused WCF may lead to a cognitive overload while prohibiting learners' processing of the feedback. On the other hand, other researchers have challenged the usefulness of focused WCF from both an ecological perspective, that is, not pertinent to the L2 classroom, and a writing process perspective, that is, more emphasis on a focus on form (see Leow, 2020, for further elaboration).

Summary of WCF findings on type and amount

In sum, the overall findings of WCF studies appear to indicate clear learning benefits for feedback over no feedback. At the same time, there are inconsistent findings for the effect of type of WCF while the value of the superiority of focused over unfocused WCF is reduced due to its lack of ecological validity in the classroom setting.

Limitations of the WCF strand of research

The recent review of the WCF strand of research (Leow, 2020) reveals several limitations that warrant future investigation, namely, 1) most studies failed to address *how* L2 writers processed the feedback provided, that is, there was a focus more on a product-oriented approach to the effect of WCF than a process-oriented one, 2) questionable measures to address what L2 writers "learned" from these interventions (typically subsumed within an overall report of several aspects of grammatical knowledge or global accuracy rate), 3) the experimental design was typically not linked to the language curriculum but largely of a one-shot laboratory-based design with minimal pedagogical extrapolations, and 4) too many assumptions made with respect to type of feedback provided and how L2 writers processed the WCF. At the same time, he also reported an uptick in adopting 1) the provision of WCF from a *writing-to-learn* perspective (e.g., Leow, 2020; Manchón, 2011; Manchón & Vasylets, 2019) that provides ecological validity to this strand of research, 2) a process-oriented research perspective (e.g., Leow & Manchón, 2020; Manchón & Leow, 2020) with empirical studies employing concurrent data elicitation procedures (e.g., Caras, 2019; López-Serrano, Roca de Larios, & Manchón, 2019; Park & Kim, 2019 for online verbal reports and Cerezo, Manchón, & Nicolás-Conesa, 2019; Manchón, Nicolás-Conesa, Cerezo, & Criado, 2020 for offline written languaging), 3) a curricular approach (e.g., Caras, 2019; Coyle, Cánovas-Guirao, & Roca, 2018; Leow, 2020; Leow, Thinglum, & Leow, 2022), and 4) an "ISLA *applied*" versus an "*applied* ISLA" approach (Leow & Manchón, 2021). ISLA *applied* comprises studies seeking to inform pedagogical practice via pedagogical intervention. To this end, these studies are not only situated within a language curriculum and seeking to inform pedagogical practice but also attempting to promote a level of learning that is successful (a passing grade) from a curricular perspective. On the other hand, *applied* ISLA studies investigate the instructed setting without much association with the language curriculum (relatively similar to controlled or laboratory-based ISLA research).

Future directions

We draw from our previous recent work (Leow & Manchón, 2021; Leow, 2020; Leow, Manchón, & Polio, 2022; Manchón, 2023; Manchón & Leow, 2020) to provide avenues for future investigation in writing and WCF.

1. There is a need for more process-oriented studies on writing as a site for learning in ISLA. Future studies need to gather as much concurrent data during the writing process, identify the cognitive processes being employed by L2 writers, and associate such processes with any potential learning. While think aloud protocols are arguably superior in gathering rich concurrent data on *how* L2 writers process during the writing and revision process, triangulation of various procedures or methods (e.g., eye-tracking, stimulated recalls, keystroke logging, screen-capture footage etc.) is clearly recommended (Leow, Grey, Marijuan, & Moorman, 2014; Révész &

Michel, 2019). In addition, data from think aloud protocols should contribute to a reduction of the need to make assumptions on L2 writers' processing.
2. Future research needs to continue addressing the writing strand of research from an ISLA *applied* (Leow, 2019) perspective if researchers are interested in the pedagogical ramifications of their findings in addition to increasing the ecological validity of their findings. To this end, researchers need to situate their research designs within the syllabus and language curriculum and, instead of the typical lab-based or one-shot or short time span design, employ more long-term or longitudinal designs to truly address the authentic classroom setting. Data gathered across the semester will likely provide richer insights into writing processes potentially linked to learning while reflecting the authentic classroom setting and syllabus. The value of such a design maximizes the benefits from theory and research by permitting pedagogical contributions to be aligned with the writing component of the language curriculum. Future ISLA *applied* studies in the WCF strand also need to conform to the type of WCF, namely, direct and/or metalinguistic, typically provided in such formal settings.
3. An adoption of concurrent data elicitation procedures leads to the need for more fine-tuned coding and analysis of the L2 writing data gathered, which would reveal not only deeper layers of L2 writers' processes but also the relationships between such processes and subsequent language learning (Coyle, Cánovas-Guirao, & Roca de Larios, 2018).
4. Future writing studies need to continue further investigations into the roles of several variables that may more clearly reveal potential relationships between L2 writers and the provision and use of WCF such as, for example, individual differences (e.g., Li & Roshan, 2019), type of linguistic item (e.g., Leow, Thinglum, & Leow, 2022), and level of proficiency (e.g., Park & Kim, 2019).
5. Future studies need to expand the scope of targeted populations. While the typical population in writing studies comprises tertiary or college-level levels of education, there is a relative paucity of studies conducted at lower educational levels (e.g., middle or high school) or even outside the formal educational environment.

Practical implications and suggestions

From a pedagogical perspective, key questions are those related to the writing tasks that students complete and the feedback provided by the teacher.

Regarding tasks, teachers must be cognizant of the range of task types and task implementation conditions that are subsumed under the umbrella of "writing" and hence make principled decisions. Among other crucial distinctions, whether writing is performed individually or collaboratively, in timed-constrained or time-unlimited conditions, in paper-based or screen-based environments, with or without the access to external sources, are key consideration for pedagogical decision-making.

Regarding feedback, the empirical support for the benefits derived from the provision of WCF to our L2 writers is undebatable. This means that L2 writers should be allowed the opportunity to do a rewrite, which views writing as a process and not a product (e.g., Horwitz, 2008). At the same time, it is important that the feedback provided is clear, consistent, and understandable to these L2 writers. For both direct and indirect WCF, this may mean that the correction provided or error flagged via a symbol (e.g., "AGR" for agreement), respectively, is supported by some explanation of the source of the error. For the metalinguistic WCF via the use of a symbol, the grammatical information sheet that typically accompanies this type of WCF should be void of much metalinguistic jargon and provide simple samples of the source and corrections of the error. Based on data revealed by concurrent online data (e.g., Leow, Thinglum, & Leow, 2022), any effort to get L2 writers to process their errors more deeply or be more cognitively engaged may lead to more robust retention of the new grammatical information associated with the errors. One strategy may be to ask L2 writers to write in their first language what they learned from their errors after their rewrite, a classic case of metacognition that is associated with deeper processing or more cognitive engagement and learning.

Suggestions for action research or case study

Based on the suggestions above, teachers can conduct an action research project or a case study to support or refute the value of metacognition, which should lead to deeper processing or more cognitive engagement, in promoting better learning. Randomly assign two language classrooms or students at the same proficiency level (ideally at a lower level) to one of the two experimental conditions: + direct WCF (or + metalinguistic WCF), - metacognition vs. + direct WCF (or + metalinguistic WCF), + metacognition. The WCF employed should be the same for baseline comparison of the value of metacognition. Create a writing prompt that targets specifically well-known grammatical points recently covered in the last chapter and upon which the composition is based. For example, in Spanish the agreement between noun and adjectives poses challenges to early stage English speakers learning Spanish and this grammatical point has been introduced in the past chapter within the context of characteristics. Here is an example of a modified composition topic taken from an authentic classroom syllabus that targets the production of the noun-adjective agreement in Spanish (Leow, Thinglum, & Leow, 2022):

Composición 1: *Yo mismo/a y mis clases*

Write a composition about yourself and your classes. Answer each point to guide your composition.

Párrafo (Paragraph) #1:
Introduce yourself including the personal information requested below.

1. Presentación de ti mismo/a (**your name** and **your personal characteristics** and **personality**. You must use at least 2 of the personal characteristic adjectives and 2 of the personality characteristic adjectives provided below PLUS any others if so desired).

[**Características personales**: *alto, bajo, mediano, guapo, bonito, delgado, gordo*]

[**Personalidad**: *simpático, introvertido, extrovertido, sincero, cómico, divertido, gregario*]

Párrafo #2:

1. Descripción de tus clases (**describe <u>each class</u> that you are taking**). For each class you describe, use adjectives from **Clases** below PLUS any others if so desired to describe the class.

[**Clases**: *bueno, aburrido, intensivo, favorito, malo, espantoso, largo (long)*]

Provide feedback and allow students to rewrite their compositions and re-submit. To assess whether either experimental condition learned this targeted grammatical item more robustly, one week later ask the students to write on their friends' characteristics and personalities and descriptions of their classes. Comparing their performances on the first and second compositions should reveal potential differences (or lack thereof) of the benefits of metacognition or deeper cognitive engagement.

Based on the available empirical evidence (including domains not covered in our synthetic review above), we would like to suggest also the following suggestions for action research:

1. Investigate whether or not performing the same task individually and collaboratively leads to differences in the characteristics of the texts produced. The students' own perceptions of the benefits of both conditions could complement the text analysis
2. Investigate the way in which our students process and benefit from different types of feedback and why.
3. Investigate how students become more apt at making the most of the feedback received on their writing as they progress in the academic program.

Conclusion

There is no question that, when viewed from a *writing-to-learn* perspective, a theoretically-driven (process-oriented) and an ISLA *applied*-based research agenda augurs well for a better understanding of L2 writing processes in the L2 classroom. This agenda allows studies to increase the ecological validity of their designs by situating them within the syllabus and language curriculum and over a longer period of time to simulate the authentic classroom setting. The agenda also permits findings to be more associated with potential pedagogical ramifications for both the teachers and writing component of the curriculum. There is also the potential investment of the teaching staff, which can also address the debatable and current issue of the researcher-teacher interface (e.g., Leow, Thinglum, Havenne, & Tseng, 2022; Sato & Loewen, 2022) given that teachers are more prone to regard the findings as pertinent to curricular learning outcomes. As noted by Leow (2020), arriving at a deeper understanding, via concurrent data, of *how* L2 writers compose and process WCF within a language curriculum is clearly challenging but with huge benefits in promoting robust learning in the instructed setting from a *writing-to-learn* perspective.

Notes

1. Readers are referred to Polio (2020) and Schmitt (2020) for an extensive treatment of current findings and future research directions on learning grammar and vocabulary through writing.

Further reading

Leow, R. (Ed.) (2019). *The Routledge handbook of second language research in classroom learning*. Routledge.

This is a comprehensive psycholinguistic account of instructed language learning. It brings together empirical studies with theoretical underpinnings and provides discussions of conceptual replications/ extensions of, and new research on, classroom learning or Instructed SLA (ISLA). The empirical studies report largely on the tenets of Leow's (2015) Model of the L2 Learning Process in ISLA that has postulated the roles of cognitive processes in the L2 learning process and do so on the basis of two major methodological data-elicitation procedures to be employed in addressing learner cognitive processes, namely, think-aloud protocols and eye-tracking). Collectively, the chapters in the handbook shed light on the manner in which L2 users process data in instructional L2 settings.

Manchón, R.M., & Polio, C. (2021). *The Routledge handbook of second language acquisition and writing*. Routledge.

This handbook offers a comprehensive, systematic discussion of recent research on the connection between L2 writing and L2 learning. Chapters in the volume synthesize and contextualize the salient theoretical approaches, methodological issues, empirical findings, and emerging themes in the domain, and collectively set the future research agenda to move the field forward. The coda chapter by leading expert Dana Ferris reflects on the implications of the SLA- oriented L2 writing research analyzed in the preceding chapters for the teaching of L2 writing.

Polio, C. & Friedman. D. (2017). *Understanding, evaluating, and conducting second language writing research.* **Routledge.**

This methodologically-oriented book provides a comprehensive discussion of the strengths of quantitative and qualitative approaches to investigating L2 writing, as well as an analysis of the manner in which these two perspectives might complement each other, covering research informed by both cognitive and socio-cultural frameworks in SLA. The book in a key resource for conducting research on L2 writing.

References

Ahmadian, M., & Vasylets, O. (2021). The role of cognitive individual differences in L2 writing performance and written corrective feedback processing and use. In R. M. Manchón & C. Polio (Eds.), *The Routledge handbook of second language acquisition and writing* (pp.139151). Routledge.

Bitchener, J. (2021). Written corrective feedback. In H. Nassaji & E. Kartchava (Eds.), *The Cambridge handbook of corrective feedback in language learning and teaching* (pp. 207–225). Cambridge University Press.

Caras, A. (2019). Written corrective feedback in compositions and the role of depth of processing. In R. P. Leow (Ed.), *The Routledge handbook of second language research in classroom learning* (pp. 188–200). Routledge.

Cerezo, L., Manchón, R. M., & Nicolás-Conesa, F. (2019). What do learners notice while processing written corrective feedback? A look at depth of processing via written languaging. In R. P. Leow (Ed.), *The Routledge handbook of second language research in classroom learning* (pp. 173–187). Routledge.

Coyle, Y., Cánovas-Guirao, J., & Roca de Larios, J. (2018). Identifying the trajectories of young EFL learners across multi-stage writing and feedback processing tasks with model texts. *Journal of Second Language Writing, 42,* 25–43. https://doi.org/10.1016/j.jslw.2018.09.002

Fu, M. & Li, S. (2022). The effects of immediate and delayed corrective feedback on L2 development. *Studies in Second Language Acquisition, 44* (1), 2–34. https://doi.org/10.1017/S0272263120000388

Gass, S. M. (1997). *Input, interaction, and the second language learner.* Lawrence Erlbaum.

Horwitz, E. K. (2008). Becoming a language teacher: a practical guide to second language learning and teaching. Pearson.

Kim, Y., & Emelivanova, L. (2021). The effects of written corrective feedback on the accuracy of L2 writing: Comparing collaborative and individual revision behavior. *Language Teaching Research, 25*(2), 234–255. https://doi.org/10.1177/1362168819831406

Leow, R. P. (2015). *Explicit learning in the L2 classroom: A student-centered approach.* Routledge. https://doi.org/10.4324/9781315887074

Leow, R. P. (2019). From SLA > ISLA > ILL: A curricular perspective. In R. P. Leow (Ed.), *The Routledge handbook of second language research in classroom learning* (pp. 485–493). Routledge.

Leow, R. P. (2020). L2 writing-to-learn: Theory, research, and a curricular approach. In R. M. Manchón (Ed.), *Writing and language learning. Advancing research agendas* (pp. 95–117). John Benjamins. https://doi.org/10.1075/lllt.56.05leo

Leow, R. P., Grey, S., Marijuan, S., & Moorman, C. (2014). Concurrent data elicitation procedures, processes, and the early stages of L2 learning: A critical overview. *Second Language Research, 30*(2), 111–127. https://doi.org/10.1177/0267658313511979

Leow, R. P., & Manchón, R. M. (2021). Expanding research agendas: Directions for future research agendas on writing, language learning and ISLA. In R. M. Manchón & C. Polio (Eds.), *Routledge handbook of second language acquisition and writing* (pp. 299–311). Routledge.

Leow, R. P., Manchón, R. M., & Polio, C. (2022). Researching L2 writing as a site for learning in instructed settings. In L. Gurzynski-Weiss & Y. Kim (Eds.), *Instructed second language acquisition research methods* (pp. 305–325). John Benjamins. https://doi.org/10.1075/rmal.3.13leo

Leow, R. P., & Suh, B-R. (2021). Theoretical perspectives on writing, corrective feedback, and language learning in individual writing conditions. In R. M. Manchón & C. Polio (Eds.), *Routledge handbook of second language acquisition and writing* (pp. 9–21). Routledge.

Leow, R. P., Thinglum, A., Havenne, M., & Tseng, R. (2022). Bridging the gap between researchers and teachers: A curricular perspective. *The Modern Language Journal, 106* (3). https://doi.org/10.1111/modl.12799

Leow, R. P., Thinglum, A., & Leow, S. (2022). WCF processing in the L2 curriculum: A look at type of WCF, type of linguistic item, and L2 performance. *Studies in Second Language Learning and Teaching, 12*(4), 653-675. https://doi.org/10.14746/ssllt.2022.12.4.6

Li, S., & Roshan, S. (2019). The associations between working memory and the effects of four different types of written corrective feedback. *Journal of Second Language Writing, 45*, 1–15. https://doi.org/10.1016/j.jslw.2019.03.003

López-Serrano, S., Roca de Larios, J. & Manchón, R.M. (2019). Language reflection fostered by individual L2 writing tasks: Developing a theoretically-motivated and empirically-based coding system. *Studies in Second Language Acquisition, 41*(3), 503–527. https://doi.org/10.1017/

S0272263119000275

Manchón, R. M. (2011). *Learning-to-write and writing-to-learn in an additional language*. Amsterdam: John Benjamins.

Manchón, R. M. (2023). The psycholinguistics of L2 writing. In A. Godfroid & H. Hopp (Eds.), *The Routledge handbook of SLA and psycholinguistics* (pp. 400-412). Routledge.

Manchón, R. M., & Williams, J. (2016). L2 writing and SLA studies. In R. M. Manchón & P. K. Matsuda (Eds.), *The handbook of second and foreign language writing* (pp. 567–586). De Gruyter Mouton.

Manchón, R. M. & Cerezo, L. (2018). Writing as language learning. In J. Liontas (Ed.), *The TESOL Encyclopedia of English language teaching*. John Wiley.

Manchón, R. M., & Leow, R. P. (2020). Investigating the language learning potential of L2 writing: Methodological considerations for future research agendas. In R. M. Manchón (Ed.), *Writing and language learning. Advancing research agendas* (pp. 336–355). John Benjamins.

Manchón, R. M., Nicolás-Conesa, F., Cerezo, L., & Criado, R. (2020). L2 writers' processing of written corrective feedback: Depth of processing via written languaging. In W. Suzuki & N. Storch (Eds.), *Languaging in language learning and teaching: A collection of empirical studies* (pp. 242–265). John Benjamins.

Manchón, R. M., & Vasylets, O. (2019). Language learning through writing: Theoretical perspectives and empirical evidence. In J. B. Schwieter, J. B. & A. Benati (Eds.), *The Cambridge handbook of language learning* (pp. 341–362). Cambridge University Press.

Papi, M. (2021). The role of motivational and affective factors in L2 writing performance and written corrective feedback processing and use. In R. M. Manchón & C. Polio (Eds.), *The Routledge handbook of second language acquisition and writing* (pp.152–165). Routledge.

Papi, M., Vasylets, O., & Ahmaddian, M. (2022). Individual difference factors for second language writing. In M. Papi & S. Li (Eds.), *Handbook of second language acquisition and individual differences*. Routledge.

Park, E. S., & Kim, O. Y. (2019). Learners' engagement with indirect written corrective feedback: Depth of processing and self-correction. In R. P. Leow (Ed.), *The Routledge handbook of second language research in classroom learning* (pp. 212–226). Routledge.

Polio, C. (2020). Can writing facilitate grammatical development? Advancing research agendas. In R. M. Manchón (Ed.), *The language learning potential of L2 writing: Moving forward in theory and research*, (pp. 381–420). John Benjamins.

Ranalli, J. (2021). L2 student engagement with automated feedback on writing: Potential for learning and issues of trust. *Journal of Second Language Writing, 52*, 1–16. https://doi.org/10.1016/j.jslw.2021.100816

Révész, A., & Michel, M. (Eds.) (2019). Methodological advances in investigating L2 writing processes. Special Issue, *Studies in Second*

Language Acquisition, 41(3).

Sato, M., & Loewen, S. (2022). The research-practice dialogue in second language learning and teaching: Past, present, and future. *The Modern Language Journal, 106*(3). 509–527. https://doi.org/10.1111/modl.12791

Schmitt, D. (2020). Can writing facilitate the development of a richer vocabulary? Advancing research agendas. In R. M. Manchón (Ed.), *Writing and language learning. Advancing research agendas* (pp. 357–380). John Benjamins.

Shepherd, R. P., O'Meara, K., Snyder, S. E. (2016). Grammar agreements: Crafting a more finely tuned approach to corrective feedback. *Journal of Response to Writing, 2*(1), 43–57.

Storch, N. (2021). Theoretical perspectives on L2 writing and language learning in collaborative writing conditions and the collaborative processing of written corrective feedback. In R. M. Manchón & C. Polio (Eds.), *Routledge handbook of second language acquisition and writing* (pp. 22–34). Routledge.

Swain, M. (2005). The Output Hypothesis: Theory and research. In E. Hinkel (Ed.), *Handbook of research in second language teaching and learning* (pp. 471–483). Lawrence Erlbaum.

Tabari, M. A. (2022). Task preparedness and L2 written production: Investigating effects of planning modes on L2 learners' focus of attention and output. *Journal of Second Language Writing, 55*, 100871. https://doi.org/10.1016/j.jslw.2021.100814

Vasylets, O., & Gilabert (2021). Task effects across modalities. In R. M. Manchón & C. Polio (Eds.), *The Routledge handbook of second language acquisition and writing* (pp. 39–51). Routledge.

Vasylets, O., Gilabert, R., & Manchón, R. M. (2017). The effects of mode and task complexity on second language production. *Language Learning, 67*(2), 394–430. https://doi.org/10.1111/lang.12228

Vasylets, O., Gilabert, R., & Manchón, R. M. (2019). Differential contribution of oral and written modes to lexical, syntactic and propositional complexity in L2 performance in instructed contexts. *Instructed Second Language Acquisition, 3*(2), 206–227. https://doi.org/10.1558/isla.38289

Wigglesworth, G., & Storch, N. (2012). Feedback and writing development through collaboration: A socio-cultural approach. In R. M. Manchón (Ed.), *L2 writing development: Multiple perspectives* (pp. 69–99). De Gruyter Mouton.

Zalbidea, J. (2017). 'One task fits all'? The roles of task complexity, modality, and working memory capacity in L2 performance. *The Modern Language Journal, 101*(2), 335–352. https://doi.org/10.1111/modl.12389

Zalbidea, J. (2020). A mixed-methods approach to exploring the L2 learning potential of writing versus speaking. In R. M. Manchón (Ed.), *Writing and language learning. Advancing research agendas* (pp. 207–230). John Benjamins.

Index

academic reading, 15–22
academic written register, 2, 5–6
accuracy, 35-37, 58, 63, 89, 115, 116, 118, 131, 132, 133, 134, 139, 140–145
  lexical, 143
  mechanical, 143
  native-like, 146
  verb, 143
ACTFL, 27
ALTE, 27
American Council on the Teaching of Foreign Languages *see* ACTFL
assessment
  literacy, 39, 45–46, *47*, 48–49, 51
  qualification, 46
  training, 47
Association of Language Testers in Europe *see* ALTE
autonomy *see* learner, autonomy
awareness, 90, 121, 129, 131

beliefs
  learner *see* learner, beliefs
  teacher *see* teacher, beliefs

CAF *see* writing, complexity, accuracy, and fluency
CEFR, vii, 27, 40
ChatGPT, xi, 169
collaborative writing, 92, 114–123
Cambridge English Assessment, 40
Common European Framework of Reference *see* CEFR

DWCF *see* written corrective feedback, dynamic

dynamic written corrective feedback *see* written corrective feedback, dynamic

EAL, xiv, 13, 15
EAP, 1–5, 7–8
EGAP, 2
engagement, xiv, xv, 38, 40, 64, 67, 101, 104, 106, 107, 109, 114, 117–121, 122, 161, 167, 187, 188
  cognitive, 67
  with feedback, 59, 62, 65, 67, 87, 90, 93
English
  as an additional language *see* EAL
  as a second language *see* ESL
  for academic purposes *see* EAP
  for general academic purposes *see* EGAP
  for specific academic purposes *see* ESAP
  for specific purposes *see* ESP
ESAP, 2
ESL, 1
ESP, 1–2, 7–8
Evernote, 169
exemplary papers, 16, 17, 19

feedback
  engagement, see engagement, feedback
  direct, 129, 130–132, 133
  indirect, 108, 129, 131–132, 133, 141
  literacy *see* literacy, feedback
  teacher, 58, 64, 90, 107, 108, 109, 127, 128, 133, 134, 135, 157, 158, 163
  peer, 20, 58, 59, 64, 91, 107, 109, 123, 127, 134, 143, 157, 159, 160–161,

Index **195**

self, 59, 64, 109, 135, 155, 157, 161–162
training, 157, 160
written corrective *see* written corrective feedback
fluency, 30, 32, 33, 34, 35, 37, 38, 40

genre-based analysis, 7
genre-based instruction, 5, 6, 91
Google Docs, 169
Google Translate, 173
grammar, 18, 29, 57, 78, 115, 116, 128, 129, 140, 141, 143–146, 148, 149, 160, 168, 169, 173, 189,
Grammarly, 173

IELTS, 57, 58, 145
IEP, *142*, 143, 145
instructed second language acquisition, xv
Intensive English Program *see* IEP
International English Language Testing System *see* IELTS

key words in context, 21, 26
KWIC *see* key words in context

L2 future selves, 89–90
LancsBox, 21, 26
LAL *see* teacher, assessment literacy
language aptitude, 87, 89, 91, 94, 181
learner
  anxiety, 91
  autonomy, xi, xv, 38, 101–107, 110, 111, 139, 160, 174
  beliefs, 90, 92
  differences, xiv, 87–95, 135
  identity, xii
  motivation, xiv, 62, 68, 73, 88–91, 92, 93, 94, 98, 101, 105–107, 109, 111, *116*, 117, 118, 120–122, 134, 161, 162, 167, 170, *see also* writing, motivation
  needs, 2–4, 133
  self-efficacy, 90–91
  self-regulation, 62, 90– 93, 98, 99, 109, 111

training, 45, 104, 107, 121, 134, 135, 141, 157, 160
learning context, 77, 78, 79, *80*, 81, 111, 114, 115, 132
literacy, 13, 14, 15, 17, 74, 167, 168, 170
  academic, 13
  assessment *see* assessment, literacy
  demands, 13, 22
  feedback, 135
  practices, 88
  training, 46, 49

machine translation, xi, 173,
motivation *see* learner, motivation
writing see writing, motivation

National Council on Measurement in Education *see* NCME
NCME, 56
Notion, 169

OneNote, 169

Pearson English Test *see* PET
pedagogical knowledge *see* teacher, pedagogical knowledge
peer
  review, 16, 17, 18–20, 107, 157, 159, 160, 163,
  texts, 18
performance criteria, 57–58
personal corpus, 17, 21
PET, 57
plagiarism, 15, 16, 17, 173

Quillbot, 173

reading, xiv, 62, 103
  academic *see* academic reading
  cognitive processing, 15
  for writing, 13–15
  global strategies, 15
  goal-setting, 15
  metacognitive strategies, 15, 16
  mining texts, 15
  skimming, 16, 18, 23

RFW *see* reading, for writing
rubric, xiii, 17, 18, 28, 40, 49, 52, 56–58, 60–65, 116, 157, 160, 161
training *see* training, rubric

Saville's model of systemic learning-oriented assessment, 60–66
scanning *see* reading, skimming
skimming *see* reading, skimming
social context, 14, 17, 47, 72, 111, 115
social networking, 169
student needs *see* learner, needs

teacher
  autonomy, xv
  beliefs, 77, 78, 81, 82, 83
  cognition, 71–73, 74
  education, 7, 9, 73, 74
  pedagogical knowledge, 45, 48–49
  language assessment literacy *see* assessment, literacy
  training, 32, 41, 48, 50, 51, 73, 74, 135
  technology, xi, 92, 116, 117, 134, 135, 167–176
Test of English as a Foreign Language *see* TOEFL
testing writing
  direct testing, xiii, 57
  indirect testing, xiii, 57
  integrative-sociolinguistic tests, xiii, 57
  psychometric-structuralist tests, xiii, 57
  quantification, 46
TOEFL, 57, 58, 145
training
  assessment *see* assessment, training
  feedback *see* feedback, training
  learner *see* learner, training
  literacy *see* literacy, training
  professional, 75
  rater, 58
  rubric, 161
  teacher *see* teacher, training
t-units, 34, *35*, 37

untreatable grammatical features, 141

vocabulary, 6, 7, 13, 18, 22, 23, 28, 29, 32, 57, 78, 89, 115, 140, 158, 168, *189*

WCF *see* written corrective feedback
word processors, xi
working memory, xiv, 89, 91, 94, 181
writing
  academic *see* academic writing
  collaborative *see* collaborative writing,
  complexity, accuracy, and fluency, 27–34, 37–40
  for specific purposes,
  in an additional language, xv, 160
  motivation, xiv, 92, 93, 97, 98
  summary, 16
  testing *see* testing writing
  written corrective feedback, 88, 89, 90, 92, 127–133, 134, 139,
  focused, 140
  direct, 129, 130–132, 141
  dynamic, 139–147, 148
  explicit, 141
  indirect, 129, 141
  unfocused, 140
  unlabeled, 141